INDIGENOUS MEDIA IN MEXICO

INDIGENOUS MEDIA IN MEXICO

Culture, Community, and the State

ERICA CUSI WORTHAM

Duke University Press *Durham & London* 2013

Library of Congress Cataloging-in-Publication Data
Wortham, Erica Cusi.
Indigenous media in Mexico : culture, community, and
the state / Erica Cusi Wortham.
pages cm
Includes bibliographical references and index.
ISBN 978-0-8223-5484-0 (cloth : alk. paper)
ISBN 978-0-8223-5500-7 (pbk. : alk. paper)
1. Indigenous peoples and mass media—Mexico.
2. Video recordings—Production and direction—
Mexico. 3. Indians of Mexico—Civilization. 4. Indians
of Mexico—Government relations. I. Title.
F1219.W67   2013
323.11—dc23
2013010724

TO PHILLIP, RICKY, ANNELIES, AND EMILIA,

my cherished husband and children,

and to my parents,

ELENA AND RICHARD WORTHAM—

for their enduring support and encouragement,

I dedicate this book to them and to the tenacious

individuals whose stories I tell.

CONTENTS

ILLUSTRATIONS

PREFACE

In June of 2006, I traveled to Oaxaca City for Raiz de la Imagen, the eighth Festival Americano de Cine y Video de Pueblos Indígenas, which my friends and colleagues in the Ojo de Agua Comunicación media collective were organizing. I had attended and assisted many such festivals alongside my friends in other parts of Latin America since the early 1990s, but seeing them host the most prominent indigenous media festival in Latin America, in their own amazing city, was a source of deep satisfaction for me. Plus, it was the first time since the festival was founded, in 1985, that it had returned to Mexico. With programs representing over twenty-five native peoples from across the hemisphere, sixty invited guests, filled screening rooms, and a balanced six-figure budget, Raiz de la Imagen was a big success, but my friends at Ojo de Agua were not able to savor their success until many months after the festival.

I was eight months pregnant at the time and remember noting how different it felt to walk (or waddle) around the city. The loaded, about to explode feeling that permeated the streets of downtown Oaxaca had nothing to do with the little one tossing around inside me, getting ready for her exit. It was the city itself that felt tense. The streets of the colonial *centro histórico* had been transformed by an intricate web—literally, like the kind spiders make—of string and rope, tethering tarps that made temporary homes for thousands of teachers and their families, who were protesting miserable wages in their familiar *plantón* (sit-in) style, while their union representatives negotiated with the government.

The teacher's plantón was an annual event, but that year's sit-in was far more extensive. My usual landmarks—the distinctive double peaks of San Felipe mountain, to the north, and the bell tower of the main cathedral in the *zócalo* (central plaza), to the south—were obscured from sight, making familiar terrain appear somewhat threatening and definitely less navigable. After long days in screening halls and nights in family-style restaurants, I would return to the step-over-creep-under obstacle course of ropes that filled many streets in the city center. I said "buenas noches" to the protestors in the streets and gave small treats to their children, who played with action figures while their parents prepared posters, held meetings in each other's tents, and listed to Radio Plantón, the teachers union's radio station. Just days after the festival ended and international guests (including myself) had left town, the "rumor" that had dominated so many conversations during the festival became a reality.

State police and special forces with armed helicopter cover entered the city on June 14, to forcibly and violently dislodge the teachers' peaceful plantón. This was a first, but so was the fact that the teachers of Sección 22 (Local 22) of the National Union of Educational Workers resisted. The teachers' acts of resistance quickly mushroomed into a wide protest movement and an unprecedented, total takeover of Oaxaca City by a broad coalition representing over two hundred civil organizations, a coalition that calls itself the Asamblea Popular de los Pueblos de Oaxaca (Popular Assembly of the Peoples of Oaxaca, APPO). The coalition's main demand was the resignation of the PRI governor, Ulises Ruiz Ortiz, who was accused by his public of committing electoral fraud, human rights abuses (including murders and disappearances), appropriating public funds, and spending public money on unwanted and unvetted public works that damaged the city's cultural heritage, while systematically ignoring the basic and pressing needs of his constituents.

My friends at Ojo de Agua jumped into action, cameras rolling 24–7 to cover the resistance and ensuing violence, until some of them appeared on "wanted" lists and were forced into hiding. They quickly and constantly circulated footage of the repression and the many "mega marches" that followed in an effort to counteract the effect of mainstream commercial media's attempt to minimize the movement and blame the protestors for the violence. Their achievement as hosts of the eighth indigenous film and video festival, while not minimized, paled in comparison to the vitality and sense of accountability with which members of Ojo de Agua recounted their role as communicators during the strife in 2006. From my perspective as an advocate-researcher who had followed the development of indigenous media since the early 1990s, this culmination of events was a complex watershed of a particular kind. Pitched in direct battle not so much against state and government armed forces but against the media the state and commercial interests control, indigenous videomakers had shed the very terms that had defined them for so many years, and moved from practicing "video indígena" to practicing "comunicación de lucha" (social struggle media).

For most of 2006, all major government offices and radio and television stations, both public and university operated, were taken over by APPO. On August 2, hundreds of women marched into the building of the state-run radio and television station and took over the broadcasting equipment, after their requests for air-time had been repeatedly denied. Ojo de Agua was there, too, providing technical assistance to the women, who soon renamed the radio station Radio Caserolas (Casserole radio), after their own boisterous march to the station, banging on pots and pans. Despite the movement's early slogan, "¡Ya Cayó!" (He has already fallen!), Governor Ulises Ruiz finished his term in office, though Oaxacans did manage to vote his party out of power in the gubernatorial elections in 2010.

The new governor (elected through a coalition of opposition parties) offers some hope that he will manage to run the state with increased transparency and accountability. Meanwhile, there is a semblance of normalcy in Oaxaca City—the tourists have returned—and members of Ojo de Agua tend to their regular lives and work again, though now they are focused more than ever on radio, as they respond to indigenous communities' desires to establish independent radio stations of their own. The importance of direct access to media that Radio Caserolas demonstrated during the 2006 protest movement in Oaxaca has rekindled the popular demand for access to media that the indigenous rebel army in Chiapas, the Ejército Zapatista de Liberación Nacional, had put on the negotiating table ten years prior, in the San Andrés Accords on the Rights of Indigenous Peoples, as a basic element of self-determination. This book recounts the struggles of indigenous communicators and their supporters in Oaxaca and Chiapas to establish their own media, and the role the Mexican government has played in helping and hindering that process.

ACKNOWLEDGMENTS

This book is based on fourteen months of field research in Mexico; many more years of experiences with indigenous media across Latin America and in the United States inform my work. My field research was funded by the Social Science Research Council, Fulbright-Hays, and the Wenner-Gren Foundation for Anthropological Research, and the Film and Video Center of the National Museum of the American Indian (NMAI) sponsored several of my trips to media festivals and workshops in Latin America. I want to thank the indigenous media-makers and their supporters, many of whom do not directly appear in this study, for having shared this dynamic arena of social practice with me. Many of the individuals whose voices and projects are included in this book have remained close friends, and I am forever grateful for their trust, openness, and patience while being subject to my inquisitive gaze.

I owe particular debts of gratitude to my academic advisers and colleagues at the Department of Anthropology and the program in Culture and Media at New York University and at NMAI. Fred Myers, Thomas Abercrombie, Jeff Himpele, and in particular, Faye Ginsburg, shepherded my studies and the development of this project in crucial ways. Jeff's invitation to write a short article for *American Anthropologist* (Wortham 2004) allowed me to begin to envision how my work could reach a broader audience, and Faye's enduring enthusiasm helped me keep the dots of field research, dissertation, manuscript, and social engagement connected and within my reach. Elizabeth Weatherford, head of the Film and Video Center at NMAI, afforded me many unforgettable opportunities to expand my knowledge of indigenous media practices in Mexico (and beyond) and to bring indigenous works from that part of the world into the museum's collection. Collectively Elizabeth, Millie Seubert, Carol Kalafatic, and my coworkers of over seven years at NMAI imparted their deep passion for and knowledge of Native American peoples and cultures to me in daily and meaningful ways. I thank them for sharing their life's work with me and for embracing indigenous mediamakers from Latin America.

The Centro de Investigaciónes y Estudios Superiores en Antropología Social-Unidad Istmo, in Oaxaca City, provided important institutional refuge and resources during my field research in 1999 and 2000. Paola Sesia is an extraordinary model of an engaged researcher, and I feel grateful to count her as a friend and colleague. I thank the Center for U.S.-Mexican Studies at the University of California, San Diego, for supporting my writing process with a Research Fellowship, from 2000 through 2001, and a second time with a Visiting Scholar Fellowship, from 2010 through 2011. Working at the center provided an unrivaled mix of intellectual stimulation, support, and friendship during both of my fellowship periods. Emiko Saldívar, Cori Hayden, and Senior Fellow Van Whiting helped me stay on track and enjoy the writing process as the dissertation took shape. More recently, Miles Rodriguez and Lara Braff, who kindly slogged through several versions of various chapters, gave me precise and tremendously helpful comments. Lara, in particular, helped me remain sane and focused as I finished the final draft of my manuscript. Justin Levitt, a research assistant at the center, helped me generate the maps for this book, and Greg Mallinger's steady presence made a group of transients feel settled and organized. Alberto Díaz-Cayeros, the center's director, spread his contagious enthusiasm for research like pixie dust, in the form of spot-on comments and penetrating questions, as he darted from meeting to meeting, airport to airport. And Graciela Platero, director of External Affairs and Fellowship Program Officer (but unofficially the vertebral column and matron) of the center, made everyone feel welcome, purposeful, and connected. Her thirty-year stewardship of the center wrapped up as I finished the manuscript and I know I speak for all my fellow colleagues in wishing her much *suerte* in her new endeavors. I am also grateful to my colleagues at UCSD's Department of Anthropology and, in particular, to Nancy Postero, whose careful reading and insightful comments of my dissertation and manuscript pushed me to clarify my ideas and believe in my perspective.

Laurel Smith, a cultural geographer at the University of Oklahoma, has been a tremendous source of support in this project. She began her field research on indigenous media in Oaxaca just as I was finishing mine. Though we approach a common subject through different disciplinary lenses, she and I share many positions and conclusions, just as we share a very specific network of friends and colleagues who practice and study indigenous media.

Ken Wissoker, at Duke University Press, with his endlessly supportive energy and positive attitude, saw me through various periods when life's demands and writing were not in sync. I am indebted to him for his patience and belief in the currency of the stories and struggles herein. It has been a lively and positive experience to live under the microscope of the staff at Duke; their careful work and thoughtful interventions have kept me on my toes.

Finally, the depth and resourcefulness of my personal support network of family and friends, new and old, sustained me through research and writing. My mother deserves special mention (don't they all?). She taught me to speak Spanish before I spoke English and kept me close to Mexico, even though I grew up in east Texas at a time when bilingualism was frowned upon as "damaging" to children. Forever critical and quick on the draw, she successfully instilled her "America is a continent—not a country" perspective in all four of her girls.

I thank my husband, Phillip Baltazar, for reminding me that this project is a "get to" not a "have to," for keeping me on track and for providing for us in ways I never dreamed possible. The sustaining smiles and hugs I received from our children, Ricky, Annelies, and Emilia while I began this project are now accompanied by complex conversations about cultural diversity and situated histories. Though I wrote this book with only a few full nights' sleep, my children and their father's daily love and growing understanding of my endeavors have been an endless source of energy. They keep my life in balance.

INTRODUCTION

Making Culture Visible

Indigenous Media in Mexico

Indigenous people in Oaxaca and Chiapas are using video, television, and radio communications media to represent themselves to their communities and regions, to the nation of which they are a part, and to broader, diverse transnational audiences. Inherently contentious and political, indigenous media matters because it is a form of self-determination, a basic human right that native peoples have been denied for centuries but are guaranteed in international law.[1] It is a well-known fact that indigenous people across the globe make up one of the poorest and most marginalized sectors of society, with a disproportionately higher number of victims of human rights abuses.[2] Mexico has nearly twelve million indigenous people living within its borders, the largest number in Latin America. They speak over sixty-five different languages despite multiple generations of Castilianization programs. Oaxaca has at least one million native people, close to a third of the state population, who speak over sixteen different languages. In Chiapas the numbers are very similar, though there is less cultural diversity.

Indigenous people in Mexico are joined by millions more across the globe—300 million, in fact, spread across 4,000 different societies (Neizen 2003, 4)—whose demands are heard loud and clear through documents and ratified covenants that are intended to hold governments accountable and safeguard not only the well-being of indigenous people, but the possibility of life on their terms. Given this situation, indigenous media matters because through these media we witness—and indigenous people themselves witness—their survival and the fact that they have managed to maintain a degree of "lived" autonomy despite the constant assaults on their ways of life, assaults from poverty, assimilation programs, military brutality, globalization and economic reforms, to mention just the most recent offensives.

In Mexico, as in most other places, the study of indigenous media is perforce a study of relations between indigenous peoples and the state. This point is particularly obvious in the Mexican case as the state, through the now defunct Instituto Nacional Indigenista (INI), effectively created *video indígena* in the early 1990s, like many other top-down development programs aimed at improving life among the marginalized, without acknowledging much less building upon indigenous media precedents taking place in other parts of the world (Evans 2008, Ginsburg 1993a, Marks 1994, Michaels 1994, Raheja 2010, Roth 1994, Schiwy 2009, Singer 2001b, Turner 1991a). But the story is far from simple or unidirectional. Video indígena was taught through the Transferencia de Medios Audiovisuales (TMA) program at a time of potential change in the institute, by individuals who were not bureaucrats, but committed artists and social activists. Their teachings steered a federally funded program (one of the only examples of the "hard transference" of government resources to indigenous ownership) directly toward a convergence with a burgeoning indigenous autonomy movement. This was as it should be—when the INI initiated the video program, in the early 1990s, the world was heading into the quincentenary celebrations that ushered in an era of official pluralism. Mexico seemed to lead the global sentiment to rethink the conquest and the rights of indigenous peoples by being the first country in Latin America to sign the International Labour Organization's Indigenous and Tribal Peoples Convention, known as ILO Convention No. 169. Affirming their resolve, the administration instituted changes to the constitution of 1917 that formally recognized Mexico as a "pluricultural nation."

True to its contradictory tendencies, however, the administration at the time also pulled the rug out from under the peasant population, with a second constitutional reform that ended the protection of peasant land from private sale. The Mexican congress amended article 27 of the Mexican constitution of 1917 in a counteragrarian reform that made it possible for half of the Mexican territory held in communal tenancy to be transferred to the private sector. Nancy Postero, an anthropologist who has written extensively on similar reform processes and paradoxes in Bolivia, aptly calls this "neoliberal multiculturalism," following the anthropologist Charles R. Hale (2007, 16; Hale 2002). Video indígena was funded under the auspices of such neoliberal multiculturalism, through an antipoverty program, Solidaridad, or Solidarity, that intended to soften the impact of neoliberal economic policies on a majority population already impoverished by one of the most severe currency devaluations in Mexican history. But after the indigenous-led Ejército Zapatista de Liberación Nacional (EZLN) declared war on the Mexican government and its neoliberal policies, on January 1, 1994—the day the North American Free Trade Agreement, between Mexico, the United States, and Canada, took effect—federal funding for video indígena practically ended. The indigenous autonomy movement in Mexico, however, was on fire.[3]

I entered the field with a few basic research questions: Why was the Mexican government, with its long history of contentious relationships with indigenous peoples, funding indigenous self-representation through video? What did indigenous peoples have to gain from participating in video production and what did this "new" form of engagement tell us about relations between indigenous and the state? How does visual self-representation fit into broader struggles for self-determination? Can video indígena assist nonindigenous people like me to further decolonize our imagination with more nuanced, nonessentialized understandings of indigenous culture and social practice? I engage these questions through detailed accounts of indigenous media initiatives in southern Mexico that are grounded in their particular and situated histories and places.

I can only imagine that from an indigenous person's perspective the overt manner in which indigenous people have been made to assimilate to dominant national society is akin to hegemony on steroids. Since the end of the Mexican Revolution, in 1917, the explicit "forging" of *lo mexicano*, as one of the leading scholars of the period, Manuel Gamio (also Mexico's father of anthropology), put it, created a unique *mestizo* identity for all Mexicans, formed from the glorious pre-Columbian, Mesoamerican cultures of the past and from European cultures (Gamio 1916). Ironically, in this scheme of building the modern nation, being Indian was no longer a possibility. To belong, indigenous people had to be peasants, and as a result their culture was relegated to folklore, split off from social and political organization through a process and set of assimilation policies known as *indigenismo*. A national system of free schools was expanded into rural areas, where the majority of indigenous peoples lived, in order to transform them into full citizens. Town plazas and government buildings were (and still are) decorated with

FIGURE I.1. "Channel 8—Culture, too, can be seen," community television in Santa Maria Tlahuitoltepec, Oaxaca. Photo: Erica Cusi Wortham.

sculptures and murals to reinforce this national identity pictorially, bridging the significant literacy gap of the postrevolutionary period. Flags and hymns and high ceremony in all things pertaining to the state became the norm. By the late 1940s, when the Mexican government was making full use of agrarian reform, creating some of the largest collective landholdings for peasants from expropriated private lands (called *ejidos*), the government also created the INI to standardize and increase the reach of indigenismo. In Mexico, the "menace of multiculturalism" in the 1990s, which Charles R. Hale wrote about to warn people against thinking multiculturalism solved inequalities (2002), was preceded by a decades of practices that set up the possibility of splitting cultural rights from political action.

The practice of making culture visible through audiovisual media strives to reposition culture as inherent to social and political life, and through the practices of indigenous videomakers, culture is mobilized to effect change. Taken directly from the field, the notion of making culture visible provides a framework for understanding indigenous media that sustains its complexity as a social activity and an oppositional category that also allows us to witness how broader notions of indigeneity, much like identity and nation, are constructed and contested in everyday, on-the-ground ways, through indigenous videomakers' programs and how they organize to produce them.

Making Culture Visible: How It "Works"

"Making culture visible" is a blended phrase taken in part from the field—from the image above (see figure I.1) as well as from some of my informants' exasperation that members of their own community didn't "see" what they were trying to accomplish with their media collective —and mixed with my own ideas, analyses, and imperatives. The phrase is best explained by separating its three parts. The gerund "making" is of utmost importance, as this study is primarily about a social activity and process. I describe several videos and television programs throughout the book with some detail, in order to give readers a sense of what indigenous media productions are like, but I am most concerned with the social activity that takes place around their production, circulation, and consumption. When anthropologists Faye Ginsburg and Terence Turner, whose early work on indigenous media (1991 and 1991a, respectively) legitimized indigenous media studies within the discipline, made the move, following Raymond Williams (1975), from understanding indigenous media as texts to be read for content to examining the social practices embedded in them, they reinforced and gave ethnographic texture to the notion that culture itself is produced in a self-conscious manner (Ortner 2006). With the help of British cultural studies scholars like Stuart Hall, practice theorists like Pierre Bourdieu (1993), and anthropology's own "crisis of representation"—which was prompted in part by the discipline's engagement with filmmaking in the 1970s and 1980s (Ruby 1991)—anthropologists began to appreciate that culture is always in formation, constantly updated, and that, as individuals and collectives, people play an inventive role in making their own cultures. In this sense, especially considering the embattled terrain of relations between states and indigenous peoples, culture is inherently political.[4] The culture concept that anthropologists have developed and redefined over many decades is actively taken up and given new life in bold and everyday ways by peoples and communities whose own cultures are constantly threatened.

Approaching the visual or the third part of the phrase "making culture visible," it is important to explain that the social and cultural processes discussed in this study rely to some measure on imagination as a force and faculty of social life (Appadurai 1990, 1991, 1996, 2000; Anderson 1991). In his ongoing concerns with flows and globalization, the anthropologist Arjun Appadurai writes, "One positive force that encourages an emancipatory politics of globalization is the role of the imagination in social life." He continues: "It is a faculty that informs the daily lives of ordinary people in a myriad of ways: it allows people to consider migration, resist state violence, seek social redress, and design new forms of civic association and collaboration, often across national boundaries" (2000, 6). Indigenous videomakers and activists employ this faculty as they make culture visible for the screen. Nations imagine, too, as Benedict Anderson so eloquently demonstrated with *Imagined Communities* (1991), but the point is that as indigenous authors "imagine," they are replacing dominant narratives that have long oppressed them with narratives of their own. In other words, they make visible narratives and realities that have long and systematically been made invisible by dominant societies.

Amalia Córdova and Juan Francisco Salazar suggest this is the "cultural logic of indigenous media," that it is "the way media practices become effective strategies for Indigenous peoples to shape counter-discourses and engender alternative public spheres" (2008, 40). A blatant example of this kind of accomplishment is how Radio y Video Tamix's television station, which I discuss in chapter 4, bumped commercial programming from TV Azteca off the air—at least in the five-kilometer radius that its transmitter reached—to present shows in Mixe, or Ayuuk, language, of local importance and made in their own community.

The potential for social change embedded within indigenous media is clear. For change to take effect it matters who sees indigenous media, but the relatively limited access indigenous-produced work has to mainstream circulation is not an accurate measure of it potential: indigenous media, as programs, but more important, in their very making, assert that indigenous people and communities are protagonists in their own stories. They move beyond the folkloric, safe versions of cultural plurality marketed by the state to include demonstrations of organized community life that valorize self-sustainability and self-government as a part of cultural richness. In other words, they repair the rift between culture and politics, a rift created over decades of misguided, positivist state policies that attempted to solve Mexico's "Indian problem."

As for the particularities of the visual, "making culture visible" also has to do with a physical process of reflection that indigenous media-makers often touch upon when discussing their work. Juan José García, a Zapotec media professional who will become a familiar figure by the end of this book, told me a story about how reflection works, drawn from his experiences teaching video in communities:

> Seeing themselves on the screen, it's like—man, I don't know. I don't know how to describe the sensation that it produces in people. They say, "Okay, we too can see ourselves on the screen or on the television" and ask, "Did María really make that video?" "Yes, María really did make it." "We can, too," the women said. Right? That is what seeing an image provokes, an image of a situation similar to theirs, because if you arrive and present a beautiful movie, say, a science fiction, to the community they are going to say, "That was an excellent movie but I didn't understand a thing. I'm not sure who died or who was the bad guy or who was the good guy." That happens a lot, but if you go and present an indigenous video, they say, "Ah, well, that's how we are, too. We make that kind of tortilla, but we do it differently. We also cut wood, but in another way—we don't carry it on our back; we bring it in a truck." So they start to make comparisons. It's where reflection starts.[5]

García, like a handful of other indigenous videomakers, came to video production via radio. A detailed and in-depth comparison between the two technologies and the practices associated with them may be the subject of my next book, but for now it is important to point out that state-sponsored video indígena in Mexico was preceded by a much more stable, well-funded, and less fraught indigenous radio program, also sponsored by the INI, which curiously never served as a model for how to build the indigenous video program.[6] Indigenous video was initiated at a moment of institutional transformation, whereas radio was instituted relatively early, in 1979, when indigenismo practices within the institution, while not unquestioned, were still the norm. The first INI radio station was placed in the severely marginalized Rio Balsas region of Guerrero state and was used "as a tool of support to government programs and of indigenous integration into mainstream society" (Castells-Talens 2004, 13). New radio stations were added steadily to the INI's indigenous radio network throughout the 1980s and 1990s, even as the institution's insistence on assimilation began to wane. In addition to the very different institutional profile given to radio, the crux of the dissimilarity between the two technologies also has to do with the visible aspect of video, and in turn with the process of reflection that García explained.

Reaching back to one of the earlier indigenous media projects in the hemisphere, Terence Turner's video work with the Kayapo in Brazil explains how reflection can be steered toward the defense of culture and autonomy through objectification: "By 'objectification,' I mean, firstly, the conception of themselves as having a 'culture' in our sense of the term, and secondly, the notion that his 'culture' is something to be defended and consciously reproduced through deliberate choice and political action in a situation where alternatives (namely, assimilation to the national culture) are conceivable" (1991c, 35). His body of work on the Kayapo positions objectification (and videomaking) as one aspect of cultural transformation that underpins the Kayapo's very survival.[7] Threatened communities' "social reproduction is [no longer] based on Kayapo themselves but on their successful negotiation with outside world" (Turner 1991b, 299). And self-representations on video play a key role in these negotiations: "By making their culture a political issue, and self-consciously making the dissemination of their cultural image in public demonstrations and news media a key aspect of their political struggle, the Kayapo not only transformed the meaning and content of their culture itself but also the political significance of documenting it and communicating about it to the non-Kayapo public" (Turner 1991b, 304–5). Unlike Turner, I did not witness such a transformation. Indeed, individuals whose lives and work I researched were not only fundamentally different than the Kayapo; their forms of social organization have been shaped by a centralized state for hundreds of years. Many also had a clear understanding of the political value of their *cultura* well before I entered the field (see the discussion about *comunalidad* in chapter 3), though my work does recover important moments in which indigenous individuals were "taught" how to defend and revitalize their culture in relation to seeing themselves on screens for the first time. In these processes of reflection and producing discourse about it, the camera is positioned as a neutral "electronic mirror" and indigenous mediamaking as a form of self-representation and self-determination: "In this reflection and in the discourse that emerges from it we find our place in the cosmos, we construct our identity" (Ojo de Agua 2001, 1). In other words, while the technology is introduced as neutral, a social and political stance or position, a *postura*, is attached to its use to give it purpose.

Situating "Video Indígena" as a Postura

For the sake of clarity, it is important to spell out that indigenous media is a global phenomenon (Wilson and Stewart 2008) and that video indígena and its short-lived predecessor *video indio* are specific media-production categories that were deliberately constructed in institutional settings in Mexico in the 1990s. That is not to say that video indígena has remained confined within the bureaucratic context of its creation; indeed, it has moved far beyond those initial boundaries, proliferating in many diverse social settings. It is an open category, subject to change and self-ascription, and, of course, it is also contested. In fact, a Zapotec group in Oaxaca claims that the INI stole the whole idea from them in the first place (see chapter 3). I do not endeavor to police the boundaries of video indígena as a category; rather, my purpose is to discuss it as an entangled project of alternative media born from state patronage as much as from indigenous demands for self-representation. Video indígena, in this case, is an example of "a community imagining its own identity after government intervention" (Guss 2000, 2).

While video indígena is an entangled project, video indígena programs themselves are many things. In this study they are edited video programs, not "home movies." They are for the most part documentaries privileging testimonials, though works of fiction are made, too, and their content includes community festivities, political events such as the changing of community authorities, marches, demonstrations, folktales, rituals such as day-of-the-dead ceremonies, or how-to processes like making raw sugar or a traditional meal. They are vehicles for reflection and education, collective dramas of social and cultural reproduction, legal testimony asserted as proof of promises or lies or acts of violence; they are organizing tools and instruments of advocacy and collective memory. Not surprisingly, what video indígena programs "look" like is as varied as what they are about.

While some scholars and practitioners have suggested that there is such a thing as "indigenous aesthetics," an intriguing if fraught exercise for sure, I defer in this discussion to my informants.[8] I often asked indigenous mediamakers, "What is video indígena?" and "What does it look like?" or "How can you tell when you see one?" The clearest answer I got, one that pervades this study, came from Juan José García. He said, "El video indígena no existe." "Video indígena doesn't exist because video is a totally foreign tool to the indigenous world."[9] It appears that the loaded, problematic term here is "video," not "indigenous." García asked, "How can one label video 'indigenous' if it is totally foreign to the indigenous world?" If anything, he conceded, there could be such a thing as "'video Zapoteco' or 'video Chinanteco' or even 'video Juan José.'" What this further explanation—the possibility of a video Zapoteco or video Juan José—pointedly expresses is a resistance to the inappropriate lack of specificity inherent in the category "indigenous."[10] Perhaps the emotional content of his words veiled what he really wanted to say, something like "el indígena no existe." This is clearly my own extrapolation, but his sentiment underscores the fact that the term "indígena" is highly problematic and underpins how he comes to settle on the definition that video indígena is first and foremost a proposal for social change.

An administrative category imposed on native peoples in the nineteenth century (Cadena 2000), with three hundred years of antecedents, "indígena" was designed to separate non-Europeans from Europeans—from a European perspective, of course, that has little to do with native people's own point of view. The term "indígena" has been appropriated and self-consciously resignified in many parts of Latin America as a positive label that asserts cultural difference in opposition to mainstream national culture—much like "Indian" in the United States. Ronald Neizen, in his book on the origins of indigeneity, stresses that this trend is rather new: "The interesting thing about the relative newness of this concept is that it refers to a primordial identity, to people with primary attachments to land and culture, 'traditional' people with lasting connections to ways of life that have survived from 'time immemorial'" (2003, 3). Once a desirable "othering" term for the purposes of empire and nation-building, "indigenous" has proven useful for peoples banded together to fight the state on many levels. But perhaps more troublesome than any vestiges of a European gaze, the term "indigenous" carries an uncomfortable tension as it attempts to collect a tremendously diverse group of peoples under one label. Ultimately, like the legal scholar Erica-Irene A. Daes, I question the "desirability of defining the concept" at all, since a single definition will not hold up in all regions of the world (quoted in Wilson and Stewart 2008, 12), though a definition like Neizen's does get at important commonalities. Thus I privilege a situated analysis from the field and return to Juan José García, for whom video indígena is a "postura"—his word —or position, more than a differentiated genre. In other words, "video indígena," like "indígena" itself, is an oppositional category that ties a term of resistance to a technology that can represent it.

Scholars of indigenous media have touched on a number of these oppositional aspects of indigenous media proposals in their attempt to define the practice. Faye Ginsburg, undoubtedly indigenous media's most celebrated scholar, ventured a definition of indigenous media in 1993. She writes:

> The first word—"indigenous"—respects the understandings of those Aboriginal producers who identify themselves as "First Nations" or "Fourth World People." These categories index the political circumstances shared by indigenous people around the globe. Whatever their cultural differences, such groups all struggle against a legacy of disenfranchisement of their lands, societies and cultures by colonizing European societies. . . . The second word—"media"— whether referring to satellites or VCRs, evokes the huge institutional structures of the television and film industries that tend to overwhelm the local cultural specificities of small-scale societies while privileging commercial interests that demand large audiences as a measure of success. (1993a, 558)

Put the words together and "indigenous media" describes a kind of media that represent rather than overwhelm "local cultural specificities." Indigenous media are also a kind of "small media," a category used by communications scholars Annabelle Sreberny-Mohammadi and Ali Mohammadi, who discuss the use of tape recorders in the Iranian Revolution, a category that differentiates local media from the large commercial and governmental media institutional structures to which Ginsburg refers.[11]

On the other hand, Pamela Wilson and Michelle Stewart, scholars of indigenous media, stress that indigenous media are defined by their authorship. They are "media expressions conceptualized, produced, and / or created by Indigenous peoples across the globe" (Wilson and

Stewart 2008, 2). Córdova and Salazar characterize this particular kind of authorship as "socially embedded self-representation," which builds on Ginsburg's earlier use of "embedded esthetics" to describe the indigenous videomaker's location in relation to his or her subject as "from the inside in" (Córdova and Salazar 2008, 40).[12] The Hopi artist Victor Masayesva Jr. frames this notion of embeddedness in terms of accountability: "A native filmmaker has . . . the accountability built into him. The white man doesn't have that. That's the single big distinction. Accountability as an individual, as a clan, as a tribe, as a family member. That's where we're at as Indian filmmakers" (quoted in Marubbio 2010, 3). More recently, Valerie Alia, in her book, *The New Media Nation: Indigenous Peoples and Global Communications*, focuses not on authorship or embeddedness, but rather on the space indigenous media as a whole has created: "I have called the fluid, constantly changing crossing from boundary to boundary and place to place—the *inter*nationalization of Indigenous media audiencehood and media production—the 'The New Media Nation'" (2010, 8). In other words, the New Media Nation, much like the concept of the Fourth World, is not a place as much as a pan-indigenous "global highway," along which indigenous peoples travel, in the words of George Manuel, who coined the term "Fourth World." Manuel said, "'The Fourth World is not . . . a destination. It is the right to travel freely, not only on our own road but in our own vehicles'" (Alia 2010, 13–14). These foregoing definitions express different key aspects of indigenous media that collectively underscore the imperative of understanding indigenous media as practice and process.

In Mexico, many formal conventions in video indígena are not embedded; they are for the most part taught by nonindigenous media professionals and the indigenous videomakers trained by them, or they are borrowed from mass media (television) formats. But, on the other hand, as García explained,

> Video indígena is loaded with symbols, codes; it is loaded with what we up there in the sierra call "comunalidad." What are its elements? Principally, collectivity, language, facial features, intimacy. That is to say, in video indígena the intimacy of a family is there in such a way that it is barely noticeable. In other words, watching the video you enter into that family, into the community and the community sees you the same; you are not a stranger but

just another person from the community with a machine stuck to your shoulder that is an extension of your body, that permits you to tape what you want. (2000)

In this sense, the videomaker is embedded even if the formal aesthetic is not, though as I discuss in chapter 4, embeddedness cannot always be assumed. Guillermo Monteforte, a close, nonindigenous colleague of García's who has made indigenous media his life's work, added another dimension of indigenous aesthetics: they have as much to do with "someone not knowing [so much] what they want to come out on tape as with [the nonindigenous viewer's] predisposition to find something that looks different."[13] Echoing a familiar modernist fantasy of finding renewal and refuge from the malaise of mechanical reproduction in something "primitive," "primordial," or authentic, Monteforte reveals his and his colleagues' Western art and film-school training (Benjamin 1978). These echoes resurface in my concluding chapter as international audiences participate in the construction of indigeneity.

There are still other, differently situated approaches to defining indigenous media, such as K-Xhon's "own way of seeing" and Radio y Video Tamix's *televisión sin reglas*, or "television without rules," that openly oppose convention and structure all together (see chapters 3 and 4, respectively). In between embeddedness and conventions taught, in between aesthetic accidents and finding what one looks for, video indígena remains first and foremost a postura that positions indigenous videomakers close to their communities and empowers their visual messages with the strength of self-representation.

As the videomakers trained under the INI's program succeeded in shaking off institutional dependency and became increasingly aligned with the Zapatista movement and, more recently, with the popular movement in Oaxaca that started in 2006, "video indígena," as a term, has fallen out of use among those involved in creating it. They now prefer more open-ended but still oppositional terms like *comunicación alternativa* as if video indígena is stained with sour experiences of government sponsorship or representative of a time in which indigenous videomakers had less control. To García, video indígena "had its moment" (2011). The popular movement in Oaxaca also seems to have eased some of the necessity of maintaining the indigenous label to describe their work, though interestingly the movement known as Asamblea Popular de los Pueblos de Oaxaca has taken key indigenous forms of social organization and collective decision making—the community *asamblea,* or "assembly"—as its defining structure. My use of the term "indigenous media" facilitates positioning this work within a particular body of scholarship, but not without engaging many of its complexities and internal dilemmas.

Locating Myself: Constructing the Multisited Field

Doing research in a country to which I "belong" and in which I have extensive family was somewhat of a mixed blessing. It was enormously satisfying to actually live in Mexico after a life of summer vacations and family visits, but at times the demands on my attention from family weighed almost as heavily on my mind as my research agenda. I owe a great deal to my mother's family, not the least of which is for helping me grow up bilingual. My grandmother's house, in the heart of one of the craziest cities I know, became even more of a refuge during my year of field research, but the comfort of familiar faces and a home where the beds and meals are made for you was transformed into a culture shock of a different order than I had ever experienced transitioning back to east Texas after a summer in Mexico. Few members of my family understood my interest in *indígenas,* and I tried not to resent them for being exemplary members of what the anthropologist Guillermo Bonfil Batalla has called "imaginary Mexico" (Bonfil Batalla 1996, xvi), but the shock of going (sometimes in the same day) from Doña Jose's modest home on a steep slope of the Mixe sierra to the walled-in, expansive gardens surrounding grandmother's house in the San Miguel Chapultepec neighborhood of Mexico City produced more than the usual dose of adjustment anxieties despite the warm "ciao, joya" my Noni (she was Italian) would greet and send me off with.

My constant comings and goings during the period of sustained field research in 1999 and 2000, in Tamazulapám, Oaxaca City, and other parts of the state, Chiapas, Mexico City, and Guatemala, not only followed paths well worn by indigenous videomakers, but also represented my own efforts to tie my "field" together. George Marcus, an anthropologist who made important contributions toward steering anthropology out of its "crisis of representation," writes that "the activist role of indigenous peoples as media producers . . . has reconfigured the space in which the ethnography of many of anthropology's traditional subjects can be effectively done; they have also made this space

inherently multi-sited" (1995). Indeed, the cultural formation and social process at the heart of my research are highly mobile and require
sustained participant-observation study in a variety of settings. Only
this way could I fully appreciate some of the problematic local-global
disconnects that emerge when indigenous videomakers present their
work to international audiences, for example. In this reconfigured
space, I have worked alongside indigenous videomakers (especially in
the exhibition of their work) as often as I have researched their lives
and work.

Working in a multisited field helps take full advantage of the recent
rethinking about the traditional "field" of anthropology—where a singular focus on the *local* has shifted to more nuanced attention to the
practice of *location* (Gupta and Ferguson 1997). Adopting a form of
ethnographic research that Marcus has described as designed "to examine the circulation of cultural meanings, objects, and identities in
diffuse time-space"(1995, 96) has allowed me to focus on the practices
of affirming and constructing both place and identity, nation and indigeneity. In other words, the "community" in my study is both a circum-
scribed place on the ground with a corresponding dot on a detailed
map of the state of Oaxaca, a dot standing for, say, Tamazulápam, and
also place constructed in the visual discourse authored by videomakers
(in dialogical manner with their audiences) who struggle to claim their
legitimacy at home but also contribute to broader notions of indigeneity beyond their home communities.

The adjustment anxieties I mentioned above, nearly constant travel
and my own process of locating myself somewhere in between being
an anthropologist, advocate, and facilitator impacted my work in significant ways. My desire to understand indigenous media practices
through their complexities sacrificed a certain amount of depth or
continuity that only daily life provides. But I saw no other way to
organize my research without a team of assistants and several more
years of funded field research. At the welcomed "risk" of writing a
history, I feel my work makes an important recuperative contribution
to understanding the changing *imagén* of indigenous people of Mexico
that has typically been considered in terms of big screen movies, during a period when self-representation became a demand and a reality.

To be concrete, my sustained field sites included Tamazulápam del
Espiritú Santo, a Mixe village in the northeastern highlands of Oaxaca
state; Oaxaca City, where Ojo de Agua Comunicación and numerous

other indigenous organizations have offices and where INI has its largest state delegation as well as the main Centro de Video Indígena (CVI); San Cristóbal de las Casas and Ejido Morelia, Chiapas, where the Chiapas Media Project has its Mexican headquarters and conducted one of many video training workshops, respectively; and, finally, Mexico City, where among many other things, the INI headquarters was located. The broader perimeters of my field encompassed Santa María Tlahuitoltepec, the Mixe community neighboring Tamazulapam (and against whom Tamazulapam has engaged in over a decade of agrarian disputes), where an incipient and rival television project was being tested in January of 2000; the region of the Rincón de la Sierra Juárez, made up of a cluster of Zapotec communities in Oaxaca's Sierra Norte, where the Zapotec videomaker Crisanto Manzano Avella hosted a video screening series in December 1999; El Pípila, a multiethnic indigenous community in the Isthmus of Oaxaca, where the CVI conducted a video workshop for members of the women's caucus of the Peasant and Indigenous Union of the Northern Zone of the Isthmus of Tehuantepec; the Chinantla region of the state of Oaxaca, where the Chiapas Media Project and the CVI organized a joint series of traveling screenings; Morelia, Michoacán, and the immediate surroundings, where the INI established the second CVI, and where several Purépecha videomakers live and work; and Quetzaltenango, Guatemala, where the sixth Festival Americano de Cine y Video Indígena took place, in August of 1999. In all these settings, I relied mostly on participant observation to gather data, though on many occasions I conducted focused (audio recorded) interviews with videomakers and media professionals involved in indigenous media, as well as with current and former employees of the INI who participated directly in the developing and running the TMA program.

Since completing my field research and dissertation (Wortham 2002), I have returned to Oaxaca on several occasions and stayed in close touch with the former director and cofounder of the Chiapas Media Project, though I have not returned to Chiapas since 1999. Before my full-time period of field research, between 1999 and 2000, I attended several important "events" in the development of the INI's TMA program. In 1994 I attended the closing phase of the last large-scale TMA workshop, held in Tlacolula de Matamoros, in the Central Valley of the state of Oaxaca. Trainees were in the editing phase of the workshop. While there, I conducted a series of interviews with trainees (with help from the French journalist José Reynes, affectionately known as "Tio Pepe") and witnessed the ceremonious arrival of community authorities summoned to the valley to receive video production equipment donated to them by the INI. The workshop ended with the inauguration of the CVI, in Oaxaca City. Later that year, the INI and several international partners organized the first Interamerican Encuentro de Videoastas Indígenas, in Tlaxcala, Mexico, not far from Mexico City. This encuentro ended with the formation of an independent organization of indigenous Mexican videomakers that never really got off the ground.

In 1996, I conducted preliminary research in Oaxaca and Chiapas. Thanks to my contacts in Oaxaca, I was able to get an "observer" invitation to sit at the communications table of the EZLN's Foro Nacional, which took place in San Cristóbal de las Casas, Chiapas, in January of that year. Discussions among EZLN guests and advisers were incorporated after the forum into the San Andrés Accords on Indigenous Rights and Culture. I also attended two introductory video-production workshops held at the CVI and assisted with the presentation and translation of the video series *Traveling with the Ancients*, curated by Sally Berger, of the Museum of Modern Art, New York City. On this trip, in early 1996, I visited the highland Mixtec region of Oaxaca with one of the rising stars of video indígena at the time, Emigdio Julián Caballero, a Mixteco from San Antonio Huitepec, and his entourage for the day, Sally Berger and Jonathan Kandell, a freelance journalist writing about indigenous media in Mexico for the magazine *Natural Science* (the story he wrote was never printed). I also journeyed to the isthmus to meet one of the other rising stars, Teófila Palafox, a Huave-Ikoods videomaker from San Mateo del Mar. Both Emigdio and Palafox are winners of Media Arts Fellowships, funded jointly by the Rockefeller Foundation and the John D. and Catherine T. MacArthur Foundation (in 1996 and 1995, respectively).[14]

I first learned about the INI's TMA project (Sámano Chong 1992) at the fourth Festival Americano de Cine y Video Indígena, held in Cusco and Lima, Peru, in 1992. I served as an associate director of the festival in 1992 and have remained as much as possible on the festival circuit since then, as a juror for their fifth festival, held in Santa Cruz, Bolivia, in 1996, and as an invited guest for the sixth festival, in Quetzaltenango, Guatemala, in 1999. In the intervening years, I was invited to participate as an international guest at the first Abya-Yala Film and

Video Festival, organized by the Quechua videomaker Alberto Mue-nala and the Confederation of Indigenous Nationalities of Ecuador (CONAIE), in Quito, Ecuador, in 1994. The Abya-Yala Festival started as a counterfestival—usurped from the Festival Americano's nonin-digenous leadership—which has become an annual program within CONAIE's cultural activities.

From 1993 through 2000, I worked as a media programmer for the Film and Video Center of the National Museum of the American Indian (NMAI), Smithsonian Institution, New York City, where I built relationships with Latin American and, in particular, Mexican indige-nous mediamakers and coordinated Latin American selections for the NMAI Native American Film and Video Festivals in 1995 and 1997. In 1998 I developed a cross-border-traveling video festival called Video América Indígena/Video Native America (VAI), in which twelve na-tive video productions based in the United States and Canada, selected in Oaxaca and Michoacán by committees made up of indigenous video-makers, were dubbed into Spanish with funding from the binational Fidecomiso Para La Cultura. The video tour was planned in institutional settings, but once the tour was underway, it took on a life of its own, subject to the unexpected pleasures (and, at times, frustrations) of indig-enous hospitality in Mexico. At each site we engaged in workshop-style exchanges about making indigenous video, watched a number of the programs, and shared warm meals and excellent company with our hosts and other community residents. We drove miles and miles—especially in Oaxaca—on asphalt and dirt roads. We rode in the back of pickup trucks (dressed with the INI's "Poder Ejecutivo Federal" logo) through lush valleys, rolling hills dotted with lakes, high rocky mountains, and cloud forests, as well as the crazy streets and freeways of Mexico City. One of our guests, Beverly Singer, a Tewa-Navajo videomaker and academic, writes, "Mexico and its indigenous people reopened my thinking about my cultural priorities. Beauty and severity, culture and poverty, clouds, mountains and volcanoes were mingled together in a context that makes the current indigenous movement in Chiapas com-pletely necessary. The presence of the government soldiers, in militia gear with automatic weapons, at checkpoints along all the roads we traveled, were strong reminders to me of the ever present danger that exists for the Native people of Mexico. The trip reawakened in my creative spirit the desire to preserve what belongs to indigenous peo-ple" (2001a, 52). All our Native American guests, none of whom had been to Mexico before, were overwhelmed by the healthy state of indigenous languages in most of the communities we visited.

Finally, my exposure to the possibilities of studying media as culture was facilitated and shaped in important ways through New York University's Program in Culture and Media and the Center for Media, Culture and History (where I worked as an assistant during its first year of operation). Both the program and the center were founded and are directed by Faye Ginsburg, who was my principal academic adviser and continues to be an important mentor.

It will perhaps not come as a surprise, after reading this long list of field sites and experiences, that the task of tying them all together in some kind of coherent manner has pulled me in numerous different directions as I wrote this book. As much as possible I attempt to write from the intersections (García Canclini 2001, 12) and represent multiple perspectives (Appadurai 2000, 8). This strategy allows me to refrain from offering rigid definitions, in favor of engaging the dilemmas, contradictions, and broader processes. If not exactly science, what I practice is what the anthropologist Néstor García Canclini describes as "a nomadic social science" (1989, 15), but either way, the following pages contain very human stories about vying for recognition and the right to have some control over the forces that shape our lives, by imagining social change or by making culture visible.

The Trajectory of This Book

I have organized this book into three parts, the first part beginning with two chapters that contextualize the emergence of indigenous video in Mexico in terms of broader issues of indigeneity constituted globally and nationally, as well as in terms of specific institutional contexts in which video indígena was "invented." Part 2 moves to the history and practices of specific indigenous media organizations that in one way or another became entangled with government-sponsored media. Part 3 examines a media organization that emerged in a binational manner from independent media communities in the United States and Mexico to service Zapatista civil communities in Chiapas. The concluding chapter reviews and reframes some of the issues and complexities discussed throughout the book, while broadening the understanding of how indigenous media play in transnational areas of festival exhibition.

Chapter 1 opens with a discussion of key documents—ILO Convention No. 169, the Declaration of the Rights of Indigenous Peoples, and the San Andrés Accords on the Rights of Indigenous People—that outline indigenous peoples' rights globally and within a specifically Mexican context. I examine the notions of indigeneity, autonomy, and self-determination, grounding them in the local settings of Oaxaca and Chiapas as well as the broader context of the Mexican nation and its history. In doing so, I suggest that indigenous autonomy is not necessarily incompatible with nationhood. Through a discussion of the history of indigenismo (as practices, policies, and programs tied to the Mexican state), I illustrate the emergence of a forced fissure between culture and politics, which making culture visible mediates. Video indígena was born as official indigenismo waned. Yet, under state sponsorship, it ultimately did not change the terms of self-representation, because video indígena was safely positioned as a "cultural" (apolitical) phenomenon. State-sponsored video indígena can therefore be seen as an example of "neoindigenismo," a new, neoliberal form of assimilationist policy (Rodriguez and Castells-Talens 2010).

Moving to the specific institutional context of video indígena in the second chapter, I argue that video indígena did not simply emerge: it was taught. I focus on the agency of individual actors—particularly the video instructors and their students. Their perspectives and experiences illuminate why video indígena in Mexico has so often taken the form of documentary and why it is vexed by particular internal contradictions (such as the tension between personal and collective authorship, which mirrors the conflict between individual and collective rights more broadly). Further, it becomes clear that what is taught is more than video techniques and practices: a social postura is also taught, as local actors engage in the project of making culture visible, they assume an activist approach to using visual media to assert indigenous autonomy. I focus on two major phases of the teaching of video indígena: national video workshops and the establishment of the CVI in Oaxaca City. Also included in this chapter is a visual intermission of sorts that illustrates video instructors' discourse about production and provides images of a community video workshop held in El Pípila, a multiethnic indigenous community in the isthmus of Oaxaca.

Part 2 shifts to particular media organizations and their activities in Oaxaca. Chapter 3 looks at several indigenous media initiatives in Oaxaca that either precede or emerged from the INI's TMA program.

Attempting to distance themselves from state sponsorship, these initiatives all complicate the notion of video indígena as a social process. I discuss three organizations: Fundación Comunalidad A.C., a community-based, nongovernmental organization involved in a regional radio project; K-Xhon Video-Cine Zapoteca, an urban-based, antigovernmental organization that sees itself as having inspired the INI's TMA program; and Ojo de Agua Comunicación S.C., an urban-based collective whose staff came directly out of the INI's TMA program, the CVI in Oaxaca City. The histories and narratives of these indigenous organizations demonstrate how communications media—radio, video, and low-power television—became central to the consolidation of regional autonomy and community in Oaxaca.

Chapter 4 focuses on Radio y Video Tamix, a community-based media initiative situated in a highland Mixe community. Guided by my ethnographic experience in Tamazulapam del Espíritu Santo, this chapter looks at how video indígena fares in a community setting. After describing the Mixe region, I detail the history of Radio y Video Tamix, discussing one video program from each of three historical moments to illustrate how the group grew and incorporated new perspectives over time. The history of this initiative did not unfold unproblematically; rather, it was punctuated by internal conflicts and tensions. I examine how producers of video indígena negotiated the dilemmas that arose in their home community as state sponsorship, foreign funding, foreign travel, and the expense of the programs spurred conflict, jealousy, and suspicion among community members. I analyze these dilemmas and how the group confronted them as a process of achieving embeddedness, showing how Radio y Video Tamix overtly constructed (rather than assumed) their representativity.

Part 3 offers points of comparison. Chapter 5 focuses on the history, strategies, and initiatives of the Chiapas Media Project/Promedios, one of the most vital indigenous media organizations in Mexico today. This binational (United States-Mexico) nongovernmental organization has provided video and computer equipment and training to members of Zapatista rebel communities since 1998. While there are important similarities between indigenous media in Oaxaca and Chiapas, there are significant differences as well. Both exemplify what Monteforte calls "comunicación de lucha" (social struggle media), but the Chiapas project was more overtly political from its inception: it began as revolutionary media, as part of the Zapatista movement.

Rather than an ethnographic introduction to the region, I provide a brief summary of some of the main factors that led to the Zapatista uprising with a focus on how the revolutionaries developed the consensual, decision-making process that the Chiapas Media Project relies on to produce media. Through Zapatista-specific community organizations and centers, the Chiapas Media Project delivers media training and equipment to members of civil communities living in *rebeldia*, in a way that ties media production directly to the revolutionary movement and structure. The Chiapas Media Project also established a sustainability and distribution model early on as a part of the project, rather than as an afterthought, as was the case with the INI's program. After discussing the project itself, I then describe videos from two distinct moments in its history.

In the concluding chapter, I offer a consideration of how indigenous media screen on the international stage, through a discussion of one last video, which I think is exemplary of indigenous media and the process of making culture visible in Mexico, *Dulce Convivencia/Sweet Gathering* (2004) by Filoteo Gómez Martínez, a Mixe videomaker whom I have come to know only more recently. The interesting and complex backstory of the documentary is evident only if we consider its making. A brief consideration of how the video has played to different audiences evidences the ways audiences are part of the process of making culture visible.

PART 1

Broader Contexts for Situating Video Indígena

ONE

Global and National Contexts
of Video Indígena

1. Governments shall have the responsibility for developing, with the participation of [indigenous and tribal peoples], coordinated and systematic action to protect the rights of these peoples and to guarantee respect for their integrity.

2. Such action shall include measures for: (a) ensuring that members of [indigenous and tribal groups] benefit on an equal footing from the rights and opportunities which national laws and regulations grant to other members of the population; (b) promoting the full realization of the social, economic and cultural rights of [indigenous and tribal peoples] with respect for their social and cultural identity, their customs and traditions and their institutions; (c) assisting the members of the peoples concerned to eliminate socio-economic gaps that may exist between indigenous and other members of the national community, in a manner compatible with their aspirations and ways of life.

**Article 2, ILO Convention 169 on
Indigenous and Tribal Peoples (1989)**

1. Indigenous peoples have the right to establish their own media in their own languages and to have access to all forms of non-indigenous media without discrimination.

2. States shall take effective measures to ensure that State-owned media duly reflect indigenous cultural diversity. States, without prejudice to ensuring full freedom of expression, should encourage privately owned media to adequately reflect indigenous cultural diversity.

**Article 16, United Nations Declaration
of the Rights of Indigenous Peoples (2007)**

With the purpose of creating an intercultural dialogue from the community level up to the national level that would permit a new and positive relationship between pueblos indígenas and between them and the rest of society, it is essential to endow these pueblos with their own means of communication, which are also key instruments for the development of their cultures. Therefore, it will be proposed to the respective national authorities that they prepare a new communications law that will allow the pueblos indígenas to acquire, operate and administer their own communications media.

**San Andrés Accords on Indigenous Rights
and Culture (1996)**

The documents quoted above were drafted in different contexts—the first two in relative peace among international counsels, the third in a war between a state and a rebel army. Taken together, they garner the collective force of countless indigenous representatives, activists, and experts who tirelessly engage the structures of power that, in turn, continue to make empty gestures that fall tragically short of the kinds of structural change many indigenous peoples seek. These documents also place self-representation squarely within the context of indigenous rights and self-determination. While making indigenous video does not lead directly to increased autonomy in ways that are easy to measure, indigenous video, as a practice, is an expression or assertion of self-determination. Gaining access to the means of audiovisual communication is an accomplishment, a victory, in the process of securing control over lives long determined and represented by others. I use these important international documents to open this chapter on the global and national contexts of video indígena in order to situate this particular media "postura" (position) amid much broader circuits of action and discourse, but also to bring these global discourses home, as it were, within the Mexican context with a brief exegesis of situated notions of autonomy and a detailed history of Mexico's Instituto Nacional Indigenista.

The possibility of the "global indigeneity" that Pamela Wilson and Michelle Stewart discuss in their introduction to *Global Indigenous Media: Cultures, Poetics, and Politics* is built on foundations and openings forged by the growing concern for human rights and the rights of once colonized peoples in the late 1960s, as well as on the civil rights movement of the same era in the United States (2008). International indigenism is a relatively new "global political entity," as Ronald Neizen asserts, that "has the potential to influence the way states manage their affairs and even to reconfigure the usual alignments of nationalism and state sovereignty" (2003, 3). Indeed, international conventions and declarations such as the ILO's Convention 169 on Indigenous and Tribal Peoples and the UN's Declaration on the Rights of Indigenous Peoples are ratified by states, signaling their legal obligation to make and maintain necessary changes in domestic practices and policies in order to fulfill the various articles. International organizations like the UN and the ILO play a key role in deciding global agendas, in channeling where resources are to be applied, and more important, they provide a powerful space (albeit mostly discursive or legal) in which indigenous activists and organizations can appeal for support and gain international visibility, leap-frogging repressive state regimes.

The ILO was founded in Switzerland with the participation of nine countries, in 1919, as part of the Treaty of Versailles, which ended the First World War, with the goal that "universal, lasting peace can be established only if it is based upon social justice" (Rogers et al. 2009, 3). As "a standard-setting agency" the ILO is a tripartite organization—"the only international intergovernmental institution in which governments do not have the exclusive voting power in setting standards and policies" (Rogers et al. 2009, 12)—and has established nearly 200 conventions on labor that have been ratified by many of its member nations. The ILO became the first specialized agency of the newly formed UN in 1946 and in 1957 adopted the first convention related to the rights of Indigenous and Tribal Populations, Convention No. 107.[1] This convention was undergirded by the familiar assumption that assimilation offers the best future for indigenous people, much as was advocated in Mexico throughout most of the twentieth century. It was not until the late 1980s, with the rise in participation of NGOs that bridged the communication and reality gap between these high-level arenas and people on the ground, in villages and communities, that scholars and government representatives began to see the need for a revised convention. In 1989 the ILO adopted Convention No. 169 on Indigenous and Tribal Peoples, which presents a human rights-based approach to indigenous policies from the "standpoint of multiculturalism" (Rogers et al. 2009, 85). The shift from "populations" to "peoples" in the title of the convention is widely seen as a positive move that opens the door for self-determination and the recognition of political rights, even though the ILO is primarily interested in mandating economic and social rights: "The ILO was the first to be able to adopt the use of this term 'peoples'—although in so doing Convention No. 169 provided that the use of the term did not determine its meaning in international law" (Rogers et al. 2009, 89). Mexico was the first Latin American member nation to ratify Convention No. 169, in May of 1990, two years into the administration of President Salinas Carlos de Gortari (1988–94). President Gortari subsequently spearheaded constitutional reforms that for the first time ever in Mexico's history formally recognized the "pluricultural" composition of the country, signaling Mexico's move to join the global sentiment to protect the rights of indigenous peoples when, in fact, calls for recognizing cultural pluralism had been vociferously made by leading scholars inside Mexico since the late 1970s. It was also under the Gortari administration that the Instituto Nacional Indigenista (INI) launched their indigenous video program.

The Declaration of the Rights of Indigenous Peoples began its journey within a context that sought to protect not just labor rights, but human rights. The atrocities of the Second World War and the subsequent establishment of the UN, in 1945, institutionalized with broad international participation a concept of human rights that had previously existed in many literate and nonliterate societies. The preamble to the Universal Declaration of Human Rights, adopted by all member nations in 1948, states that "the recognition of the inherent dignity and of the equal and inalienable rights of all members of the human family is the foundation of freedom, justice, and peace in the world."[2] The nongovernmental organization International Work Group for Indigenous Affairs, which was founded by human rights activists and anthropologists in 1968 who shared an awareness of the need for special measures to protect the rights of indigenous peoples, urged the UN to establish the Working Group on Indigenous Populations in 1982. In 1988, the UN requested that the group begin putting together a set of principles for a draft declaration of rights specific to indigenous peoples. The first draft of the declaration was completed in 1993, but it took another fourteen years of reviews, debates, and negotiations between independent experts, government representatives, indigenous activists, and participating NGOs before the document was finally ratified by the global assembly, in September of 2007. In the intervening years, the UN launched the first International Decade of the World's Indigenous Peoples (1995–2004), in order to bring global awareness to indigenous peoples' struggles. Now, approaching the end of the second Decade of the World's Indigenous People (2005–15), the declaration remains without covenants to transform its articles into international law. Nevertheless, the document stands as an important global referent to which indigenous peoples can appeal when seeking protection of their rights, to strengthen and maintain their own institutions, cultures, and traditions, and to pursue their development in accordance with their aspirations and needs. Mexico and 143 other member nations ratified the declaration while eleven nations abstained and four voted against it.[3]

The Universal Declaration of Human Rights, like the Universal Declaration of Rights of Indigenous Peoples, attempts to guarantee our rights as individual persons, independently of what the governments under which we live do or say, allow or do not allow. The authority of the nation-state is bypassed as our individual rights are deemed indivisible and inalienable, and, of course, universal. The declarations provide a higher order to which we can appeal when our individual rights are violated, but there is less recourse for asserting and protecting collective rights. The rights of collectives, as peoples, continue to be a primary concern of many indigenous groups and, without a doubt, are a fundamental issue in any struggle over self-determination and autonomy, as collectives with rights not only pose a radical alternative to the primacy of the individual in Western democratic culture, but tend to directly clash with issues of national sovereignty (Anaya 2004). Indeed, the nation-state plays a critical role as the protection of our rights cannot be achieved without the cooperation of nations and their governments, and sadly, the nation-state remains the most enduring obstacle to real change in favor of indigenous peoples, as the unfulfilled San Andrés Accords remind us.

The San Andrés Accords on Indigenous Rights and Culture are specific to Mexico but resonate directly with the documents discussed above. The accords were signed by both the Mexican government (at the time headed by President Ernesto Zedillo) and the Zapatista Army of National Liberation (EZLN), on February 16, 1996, in the village of San Andrés Larráinzar, after many rounds of dialogue between the two parties and among broader audiences and experts consulted by both sides. Based on principles of respect, participation, and autonomy, the

San Andrés Accords were intended to be the first in a series of accords that outlined a new relationship between indigenous peoples and the state of Mexico. The second set of accords, on land, were never debated, however, as the EZLN broke off negotiations with the Mexican government after the Zedillo administration introduced a flawed and watered-down counterproposal later that same year. The "Indigenous Law," known as the COCOPA proposal, which the Mexican congress did pass in 2001 after the opposition president Vicente Fox promised to renew the peace process, was loosely based on the accords but was emptied of all their potential for structural change. The Indigenous Law passed under Fox—which the Zapatista spokesperson renamed the "Constitutional Recognition of the Rights and Culture of the Landowners and Racists"—put the possibility of any indigenous autonomy onto the states.[4] The Mexican supreme court ruled, in 2002, on the hundreds of objections filed against the law: "The Magna Carta should always prevail, and any secondary laws (such as those proposed in the original COCOPA legislation) which opposed it should not be obeyed by any authorities" (Stephen 2009, 130).

Forms of indigenous autonomy—already and for many centuries practiced in Mexico—are not inherently incompatible with nationhood or state sovereignty. Indeed, these documents outline specific ways in which indigenous self-determination and "nation" can openly and manifestly co-exist, just as today's forms of indigenous autonomy such as self-government and self-representation offer situated and daily evidence of such a co-existence. However Convention No. 169, the Universal Declaration of Rights of Indigenous Peoples and the San Andrés Accords on Indigenous Rights and Culture come on the heels of nearly a century of assimilation practices and programs—known as indigenismo—that are deeply engrained in relations between the state and indigenous peoples, and therefore difficult to reverse. Video indígena emerges at the end of official indigenismo as if to deal it its final blow. Conceived in an experimental moment within the very institution that embodied indigenismo, video indígena, as state-sponsored indigenous media, nevertheless ultimately fell short of changing the terms of self-representation. The history of unequal relations between the state and indigenous peoples, so heavily shaped by assimilation programs which pitted culture against political action and structural change, weighed too heavily, and video indígena was brought back in line with safe versions of cultural expression and pluralism, in response to the Zapatista movement in 1994. Indeed, in a recent study on indigenous media sponsored currently by the Comisión Nacional para el Desarrollo de los Pueblos Indígenas (CDI), which was created in 2003 to replace INI, communication scholars Jorge Rodriquez Ramos and Antoni Castells-Talens conclude that the CDI practices *neoindigenismo*, a new form of an old assimilationist policy with a neoliberal bent (2011).

It is important to note that global, national, regional, and local arenas of social activity and discourse constantly intersect and interact; and while this level of complexity is critical to understanding video indígena, I feel it is my obligation here to thread the needle through the local, to assert the most particular examples of indigenous self-determination and the specific struggles indigenous actors face, while sewing up as many loose ends as possible. Videomakers like Juan José García and others have never traveled to Geneva to participate directly in discussions and draftings of declarations and conventions that have come to define the imperative of indigenous self-determination for the broadest audiences. Some of them, however, have sat at the table with Zapatista authorities at conferences and workshops where the San Andrés Peace Accords were vetted. And all of them, in one manner or another, live forms of self-determination and autonomy on a daily basis as members and leaders of their communities, as activists and as videomakers whose work it is to make their culture visible.

Proposals from Indigenous Activists and Scholars in Mexico: On Autonomy and Self-Determination

Most activists and scholars agree that the question of indigenous autonomy calls for significant structural changes in the organization of the Mexican state, but it is important to consider from the outset that the community-based proposal calls for recognizing what has always existed within the Mexican state: indigenous autonomy at the community level. The *comunalista* proposal relies on notions of autonomy as "lived" or, as the Zapotec videomaker Juan José García put it, as "esquemas que hay" (schemes that exist). For García and other videomakers in Oaxaca engaged in the autonomy movement, community-based autonomy is seen as natural. Indigenous autonomy is composed of "community practices that are real, that permit us to make and carry through decisions on our own, in practice."[5] For one of García's Zapotec colleagues, Francisco Luna, autonomy is more about self-sufficiency, "about being able to generate and carry out projects rather than depend on government assistance."[6] Like García, Luna believes that "autonomy exists in various aspects of community life." Rather than something to be achieved, in the words of the Zapotec K-Xhon collective, autonomy is more about "respect for what is now": "There will be and should be many, many autonomies, all of them respectable and respected. Autonomy is to become responsible to ourselves. In each family, in each neighborhood or street, in each community or subdivision, from deciding what to do with our trash and other waste to deciding what kind of education we want for our children" (Topil 1994, 1).

In Oaxaca's Sierra Norte, indigenous intellectuals, with the help of the anthropologist Juan José Rendón, who organized "cultural dialogue" workshops in the region in the late 1980s, have distilled community life down to four components, which include (1) land "as a physical collective space conceived as mother and creator of life"; (2) *tequio*, or "communal labor," which is the manner in which "indigenous pueblos relate to land and nature"; (3) the general community assembly, which is the supreme power and collective decision-making body of the community; and (4) the fiesta, which "contributes to the articulation and cohesion of community life" and has its frame of reference embedded in agricultural and religious cycles (Regino Montes 1998). This four-part definition of community life—land, tequio, assembly, and fiesta—underwrites the concept of community-based *comunalidad*, or "autonomy" (Martínez Luna 1995). "To reconstruct [indigenous pueblos] we have to start with reinforcing what we already have," writes the Mixe leader Adelfo Regino Montes (1998, 420). Luna agrees: the problem is "getting people to realize this, to revalorize more than anything else that they have their own resources to work the land without having to depend on someone."[7] As activists and videomakers, their task is "about giving [people] a little help, to orient them and revalorize what they have and the work they have been doing all along, to know that the knowledge the grandparents have is not lost, on the contrary, that it needs to be recovered and applied."[8] Securing or building community autonomy is a kind of consciousness-raising process and provides the necessary foundation from which broader forms of autonomy can be envisioned. Regino Montes believes that "communities should be the point of departure for relationships with the nation-state"; rather than preclude the possibility of regional autonomy, community autonomy forms its basis (1998, 421).

Community-based autonomy, however, is not applicable in every part of indigenous Mexico.[9] At a day-long conference in 2001 on indigenous and migrant rights, at the Center for U.S.-Mexican Studies at the University of San Diego, California, the anthropologist Rodolfo Stavenhagen, one of the foremost scholars on autonomy in Mexico, conceded that "autonomy" had remained somehow beyond description (Stavenhagen 2001). Autonomy is difficult to define, in large part because it is a deeply contentious issue that threatens notions of national sovereignty, but also because it must be conceived in a site-specific manner attuned to historical, geographical, as well as sociopolitical and cultural specificities. Complicating matters, there is no known indigenous word for "autonomy," though equivalents have been suggested, such as the Mixe concept of *pöjxün kajpün* (force of the people) or *nuestra propia palabra* (our own word).[10]

Self-determination is a legal right conferred to peoples in international law. Self-determination covers several kinds of rights, according to Stavenhagen: "The right to preserve and develop their own cultures, the right to land and territory and the development of economic resources on their own terms, yet within the context of existing nation-states" (1992, 436). Rather than coterminus, the relationship between autonomy and self-determination is best understood where autonomy is a "system through which sociocultural groups exercise their right to self-determination" (Díaz Polanco 1997, 98).[11] What that particular system is—what it looks and feels like, how it is structured and legally protected, or not—however, is up for grabs.

The anthropologists Miguel A. Bartolomé and Alicia M. Barabas write, "Autonomy is none other than the recognition of the right to self-determination of the pueblos that supposes not only the transference of a series of powers of the State to ethnic regions but also the acceptance of cultural difference in the organization of those powers" (1998, 13). Stavenhagen's two-part strategy to defend (if not define) indigenous autonomy has been to discuss indigenous rights in terms of human rights, and to promote the study of indigenous customary law. In 1988, with the publication of a detailed book on indigenous rights and human rights, Stavenhagen anticipated the EZLN's call for a new pact with the government:

The principal thesis of this work is that the violation of indigenous populations' human rights in Latin America is not an isolated or fortuitous phenomenon, rather one that responds to structural conditions of the economic and political history of the region. Moreover, the legal and institutional structure of our countries, rooted in a colonial system of government and economic and political liberalism of the nineteenth century, is the frame that permits precisely—though not intentionally—the violation of indigenous peoples' human rights. The national legislation, in so far as they effect indigenous populations, have contributed in great measure to the critical situation of these peoples. This legislation emerges from a concept of State and national society that favors such a situation. And, thus, it is in the same legislation and in the philosophy of the State and nation that we find part of the explanation for the problematic situation of indigenous human rights. (1988, 10)

Once the liberal nation-state of the nineteenth century (and by extension the neoliberal one of the twenty-first century) is identified as the leading explanation for indigenous peoples' continued subjugation, Stavenhagen proceeds to identify flaws in the construction of the nation, flaws that in turn present possibilities for alternatives to be imagined.

In the introductory chapter to an edited volume on indigenous customary law, Stavenhagen makes a plea for scholarly research on indigenous customary law because as he argues, "The recognition of customary law by the state, opening a space for the acceptance of legal and judicial pluralism, would bring an indispensable element to better defend the human rights of indigenous peoples" (1990, 43). "Law (customary or otherwise) constitutes a basic element of the ethnic identity of a pueblo, nation or community," but customary law is of particular interest to Stavenhagen because it is prior in historical terms to codified law, and moreover, deeply "conditions relations between peoples and the state" (Stavenhagen 1990, 27). Indeed, it is through the recognition of customary law that indigenous communities can be seen as autonomous already. The recognition of customary law was a key ingredient in the constitutional reforms of the state of Oaxaca in 1995 and 1997. Considered the one of the most progressive pieces of legislation in Mexico, the Law of the Rights of Indigenous Peoples and Communities in Oaxaca recognizes "indigenous rights and self-determination not only in elections, but in forms of justice and other arenas of community and municipal (county-level) administration" (Stephen 2009, 130). Known as *usos y costumbres,* this law doesn't bring a new practice into being, but rather recognizes long-existing practices that are at the core of indigenous community life in Oaxaca, and in so doing, these practices are aligned with indigenous autonomy (Recondo 2001, 2007).

Héctor Díaz Polanco, an anthropologist who has written extensively on indigenous autonomy in Mexico, understands autonomy as an "articulating demand" of organized indigenous peoples that is intimately linked to national democracy: "Imperatives of national democracy make autonomy unavoidable. Thus it is through a larger democratic project that ethnic groups find a foundation for their demand for autonomy" (1997, 90). However, Díaz Polanco is wary of what he calls "laissez faire" conceptions of autonomy, based on "broad permission for ethnic groups to tend to their own affairs or to retain their customs," because this kind of autonomy "depends on the permission of the powerful" and as "prerogatives, grants or favors are sooner or later withdrawn by the same whim that bestowed them" (1997, 95). Instead, Díaz Polanco insists on autonomy as "a political-juridical regime, agreed upon and not granted, that implies the creation of a true political collectivity within the national society" with constitutional and legal protections (1997, 98). Consistent with the way he links autonomy to national democracy, Díaz Polanco claims, "The regime of autonomy aims at finding means for the political integration of the nation-state based on coordination rather than subordination of its partial collectivities" (1997, 96). Autonomy, rather than a threat to national sovereignty, can bring about the "harmonization of national life" and, in his vision, the state takes on the role of the "arbiter of common and plural interests" (Díaz Polanco 1997, 97).

Díaz Polanco supports the creation of pluriethnic autonomous regions (RAPs), a proposal that emerged from discussions leading up to the San Andrés peace talks in Chiapas, and was more fully developed through the National Assembly of Indigenous Peoples in Support for Autonomy. Based on the "notion that different ethnic groups, with historical claims to the land they inhabit, would live together under regional governments," the RAP proposal entails the creation of a "fourth level of government" (the first three being federal, state, and municipal) and "must be understood within wider national context of social movements demanding democracy and the transformation of the state" (Mattiace 1998). Since the Zapatista uprising, thirty-eight pro-EZLN municipalities *en rebeldia* have declared themselves "autonomous" and have formed de facto RAPs (Stephen 1999). Though the federal government has conceded "transitional municipal" status to some of these rebel municipalities, it has generally responded by physically dismantling these municipalities, removing autonomous governments and replacing them with those sympathetic to the Partido Revolucionario Institucional (PRI).

Both Shannan Mattaice and Lynn Stephen, in their ethnographic analyses of indigenous autonomy, discuss a second autonomy proposal that is based on "the idea that Indian identity is best maintained within the structure of the local community" (Mattiace 1998, 2). These two autonomy proposals, regional and community-based, emerge from Chiapas and Oaxaca, respectively, for reasons Stephen attributes to different regional histories of land distribution, colonization, and interactions with the state. Chiapas's long history of large landholdings and forced labor migrations created multiethnic regions, whereas Oaxaca's history of land tenure continues to be based largely on monoethnic communal land holdings that have been fiercely guarded from neighboring communities (Stephen 1996). Though not uncontested by leaders in the autonomy movement in Mexico, regional and community-based autonomy proposals characterize the major efforts to pin down indigenous autonomy in Mexico, to make it "real."

The kind of autonomy proposed and lived by the Zapatistas and Oaxacan indigenous peoples does not contradict being Mexican, but rather exists alongside it or in a tiered relationship, much as the Mixe express it in their television broadcasts by playing the national anthem before the Mixe anthem, to show respect for and honor the nation in which they live while at the same time insisting on their own position as a distinct and organized people. A love of Mexico, along with a sense of national identity, permeates Zapatista discourse and performance; Subcomandante Insurgente Marcos is famous for kissing the Mexican flag. Yet some groups oppose such accommodations. The K-Xhon collective see constitutional reform in Oaxaca as yet another attempt to integrate indigenous peoples. "Some leaders of the so-called *Indian* or *indigenous movement* have proposed modification to the Constitution. For example, the state Constitution of Oaxaca 'recognizes' the tequio as a form of labor [making] the tequio one more element of oppression" (Topil 1994, 6). Not only does the constitutional reform presuppose a condition of "constitutional illegality," according to the K-Xhon collective, "what they have accomplished with their efforts is that the state and its ideologues fine tune their programs to—once and for all!—integrate us into Mexican-ness" (ibid.). Integrating regionally specific forms or "systems" of indigenous autonomy into the state would certainly create bureaucratic and administrative headaches of epic proportions for the Mexican government, which despite liberal trends has historically never had a "hands-off" style of governing at any level, but it is not impossible, as indigenous communities and autonomous municipalities prove every day. What dissenting voices like K-Xhon's point to, however, are the to-be-expected problems of legalizing any system of governance—often times the system being legalized has internal shortcomings, such as the fair and equal treatment of women or the lack of checks and balances that prevent abuses of power (Stephen 2002, 2009). The coexistence of individual rights and collective rights can also be problematic—an urban worker can blame tequio responsibilities in his or her home community as a legitimate reason for not going to work, just as a community member can assert his or her individual rights when choosing not to participate in a tequio. The K-Xhon collective rails against how the post-Revolutionary nation-state has attempted to integrate indigenous peoples into "Mexican-ness" through the creation of the INI and the *dirección de antropología* that came before it.

Many indigenous videomakers in Mexico today have been trained through the INI's video program (the subject of the next chapter). Their social roles as cultural brokers who actively shape how members of their communities understand identity are part of an older INI legacy of cultural promoters who pitted cultural recovery against political action. Indigenous videomakers who make culture visible today insist on the compatibility of the two processes, asserting cultural identities in a way that connects them to notions of community and autonomy. As the Zapotec videomaker Juan José García explains, the challenge of video indígena is to make "schemes" of autonomy that indigenous peoples already live visible and self-conscious, so that they can be overtly defended. The Mexican state, on the other hand, through the INI, enlists indigenous people to construct "a visual memory" that corresponds to Mexico's diversity (INI 1994b, 2). The state builds its patrimony of pluralism as indigenous activists assert autonomy from culture. What emerges from a closer look at the INI's history and practices is an understanding of how culture was stripped of its political impact through a process of folklorization. Making culture visible re-empowers culture with its political role as indigenous mediamakers represent their cultures in complex ways.

Mexico's Instituto Nacional Indigenista: From Indigenismo to Video Indígena

When the ILO first convened to discuss the possibility of holding nations accountable for the "decent treatment of working people," in 1919, Mexico, on the other side of the hemisphere, was just coming out of the revolution of 1910–17. Its constitution of 1917 included official support for agrarian reform and worker protection provisions that the ILO deemed essential to civilized nations just two years later. During a period of intense and confusing institutional consolidation following the revolution, scholars and intellectuals were busy building a national society based on the idea of a *mestizo* nation that would recognize its indigenous roots, giving Mexico a unique American (non-European) composition that would also be committed to the "elevation" of indigenous peoples to modernity (Gamio 1916). To achieve this end, Mexican anthropologists founded the notion and practice of *indigenismo*, a public policy that put anthropologists and the notions of cultural relativity to work for assimilation. Like many things revolutionary about the Mexican revolution, indigenismo wasn't put into wide practice until the 1940s, through the creation of the INI.

In broad strokes the INI's narrative is about creating an agency and series of policies and practices to overtly locate indigenous peoples within Mexico's postrevolutionary nation. As anthropologist Emiko Saldívar reminds us, however, the role of indigenismo in Mexican history should not be underestimated: "Indigenismo is not only a series of practices and policies that define the indigenous person as an object of integration, entertainment and education, it is also a process through which mestizo identity is defined as the redeemer and promoter of development" (2004).

I have organized the INI's narrative into four periods of decreasing lengths. The first period covers the postrevolutionary moment and the INI's foundation, in 1948, as well as its first two full decades of operation, through 1970. This period is characterized by a desire to unify Mexico under a mestizo national identity and assimilate indigenous peoples into that project. What interests me about early indigenismo are two institutional currents that are relevant to my analysis, namely the creation of indigenous and nonindigenous cultural "brokers" (mostly INI staffers) and the tendency to folklorize indigenous cultural expressions and representations through a practice the INI calls "cultural promotion." The second period, from 1971 through 1988, covers a period of intense criticism and crisis as the INI's practices of assimilation were called into question.

From 1989 through 2000, the INI underwent significant changes, infrastructural expansion, including the creation of a system of indigenous radio stations and the urban-based film production unit, and a marked shift to pluralist discourses. During this time the institution was not only repositioned administratively within the Mexican government, but President Carlos Salinas de Gortari's National Solidarity Program reconfigured its relationship to its constituency in terms of neoliberal economic philosophy, in 1988. With the sweeping new anti-poverty program, the Programa Nacional de Solidaridad (PRONA-SOL), known simply as solidaridad or Solidarity, the president promised to rewrite state-society relations through "social liberalism" and "direct democracy." Solidarity "was intended to remind the Mexican people as well as the outside world of governments . . . that the technocrats presiding over Mexico's so-called neoliberal economic revolution were not insensitive to the social costs of the market-oriented policies that they espoused" (Cornelius, Fox, and Craig 1994).[12]

Of the post-1970s period, the years from 1989 through 1994, which correspond to the Salinas administration, are of central importance to this study. Not only was the INI's video program created in those years, but INI leadership played an active role in the constitutional reform process of 1991–92, which culminated with the much celebrated "pluricultural" amendments to article 4. Scholars of the INI were not asked to participate, however, in the amendments to article 27. Article 27—"without a doubt, the most enduring legacy of the Mexican Revolution" (Stephen 2002, 3)—allowed for and protected "the formation of *ejidos* as collective entities with legal stature, specific territorial limits, and representative bodies of governance" (ibid.).[13] The reforms to article 27 dismantled the protection of communal land ownership, opening the door for its sale as private property, a key step in the administration's plan to "prepare" Mexico for entry into the North American Free Trade Agreement with the United States and

Canada. Whereas the Solidarity years were about revitalizing and reinventing the institution, after 1994 and in response to the Zapatista uprising in Chiapas, the INI entered a stagnant, inactive "holding pattern" that characterized the institution until its reinvention in 2000 under the Fox administration.

In 2003, President Fox dismantled the INI by presidential decree, creating in its stead the Comisión Nacional para el Desarrollo de los Pueblos Indígenas (CDI). Fox promised to end indigenismo and embarked former INI employees on a massive national *consulta*, or query, to gather recommendations for the new agency (CDI 2004). The query was called "Consulta a los pueblos indígenas sobre sus formas y aspiraciones de desarrollo," or the "Query to indigenous peoples on their forms and aspirations for development" (my translation). In a book called *El Estado y los Indígenas en Tiempos de PAN* (The state and indigenous people in the time of the PAN), scholars evaluate Fox's efforts to address indigenous peoples' most pressing issues with a grim warning that little has changed (Hernández et al. 2004). Despite the advances in legalizing certain kinds of autonomy at the state level, Oaxaca has become a militarized state where "a wide range of social movements, including those of indigenous peoples, are being held hostage by the presence of multiple state and local police as well as by the presence of paramilitary forces in increasing numbers of communities" (Stephen 2009, 130).

Positivist Dilemmas, Revolutionary Redemption and Social Justice: Founding and Fixing Indigenismo, 1917–1970 • With the creation in 1917 of the Dirección de Antropología y Poblaciones Regionales under the direction of Manuel Gamio, Mexico's "father" of anthropology, along with Moises Saenz and Gonzalo Aguirre began to formulate a solution to the country's perceived "Indian problem" and forever entangled cultural anthropology—deemed the "science of good government" by Gamio—with state building (Herrasti 1989).[14] Their solution was indigenismo. Cobbled together and given life through numerous conferences, ministries, and institutions that I briefly discuss in this section, and variously described as official policy, ideology, and practice or later, *acción*, indigenismo's principal goal was to enact the homogeneously mestizo Mexico imagined by its post-Revolutionary national leaders. In other words, indigenismo was created to "Mexicanize" indigenous people.[15] Through assimilation, Mexico's indigenous peoples were going to be brought out of their backward marginalized state and incorporated into the country's project of building a modern nation.[16]

Gamio is indisputably indigenismo's principal architect. As a cultural relativist who studied under Franz Boas in the United States, Gamio wrote fiercely about the indigenous person's equal capacity as a human—in fact, he accorded indigenous people superiority in moral matters—in order to combat rampant racist attitudes of the time, but identified their "cultural inferiority" in terms of progress and modernization (Herrasti 1989, 241). As he addressed this presumed inferiority, he also carved out the life work of many anthropologists in Mexico: redemption. To the Indians, Gamio said: "You will not awaken spontaneously. It will be necessary for friendly hearts to work for your redemption" (Knight 1990).

Turning theory into practice, Gamio enlisted ideas of acculturation as well as a handful of ethnographic researchers to study indigenous cultures in order to "liberate" indigenous peoples from the roots of their "backwardness" ("substitutable" aspects of their cultures). Through managed acculturation, indigenous peoples were to preserve "positive" aspects of their cultures while shedding "negative" or backward cultural traits (Knight 1990, 87). The positive aspects of indigenous cultures were basically expressive (such as dance, music, dress, and to some extent ritual), aspects that were later "rehabilitated and woven into a new tapestry of folkloric nationalism" (Knight 1990, 82). These early and rather bizarre (in their frankness) practices of selective cultural change were essential to the production of representations of indigenous identities that were "safe" for the nation-state. They were also easily consumable and performed aspects of indigenous culture.

Díaz Polanco narrates the story of forced culture change as one that attempted (but ultimately failed) to resolve inherent contradictions in the liberal project of the nineteenth century. Culturally differentiated peoples were incompatible with liberalism's blind faith in positivist, evolutionary notions of progress that saw Western civilization and the primacy of the individual as its climax. "Not surprisingly, liberal governments put policies in practice that proposed including indigenous peoples in the national life but were based on excluding the maintenance of their cultural particularities" (Díaz Polanco 1991). Cultural homogeneity was the solution, and it was achieved in the nineteenth century by elevating Indians to the status of citizens, the epitome of the liberal project: "From then on, there were no Indians, only citizens" (Díaz Polanco 1991, 89). Arturo Warman, anthropologist and former head of INI, agrees with the assessment, "The Indian problem only allowed for one response: that Indians cease being Indians" (1968).[17]

Thus early indigenismo turned the incompatibility of "backward Indians" and liberal ideals of modernization into an affinity with the concept of cultural relativity. Indigenous peoples could be integrated into national life while they were accorded human dignity and their cultural values were respected (Díaz Polanco 1991, 92). They simply needed to be given the "instruments of civilization necessary for their articulation within modern society" (Aguirre Beltrán, quoted in Díaz Polanco 1991, 92). The internal contradiction between cultural relativism and evolutionary thinking resulted in a tragic failure of destruction and oppression, according to Díaz Polanco, and only served to stimulate ethnic-national conflicts that are still unresolved today. As Díaz Polanco argues, the logical application of a relativist position would be to respect the self-development of differentiated cultures, but the imperative of integration led early indigenistas to rely on positivist notions of the previous century, as is evident in Gamio's discourse (Gamio 1916, 1935). Similar positivist and evolutionary underpinnings were also at work in the construction of article 27 of the Mexican constitution, according to the historian Emilio H. Kourí (2002). Kourí recovers how Andrés Molina Enríquez, the principal author of article 27, resurrected the imperative of communal land as a solution of Mexico's Indian problem. He writes, "Given the Indian's 'evolutive backwardness' no other form of organization could have better served their interests" (2002, 102). Indigenous people were deemed not ready in a developmental or evolutionary sense to handle the private property that was forced onto them during the nineteenth-century wave of liberal reforms that dismantled communal land protections. Nearly a century later, President Salinas, it seems, thought they were.

If anthropologists were the ones equipped to identify (through ethnographic research) aspects of indigenous cultures that needed to be changed, it was through education, delivered to indigenous communities through a broad system of rural schools and "cultural missions" in the 1920s and 1930s, that Gamio's vision of redemption was to take effect. The rural school was conceived as an agent of change that could "implant positive Western values and uproot negative values of [indigenous] tradition" (Warman 1970, 30). Along the way, the schools also consolidated the nation into an imagined community: "The *maestro rural*, acting, like his French Republican counterpart, as the front-line soldier of the secular state, was expected to counter the influence of the church and to stimulate sentiments of patriotism, to inculcate, as one study put it, 'the new "religion" of the country—post-Revolutionary nationalism'" (Knight 1990, 82).

Such sentiments of patriotism were inculcated in practice through *castellanización*, the main thrust of the rural education program (Stavenhagen 1978). Following Díaz Polanco's argument, the cultural traits deemed "negative," and therefore most incompatible to the new mestizo nationalism, such as language, were ones most intimately constitutive to indigenous cultural identities. From these early years, indigenismo, as a practice, was intrinsically linked to education, and accordingly, "castillianizing, literacy and technologizing the Indian were clearly conceived as the work of anthropology" (Warman 1968, 30–31). The following passage clearly delineates the institution's work and the role Castilianization plays in solving Mexico's "Indian problem": "The Federal Government considers that the indigenous problem is a special aspect of the problems of the peasant population of Mexico; but the indigenous problem needs special treatment precisely because of the cultural backwardness of indigenous communities and, especially due to their exclusive or predominant use of indigenous tongues, they are not incorporated in to the social, economic or political life of the country" (INI 1955a, 15). Through forced Castilianization, and later through the training of bilingual indigenous teachers, indigenous people throughout Mexico were relocated somewhere in between their indigenous communities and the nation-state, made to bridge between two worlds through a kind of lived or learned cultural *mestizaje* that underwrote one of Mexico's most overt nation-building schemes.[18]

Indigenismo took further shape as policy and practice in the 1920s and 1930s, under Gamio, at the Dirección de Antropología, and Moisés Sáenz, at the Ministry of Education, but it was not until the election of populist, socialist president Lázaro Cárdenas that indigenismo was fully bureaucratized within the government. Cárdenas had already established the country's first official government agency dedicated to indigenous "problems," the Autonomous Department of Indigenous Affairs, by the time Latin American leaders met at the first Interamerican Indigenous Congress, held in Pátzcuaro, Michoacán, Mexico, in

1940. Gonzalo Aguirre Beltrán, who became the INI's chief theoretical architect under Alfonso Caso, believed indigenismo (which he describes as a "popular ideology promoting social justice") reached its climax in 1940 at the famous Pátzcuaro Congress (Aguirre Beltrán 1969). Cárdenas's articulation of Aguirre Beltrán's notion of "social justice" has a familiar face: "Our indigenous problem is not in preserving the Indian as Indian or in indianizing Mexico, but rather in Mexicanizing the Indian" (quoted in Warman 1970, 32).

The Mexican delegation at the Pátzcuaro Congress played a leading role at the congress and spearheaded the foundation of the Interamerican Indigenous Institute during that same year (Masferrer Kan 1989). While proposals from other countries were on the table—such as that of José Carlos Mariátgui (founder of the Peruvian Socialist Party), who insisted that the restoration of lands was the solution to the indigenous "problem," and others who invested in ideas of cultural revitalization and self-determination (Masferrer Kan 1989, 156–57)—Mexican indigenismo underwrote the international institute's indigenous policy.[19] One of the resolutions of the congress was for each participating country to establish its own indigenous affairs department, something Mexico already had. By the late 1940s, the Autonomous Department of Indigenous Affairs had been subsumed under the Ministry of Education and was deemed basically ineffectual by the leading anthropologists of the time (Herrasti 1989). The prominent archeologist and attorney Alfonso Caso petitioned then president Miguel Alemán to create an institution that specifically focused on indigenous peoples and the resolution of their problems. In 1948 the Instituto Nacional Indigenista (INI) was created by executive mandate, and Caso was appointed as its first director, a post he held until 1970, the year of his death.

Though official INI history describes the INI's establishment as a direct response to fulfill Mexico's obligations to the agreements reached at the historic Pátzcuaro meetings in 1940, the institution's foundational narrative is often written as a way to make revolutionary ideals reach the country's most isolated and marginalized population. INI historian Lourdes Herrasti describes those ideals as including "building an integrated nation, a modern civilization and a fundamentally mestizo society characterized by the determinant presence of 'social justice'" (1989, 240). Caso's vision for the INI emerges through a series of sometimes combative opinion pieces that begin the move from assimilation to social justice, published in journals such as *América Indígena* and *Acción Indigenista* of the Interamerican Indigenous Institute and the INI, respectively. In one piece entitled "Beneficence and Indigenismo," Caso argues that Mexico's Indian problem is not going be solved through charity: "Indigenous populations live in great cultural backwardness and lack adequate means and technical skills to elevate themselves, by themselves, to a better life plan, but they present a totally different problem than those individuals or groups that need beneficence. Their conditions are not due to advanced age, illnesses or failures that might have lead them to indigence. They are social and economic conditions that have cast indigenous people to the most inhospitable places of the national territory" (Caso 1953). Resonating with Aguirre Beltrán's famous treatise on "regions of refuge," Caso's solution was to modify indigenous peoples' economic conditions with their collaboration. "They are energetic, hardworking individuals who try harder than anyone else to make unproductive land produce" (Caso 1953, 260). Caso defines indigenismo "acción" as explicitly social rather than cultural and one that must always count on the full participation (implying not only labor but, to some extent, consent) of the communities (1953, 262). He dismantles stereotypes of the lazy, unproductive Indian and simultaneously upholds the interventionist role of the state in bringing "positive" change to indigenous communities. Under Caso, the INI was constructed as an agency entrusted to "speak for" Indians (with their cooperation), creating a kind of dependency on the state even though indigenous people were not invited to cooperate in setting indigenista policy—"chicken soup without the chicken," as one enlightened senator described the INI back in 1948 (Herrasti 1989, 243). While Caso and Aguirre Beltrán's discourse does not stray too far from Gamio's redemptive vision, they (especially Aguirre Beltrán) introduce notions of social justice and indigenous collaboration that resonate in later periods of INI history.

Given that the indigenous "problem" was seen as cutting across all sectors of government, the INI was established as an "autonomous" body, funded entirely by the federal government but not administratively dependent any single government ministry. Up until its last decade, its director reported to and was directly appointed by the president of the republic (INI 1955, 16).[20] Its board of directors was made up of heads of cabinets as well as leaders of cultural and financial institutions that directly served indigenous or peasant constituencies.

The INI's budget was created through "subsidies" from other government ministry budgets: "It is not up to a single department, like the previous Department of Indigenous Affairs, but up to the federal government as a whole to work in a coordinated manner to resolve the problems of the indigenous population" (INI 1955a).

Herrasti describes the INI's first decades as ones of "learning and pilot projects" (1989). Indeed, one of the institution's first tasks was to measure or take stock of what was called the "magnitud del problema indígena" (INI 1955a, 23). The first four studies to be published by the INI—all conducted and written by ethnographers who have come to be some of Mexico's best known anthropologists—incorporated "problem" in their title, as in *Problemas sociales y económicos de las Mixtecas* and *Problemas indígenas de la cuenca del Papaloapan*.

Even though Warman describes the INI from the time of its founding through 1970 as functioning in a "state of paralysis," there are a few developments during the institution's first years of operation that are of interest (1968, 35). The principal "pilot project" during the period was the establishment of the first regional coordination center, or Centro de Coordinación Indígena (CCI), in San Cristóbal de las Casas, Chiapas, in 1951.[21] Headed by Aguirre Beltrán himself and later by Julio de la Fuente and Ricardo Pozas, both major figures in Mexican cultural anthropology, the CCI in San Cristóbal was modeled after the rural schools run by the Ministry of Education (Herrasti 1989, 248). An essential part of the CCI was the selection of indigenous *promotores*, who were to serve as insiders or informants for INI staff that at times also included agronomists, lawyers, economists, medical doctors, and professors. The promoters were selected for their knowledge of indigenous languages and for their solid position in their communities, but they also had to be at least somewhat bilingual. Cultural promoters, "extracted from their own communities, were conscientiously prepared to take the new teachings, like writing, reading and numerals, to their native places in their own languages" (INI 1955b, 45). They were informants endowed with a purpose: to "carefully induce" the cultural changes the INI had in mind (ibid.). Caso describes the work of the CCIs, its staff, and promotores as the opposite of imposing: they "never employed coercive or compulsory methods. [Their] technique [was] to invite and demonstrate by example" (Caso 1978).

The first group of forty promoters at the CCI in San Cristobal consisted of Tojolabal community authorities and youths, none of whom had completed primary school (though some promotores had at one time been through the Ministry of Education's boarding schools). The activities of the CCIs were diverse, from technical support for agriculture, to road and school building, the establishment of medical clinics, vaccination programs, and literacy. Slide films, motion picture films, and even an indigenous-language puppet theater called Teatro Petúl were employed as "a step to teach them to speak, read and write in Spanish" (Caso 1978, 86).[22] By 1970 the INI had established ten more CCIs in indigenous areas throughout the country (three of them in Oaxaca state). Many of the cultural promoters selected and trained by the INI, who in 1955 were celebrated as "universal indigenous teachers" (INI 1955b), had become bilingual teachers and were transferred, in 1970, to the Ministry of Education, where they had more opportunities for professional advancement, union representation, and better salaries, even though the bilingual teachers had to struggle for equal pay continually from within the ministry, until the 1980s (Herrasti 1989, 252).

The INI's practice of forming cultural promoters is an important aspect of how the state penetrated indigenous communities in the name of their own "redemption," creating in the process individuals who were asked to live "in between" their own communities and the state. Also, the concept of separable "positive" and "negative" aspects of culture, which undergirded the INI's position on cultural change, where the positive aspects were destined for preservation and the negative ones for extermination (or at best replacement), laid the foundation for representations of indigenous culture, based on dress, dance, or food—in short, folklore—that were considered "safe" or not threatening to the state. Furthermore, as indigenous pluralism became official toward the end of this narrative, through processes of constitutional reform in which the INI participated, political autonomy was "contained" by the state as cultural autonomy (Hindley 1996, 230).

On the Air with the INI's Indigenous Radio System: Expansion and Crisis, 1971–1988 • I have grouped together several presidential administrations and upheavals in this section of the INI's narrative. Aguirre Beltrán took the helm of the INI after Caso's death, in 1970, and sent the INI into a period of infrastructural expansion. In this period, the INI opened seventy-nine new CCIs throughout the country, launched its Proyecto Radiofonico, in 1979, with the first of six radio stations, WEZV, "La Voz de la Montaña," in Tlapa, Guerrero, and established the Archivo Etnografico Audiovisual in 1977, in Mexico City. The archive (renamed the Departamento de Imagen y Sonido in 1994) is the filmmaking and visual archive branch of the institution, created for the purpose of "preserving and distributing cultural expressions of indigenous pueblos though audiovisual media" (INI 1994a). This kind of "national" expansion that increased the INI's presence throughout indigenous regions in the country, abruptly ended the INI's developmental period of "learning and pilot projects" (Herrasti 1989). The INI historian Andres Fabregas labels this expansion "artificial" because the INI no longer had a theoretical basis: "It was more of a pragmatic policy of the state" (1978). The INI's theoretical basis had come under severe attack as Mexico's most prominent anthropologists and former INI staff, such as Arturo Warman and Guillermo Bonfil Batalla, "satanized indigenismo" (Herrasti 1989, 256). Additionally, the growing indigenous rights movement and the flight of the INI's cultural promoters to the teacher's union, the Sindicato Nacional de Trabajadores de la Educación, left INI staff to fend for themselves in the communities, forced to establish "direct" relations just when they "found that the communities had been transformed and it was no longer easy to find interlocutors for their programs" (ibid.). The INI's infrastructural expansion into radio broadcasting and film production came just at the time when the indigenous rights movement was picking up speed and more organizations and unions were representing indigenous interests, perhaps evidence of the state's trying to service as well as maintain its grip on and presence in the rural indigenous population.

The most overt "satanization" of the INI was made by a group of anthropologists and professors—the "dissident" scholars to whom the human rights scholar Alyson Brysk attributes the origin of the transnational indigenous autonomy movement (2000)—at the National Anthropology School in Mexico City through a provocative little book entitled *De eso que llaman antropología Mexicana* (So-called Mexican anthropology) (Warman, Nolasco Armas, Bonfil Batalla, Olivera de Vazquez, and Valencia 1970). Warman and his coauthors place the foundations of anthropology firmly within a white, Western, expansionist tradition essential to European imperialism, and those of Mexican anthropology within the context of the conquest and later Mexico's own expansion and industrialization. He locates Mexican anthropologists' forefathers as intermediaries between conquistadors and natives but is careful to remind his readers in at least a few places in his narrative of the potential for dissent that such a position implies (offering the example of Fray Bartolomé de las Casas, known as the "defender of the Indian," who was one of the only contemporary and vocal critics of the conquistadors) (1970, 13–14). Warman calls for anthropologists to rebel against or at least move beyond the bureaucratic confines that have shaped (and have severely restricted) the discipline historically in Mexico (1970, 37), but other contributors formulate potential alternatives.

In particular, Bonfil Batalla introduces what he calls the "unavoidable conclusion of a critical anthropology": the recognition of Mexico as a "pluricultural state" (1970). Addressing indigenismo's obsession with national integration, Bonfil Batalla insists that cultural diversity per se is not incompatible with the idea of the nation (1970, 57). And Nolasco affirms that cultural diversity is "perfectly compatible" with modernization (Nolasco Armas 1970). The Indian still has to be "liberated," not from his internal cultural backwardness but from national society. Once he is liberated, it will be possible to construct a *nacionalidad*, a common nationality, where cultural differences are not an obstacle, "not because they will no longer exist, but because they will exist without a system of asymmetrical relations that frames them today" (Bonfil Batalla 1970, 59). These "dissident" scholars systematically dismantle notions of integration and attack practices of assimilation that constituted the INI's *acción indigenista*, and in doing so, they relocate indigenous peoples within a nation-state that celebrates cultural difference.[23]

Discourses of cultural diversity and plurality, which characterize the critique of the INI and indigenismo during the late 1960s and early 1970s, are adopted by the INI by the time the institution publishes its thirty-year memoir, appropriately subtitled *Revisión crítica* (INI 1978), which is also the first time in its history that the INI is not headed by an anthropologist. The Mexican president José Lopez Portillo begins his entry in the INI's 1978 *memoria* with the following statement: "The Indian, proud essence of the county and bad conscience of society . . . herein lies the struggle for our identity and our independence" (INI 1978, 5). Notions of indigenous participation ("por si mismos") and cultural plurality are already explicit in the introductory greeting written by the education secretary, Fernando Solana Morales. In a democracy like

Mexico's, Solana writes, it is "unacceptable that [their] education consider a human group merely as receptors, incapable of participating in the decisions that concerns them . . . national unity will only happen through the respect for cultural plurality" (INI 1978, 7). Indeed, Solana goes on to say that paying the nation's debt to indigenous people is precisely what will allow Mexicans to be "even more Mexican" (ibid.). Being Mexican still hinges on the role indigenous people play in national identity (Saldívar 2001). The 1978 memoria pays homage to the INI's founding fathers with reprints of key texts by Gamio, Saenz, Cárdenas, Caso, and Aguirre Beltrán (among others), but the bulk of the publication is dedicated to contemporary position pieces (with titles like "Integration and Ethnocide" and "Let Us Admit that Indians Were Not Born Wrong") by Warman, Bonfil Batalla, Stavenhagen, Nahmad, Esteva, and still others among those anthropologists who satanized indigenismo a decade earlier.

Warman writes his contribution to the INI's thirtieth anniversary as a letter to the director, declaring that the idea of a social homogeneity is an "outdated concept of nationhood" (Warman 1978). He frames his letter with a historical review of indigenismo similar to his acerbic essay from 1970, but this time offers a possible solution: self-determination (1978, 144). The "pluralist declaration," according to Warman, has not been sufficiently linked to its prerequisite, self-determination: "Today there exist demands, with groups and organizations that backing them up, that mark the new route of indigenismo. These demands, which call for pluralism, do not locate the Indian's problem at the margin of the national project. On the contrary, they situate it in the center of the debate about what kind of country we want. Pluralism is not only an indigenous demand, though they are the ones expressing it with most clarity and urgency, but of many other social groups in our society" (ibid.). Bonfil Batalla's contribution, also in the form of a letter to the director, pushes the director to think beyond an INI "for" or even "with" indigenous people to one "by" indigenous people, an institution "under their control and responsibility" (Bonfil Batalla 1978). His vision for the INI is based on a specific end: "That indigenous peoples take into their own hands the management [*gestión*] of their own destiny" (1978, 149). He specifies that the problem of self-determination is not a technical one, but a political issue that "implies a radical change in Mexican society's reality and future" (1978, 150). "Indigenous peoples," he writes, "have now passed from the defensive to the offensive: they are organizing, reclaiming, proposing and affirming that they too want a place in the future" (ibid.). Herrasti affirms that the INI's official response to its satanization was the adoption of words like *autogestión* and *participación* to define its vision, but she adds that notions of self-development and participation stayed at the level of discourse instead of serving to redefine institutional practice, a pattern that has continued to be repeated (1989, 257).

By 1982 Mexico was in a deep economic crisis and the INI's expansion was halted. The institution's directorship was given "back" to an anthropologist, Salomón Nahmad, who was trained in INI practices since his first fieldwork, in the 1950s, with the Mixe of Oaxaca (see chapter 4). Nahmad inherited an institution without clear goals, a frozen budget, and an indigenous constituency that was well organized and making demands of the government (Herrasti 1989, 258). With close ties to emerging indigenous leaders, Nahmad steered the INI toward fulfilling its promises of "ethnodevelopment," a notion that, according to Herrasti, emerged from indigenous intellectual elite (ibid.). Nahmad's vision for the INI was more along the lines of what Bonfil Batalla imagined, an institution by indigenous peoples, but his efforts to hand over control of the INI's CCIs to indigenous organizations cost him the directorship, not to mention his freedom and professional reputation within certain circles. Recent INI publications state the truncated dates of Nahmad's term (four of the six years) with little explanation, but Herrasti hints at some of the circumstances of his "violent" departure. Accused of fraud, "the state did not take into account any arguments in his favor, not Nahmad's prestige, his clean trajectory, or the political pressure from indigenous peoples and intellectuals" (Herrasti 1989, 259).[24]

Nahmad was replaced by Miguel Limón Rojas, a lawyer who designed and implemented an extensive diagnostic aimed at solving the INI's crisis, which included a severely reduced budget, a lack of impact in indigenous communities, and a chronic lack of indigenous participation within the institution itself (Herrasti 1989, 259). To address these problems, the INI focused its efforts on creating community planning committees that were to have their basis in already existing forms of community organization and authority. These committees would serve as intermediaries empowered to select and modify projects the INI proposed and were woven into participatory positions within the institution's hierarchical structure, through representation on the boards of directors at local (CCI), state (delegations), and national levels. During the Limón years, places for indigenous representatives were opened on the INI's national board of directors for the first time in the institution's history. But while some chicken was finally added to the soup, to follow the metaphor, indigenous representatives on the board functioned in a consultative rather than decision-making capacity.

This period of crisis in the INI's history demonstrates a dynamic that is to be replayed in more recent times. The state attempts to deliver services to the country's entire indigenous population through the creation of CCIs and adopts, even celebrates, notions of plurality and cultural diversity, but as Nahmad's directorship of the institution shows, the federal government remained unwilling to cede control. These community committees, which represent a much more mediated effort to bring indigenous peoples into decision-making sphere of the institution than what Nahmad had in mind, were later seen as the precursors to the next administration's Fondos Regionales de Solidaridad. In the INI memorias from 1988 to 1994 the institution's experience with the committees "demonstrated [to INI staff] that indigenous organizations had full capacity to administer resources designated for their development as well as to design and execute their own projects" (INI 1994a). Indigenous participation in the institution was rearticulated in the period that followed, in terms of neoliberal economic policy and the new president's vision for "social mobilization" (Fox 1994).

Embracing Neoliberalism: Solidarity's "New" INI, 1989–2000 •
Banking on the magic of nationalism that turns "chance into destiny" (Anderson 1991), President Salinas de Gortari employed the "magic" of bureaucratic political language to claim to undo the Mexican government's paternalistic stance toward indigenous peoples, while in fact perpetuating it: "Still today Mexican society is far from accepting living together with indigenous peoples under conditions of respect and equality. This is why, the dedicated and daily push to develop indigenous peoples with respect to their cultural identity constitutes a determining action of the Executive branch towards constructing a new system grounded in tolerance, respect for difference and plurality" (INI 1994a, 11). This "new system," which promised to rewrite the relationship between the state and society was President Salinas's

Programa Nacional de Solidaridad. Solidarity was a presidentialist program par excellence (Cornelius, Fox, and Craig 1994, 6). Based on the idea of empowering citizens to help themselves and billed as an antipoverty program, Solidarity had tremendous impact in its sociopolitical role, though scholars agree that it ultimately served a political goal of rebuilding electoral support for the PRI, which until 2000 was Mexico's only ruling party (Cornelius, Fox, and Craig 1994).[25] Salinas directed huge amounts of the federal budget (plumped by recent privatizations) into Solidarity in order to implement the social change he envisioned, but in the end Solidarity was a "modern" form of government patronage unable to "defy its paternity," rather than a program of structural reform (Knight 1994, 37).

In order to contextualize how the INI is transformed under Solidarity, it is worth reiterating changes that occurred on the national level during the Salinas administration's adoption of pluralism, in the early 1990s. Well before the deeply contentious quincentenary "celebrations" were turned upside down (or right side up) by indigenous organizations and spokespersons like Rigoberta Menchú, who used the historic event to galvanize global support for indigenous peoples' rights in the Americas, Mexico had passed a series of reforms related to indigenous rights. These reforms, which constituted an important aspect of Salinas's "new indigenismo," according to the anthropologist Jane Hindley, included the ratification of the ILO's Convention 169, which outlines new international standards for relations between states and indigenous peoples based on the rejection of assimilation and the recognition of pluralism. Hindley argues that signing the ILO convention in turn created the "responsibility" to amend Mexico's constitution of 1917 to recognize the pluricultural composition of the Mexican nation, but in the context of the harsh criticism coming from within Mexico, criticism of the country's failure to promote the wellbeing of indigenous peoples, it is evident that Mexico had a clear responsibility prior to 1989. For its part, the INI wrote "new policies . . . oriented to promoting justice, training, self-reliance and the transfer of resources" (Hindley 1996). Hindley concludes that Salinas's reforms were "politically expedient" in light of increasing international attention to indigenous issues, but signals Salinas's "political will" in naming Arturo Warman the director of the INI, and in creating the Comisión Nacional de Justicia para los Pueblos Indígenas (CNJPI) (1996, 230).

The INI was heavily involved in the constitutional reform process regarding article 4 (see INI 1994, 48–56), arranging hundreds of consultations, meetings, and surveys with indigenous and nonindigenous groups, opinion leaders, unions, anthropologists, governors, and federal deputies before the amendment was drafted and approved by congress, in 1992 (Hindley 1996, 233). But the INI did not consult with indigenous political organizations and no indigenous representatives were included on the CNJPI commission, an exclusion that was "indicative of [the state's] continued paternalism toward indigenous peoples," according to Hindley (ibid.). Functionaries from the INI attempted to push far more reaching reforms, including the right to territory, which remains one of the most contentious issues of indigenous autonomy, but they were thwarted by the administration. "Thus the terms of the reform reflect not the INI's position with regard to the extension of rights, but its political position within the State as the appointed representative of the weakest social force in society" (Hindley 1996, 234). As Hindley argues, while the reform of article 4 signals an "explicit reversal of the revolutionary legacy of assimilation and the abandonment of the goal of creating a homogeneous nation," the reform "succeeds in containing the indigenous question within the parameters of culture: thus it reproduces the revolutionary nationalist framing of the indigenous problem as a *cultural problem*" (1996, 236). Additionally, framing the indigenous issue as one of justice and injustice rather than rights effectively weakens any potential for real change (Hindley 1996, 230). Changes to article 27 represent an "explicit reversal of the revolutionary legacy" of a different order, effectively ending land reform and eroding the foundation of communal land in Mexico.[26]

If the Salinas administration's initiative to plant pluralism firmly within Mexico's constitution was at best a symbolic gesture, the administration's transformation of the INI was Salinas's attempt to make pluralism "trickle down." In the introduction of the INI'S memorias covering 1989 to 1994, the institution is portrayed as a lonely agency with few resources, little support from the federal government, and a massive constituency (INI 1994a, 27). Under Solidarity, however, the INI was given new life. First, the appointment of Warman to be the institution's director signaled an end to the "whole indigenist debate about integration/assimilation" (Hindley 1996, 239). Warman's move to decentralize the INI and focus on transferring its functions and resources, which adhered to his own previous criticisms of the institution (1970), was surprisingly compatible with the administration's official goals for indigenous peoples development that are as follows:

- To strengthen the autonomy of indigenous organizations and communities so that they can manage, directly and independently, their resources.
- To encourage the indigenous organizations and communities to participate actively in the planning, programming, execution, oversight and evaluation of all the projects oriented toward their development.
- To promote organizing processes in the weakest communities and strengthen them where required, to avoid the concentration of resources in the most organized communities, which often already have access to diverse funding sources.
- To establish profitable, self-sustainable productive projects, based on true co-responsibility with indigenous communities.
- To encourage productive diversification and to increase the productivity of indigenous communities through the delivery of resources and training of their members.
- To encourage the formal recognition of the associational figures that communities choose, so that they can have access to other existing funding sources.
- To support the tendency for the benefits of the productive actions to capitalize the indigenous organizations and communities.
- To generate more employment in the communities, to improve the standard of living of the indigenous population.
  —From the *Manual de Operación de los Fondos Regionales de Solidaridad* (quoted in Fox 1994, 195)

Warman headed the INI until 1992, when the institution was repositioned administratively from the Ministry of Education to Mexico's new Ministry for Social Development, a move that was based on the sweeping conclusion that the "institution's activity in indigenous regions was no longer an educational issue" (INI 1994a, 27) and coincided with reforms to article 27. According to Jonathan Fox, a political scientist who specializes in Mexico and transnational civil society, "with Solidarity funding, INI transformed itself from a service provider into an economic development agency" (1994, 189). To fund this new development agency, the INI's budget was increased eighteen-fold during the first three years of the new administration, to about $140 million (Fox 1994) with only a 30 percent increase in staff. By 1994, the INI had a staff of 4,691, spread throughout its central offices in Mexico City (where one quarter of the staff lives and works), ninety-six CCIs, twelve state delegations, a "mixed" hospital (where both Western and traditional medicine are practiced), fifteen radio stations, three training centers, and over one thousand boarding schools, for 58,000 primary-school-age children (INI 1994a).[27]

Fox believes that the INI carried out Solidarity's most successful and innovative programs: revolving credit funds managed by councils of community-based indigenous groups, known as Fondos Regionales de Solidaridad (1994, 188–89).[28] Community-based indigenous organizations (called "Solidarity Communities") apply to the regional funds for a variety of productive and improvement projects, and their proposals are funded to the extent they are deemed "self-sustainable, profitable and recuperative" (INI 1994a). Part of their success, according to Fox, has to do with the funds being distributed directly to indigenous organizations rather than through municipal or state governments (1994, 191). However, it has been noted that because the funds are coordinated through the INI's network of CCIs, their success in promoting the incorporation of indigenous peoples in the decision-making process of the institution often depends on the openness and attitudes of CCI staff (Quintana 1998). As Fox notes, "CCI directors must co-sign Regional Fund checks for development projects when leadership councils were supposed to be empowered to allocate the resources" (1994, 205). Monteforte criticized the funds program for further bureaucratizing indigenous participation: "I believe that more than anything else, instead of having more access to funds the whole thing is bureaucratized, and indigenous people become functionaries themselves. What is transferred is corruption, inefficiency, and verticalism."[29]

The convergence of indigenous autonomy proposals and a federal "Indian" institution poised to transform its practices set the stage for the emergence of the INI's video program, the Transferencia de Medios a Comunidades y Organizaciones Indígenas (TMA). Funded entirely by Solidarity, the TMA is one of the only examples of "hard" transference (donated, not loaned, video equipment) within the INI and, while developed concomitantly alongside the Fondos Regionales program, the TMA pushed the limits of the institution's transformation. The video program emerged from the specific context of the institution's Archivo Etnográfico Audiovisual, in Mexico City, and was shaped by a handful of individual media professionals employed by the INI. By the time the Fox administration conducted the *consulta* regarding the future of the new CDI, those trained during the INI's original video program were for the most part working independently, outside the prevue of the new institution. The *Informe Final* of the consulta states that 93 percent of the proposals the CDI received suggested "the use of communications media in favor of indigenous peoples" (2004, 67). The proposals reiterate the demand that indigenous peoples participate directly in the creation of television programs as well as be guaranteed access to produce their own television and radio programming. Some proposals also detailed the need to ease the process of acquiring phone services and asked for mail and telegraph services to be made available. Others centered on the "promotion and opening of spaces for the participation of indigenous women in communications media" and on the priority of implementing the federal "e-México" program, aimed at the creation of digital community centers that would help connect indigenous people across the country through the Internet (CDI 2004, 62). The CDI writes in the informe that it is "committed to walk towards a new pact, a new relationship between the state, society and indigenous peoples" (CDI 2004, 9) as is mandated by the Mexican Constitution and by ILO's Convention 169. But many scholars and indigenous activists agree that a "new pact" cannot exist unless the government fulfills its promise to pass the San Andrés Accords of 1996.

TWO

Inventing Video Indígena

Transferring Audiovisual Media to Indigenous

Organizations and Communities

> The objective of transferring audiovisual media is for indigenous
> peoples to represent their reality through their own eyes ... [a]s
> the first step toward the development of their own visual lan-
> guage on video.
>
> ***Encuentro Interamericano de Videoastas Indígenas:***
> ***Transferencia de Medios Audiovisuales a Organizaciones***
> ***y Comunidades Indígenas* (INI 1994, 2)**

Indigenous self-representation on video in Mexico would seem to flow
somewhat naturally from a confluence of factors in the late 1990s: the
availability of relatively inexpensive video production technology; a
fertile mix of prodemocratic possibilities resulting from constitutional
reforms, ratified international agreements, and increased institutional
budgets; and the fact that several important initiatives in indigenous
media production were well underway in Brazil, Canada, and Australia by this time. However, video indígena did not just happen in
Mexico; it was taught.[1] In other words, video indígena was "invented"
within a specific institutional program that necessitates a focus on the
agency of individual actors, on the video instructors in particular.

A close look at how video was taught (and to whom) allows us to
understand why video indígena in Mexico, at least (but generally elsewhere, too), has been so closely aligned with the documentary genre,
as well as to understand some of the internal contradictions that vex
video indígena in general, such as the tension between personal and
collective authorship that resonates directly with the conflict between
individual and collective rights on the level of national and international law, or the tension between "indigenous ways of seeing" and

making culture visible. The social postura that bolsters video indígena is also taught, if indirectly at first. In the case of the government's video program launched in Oaxaca, the social project is taught on the heels of video production. Focusing on how the program was developed and how video was taught to members of indigenous communities permits us to see how a nominally monolithic and highly bureaucratized institution like Mexico's Instituto Nacional Indigenista (INI) functions on the ground with a surprising amount of spontaneity and serendipity at a time of potential change that this period of official pluralism seemed to promise.

The creation of the video program was achieved in two major phases: national video workshops and the establishment of the Centro de Video Indígena (CVI) in Oaxaca City. Video indígena was taught as a tool for representing indigenous identity through national video workshops, and this, in turn, hinged on documentary realism. The project's directors attempted to address community obstacles to video production by building an infrastructure and support system for sustaining video indígena beyond government sponsorship. Individuals and social relationships continue to sustain video indígena as a social process outside government sponsorship, more than twenty years later.

The images placed at the end of the first section of this chapter, on the national video workshops, were selected from photographs I took at a community video workshop held by the CVI in El Pípila, a multiethnic indigenous community in the isthmus of Oaxaca. The text that runs under the photographs is taken directly from the introduction of the CVI's video-production teaching manual, published in 1999. The manual expresses an open-ended approach to video production that leaves room for the expression of "indigenous ways of seeing." As the project developed, however, the priority of finding or providing the conditions for indigenous ways of seeing to emerge gives way to making culture visible, a more activist approach to using visual media to assert indigenous autonomy. In other words, the question of an aesthetic possibility that the language in the manual asserts is replaced in practice by the imperative to position visual self-representation as a postura at the center of indigenous struggles for self-determination.

Building the Program: Transferencia de Medios
Audiovisuales a Organizaciones y Comunidades Indígenas

The quote that opens this chapter is taken from the printed brochure of one of the first pan-Mexican indigenous media festivals. The brochure was written in the offices of the INI's Archivo Etnográfico Audiovisual, in Mexico City, and speaks of this familiar, if outdated, interest on the part of nonindigenous people in finding a different ("their own") visual language that might breathe new life into stagnant Western art forms, much as modernist painters of the 1920s were interested in non-Western, "primitive" art. There is also an important precedent in anthropology from the 1970s, when Sol Worth and John Adair taught Navajo individuals how to make 16 millimeter films in the hope that a Navajo worldview would produce a different visual language on film (Worth and Adair 1997). The point in bringing these earlier experiences into a discussion of indigenous media in the twenty-first century is that vestiges of the way they position indigenous peoples as "other" are still at play in how indigenous media is interpreted, consumed, and discussed. Focusing on how indigenous videomakers might produce a different visual language also situates indigenous media production within a safe, fairly nonpolitical arena of cultural expression, rather than that of political and social change, which is the proper place to locate the indigenous media initiatives I discuss in this book. In Oaxaca, this incipient search for an indigenous visual language was transformed relatively quickly into the possibility for a "comunicación de lucha," or social struggle media, especially once the Ejército Zapatista de Liberación Nacional (EZLN) put indigenous struggles center stage.

As the bureaucratic title of the program suggests, Transferencia de Medios Audiovisuales a Organizaciones y Comunidades Indígenas (TMA) was created to fulfill the INI's new institution-wide directive to shift more functions and control over institutional resources and programs to indigenous people, as described in the *tareas*, or "tasks," set forth by the INI director Arturo Warman for his directorship, from 1989 to 1994.[2] The notion of transference also indexes the institution's paternalistic stance toward indigenous peoples by carrying an implicit suggestion that indigenous peoples are beholden to the INI's benevolence for their access to audiovisual media when, in fact, urban and foreign migration is probably more responsible than the INI for the proliferation of video technologies in indigenous communities. Juan

José García, who was one of the TMA's key figures, pointed out in 2000 that the TMA had strengthened "naturally occurring" processes in communities.[3] In his view, indigenous video production would clearly exist without the INI: "It would just have been a lot harder" (ibid.). One "naturally occurring" process García refers to specifically is community organizing around notions of "comunalidad," a notion that underwrites indigenous autonomy (chapter 3), but other processes include the very human practice of storytelling. The point to understand here is that the INI program did not simply put a technology to a social process already underway, the INI created video indígena and along with it the social role of indigenous videomakers.

The transference program emerged in 1989 as Warman's *proyecto consentido*, or "pet project." Warman dabbled in filmmaking early in his career as an anthropologist, and he steered the project to fulfill many of the transformative directives he planned for the institution as a whole. His close friendship with the director of the Archivo Audiovisual Etnográfico, filmmaker Alfonso Muñoz Jimenez, further solidified the necessary conditions for the program to take off with unprecedented autonomy within the INI, which had advantages and disadvantages. Unlike the system of indigenous radios, the TMA was never given a structural place within the INI, and the program had to rely instead on the relative security and effectiveness of individuals committed to the project's survival. A major crisis in the project following Warman's (and later Muñoz's) departure from the INI left the project vulnerable to the political whims of the upper-level management, who felt threatened by the "independence" of the TMA, especially after the EZLN launched its rebellion, in January of 1994.

One member of the original TMA project-development team, Carlos Cruz, attributes the team's rupture to the team's own level of "insolence, liberty or distance from the canons of the institution."[4] Following Warman's and Muñoz's lead, the project developers inadvertently limited the project by threatening the INI's hierarchical power structure: "Perhaps the danger [the project] represented, above all, was that we were breaking out of the ignorant schemes of authority among medium level bureaucrats at INI who consciously or unconsciously create groups of power in the communities. 'Those dummies who come to teach video, who even say the equipment is for the indigenous people and not for themselves, that it should be at the service of indigenous people and not at the service of the institution.' We were not in agreement. We stayed outside the power structure" (ibid.). This overtly contentious dynamic fostered by locating an independently minded program within the thick and decidedly hierarchical bureaucracy of an institution like the INI is particularly relevant for understanding how the TMA developed in Oaxaca and prefigures the limits to *transferencia*.

By the time the TMA organized the last large-scale, extended video production workshop, in May of 1994, upper-level INI bureaucrats had ousted Warman and Muñoz, and the program's original development team was barely functioning. Nevertheless, the second phase of the TMA project was underway with the inauguration of the first of four CVIs in Oaxaca City, a postproduction and training facility that became the single most important space for video indígena in Mexico (thanks to Guillermo Monteforte, the center's first director).[5]

In 1989, the INI's Departamento de Investigación y Promoción Cultural and the Archivo Etnográfico Audiovisual organized a joint seminar called "Antropología y Comunicación," in which nonindigenous anthropologists and filmmakers were invited to discuss how to implement Warman's vision of transferring institutional functions to indigenous peoples within the archive. The seminar presentations were published in a small book, entitled *Hacia un video indio* (Toward an Indian video) (INI 1990a). Though there were voices in opposition—mostly those of filmmakers who felt their jobs were threatened by the very idea of transference, and a minority of anthropologists who insisted on literacy as a prerequisite for learning a visual language, or who were suspicious of the imposition of audiovisual technology on traditional communities—the fundamental idea of transference was not questioned. In his introductory words at the seminar, Muñoz articulated the rationale behind "un video indio":

> It is true that video, television, radio and photographic cameras, satellite antennas and cinema, are technological instruments of urban, industrial and dominant society, but these are also part of asymmetric conditions of the reality of indigenous peoples. It is a fact that these technologies are operating in indigenous regions, fulfilling a communicative function between disymbolic realities, a unidirectional communication without any regard for other necessities, of other forms of seeing, of feeling of self-representation. There is a need and desire to generate spaces in the arena of more

direct communications, less persuasive that respond to the needs and realities of an unprotected sector of the population. (Muñoz Jimenez 1990, 9)

This democratic imperative to correct the asymmetrical, single direction of mass media was accompanied by a more specific institutional incentive that Muñoz explained to me in an interview. The potential fiscal efficiency of having a permanent fieldworker on hand to tape from an "insider's perspective" appealed to INI anthropologists as a sound research strategy. In other words, having community people with video equipment would reduce the research expenses of the institution and allow much longer shooting periods.[6] Building on the idea of the cultural promoter, discussed in the previous chapter as someone attuned to the INI's objectives but working inside his community, the video program sought to train indigenous peoples to "do the institution's work." However, this kind of pragmatic rationale does not appear in any official descriptions of what became the TMA. Instead, the democratization of mass media and the overarching institutional current to represent the pluricultural composition of Mexico, along with the goal of developing an indigenous visual language, were stitched together to form the legitimizing rationale of the TMA, as the opening quote to this chapter emphasizes.

Muñoz was given full authority by Warman to turn the TMA into a reality, and he, in turn, handed the task over to a group of hand-picked, nonindigenous Mexico City-based media professionals with healthy skepticism toward government projects: Carlos Cruz, Guillermo Monteforte, and Juan Cristián Gutiérrez. Gutiérrez held a Master's in philosophy and had worked for Mexican television and for the BBC in London. Cruz and Monteforte were both graduates of film school—Cruz in Mexico City and Monteforte (an Italian-born, Canadian national) in Toronto. Cruz was working as a documentary producer for the National Autonomous University of Mexico at the time he was approached by Muñoz. He was poised to solidify his career in more commercial circuits of media production when he decided to join the project. His description of his decision to join the project is common to many INI workers who begin their work with the INI with little or no knowledge of, much less direct experience with, indigenous peoples and yet feel a calling that seems very exciting (compare Saldívar 2001). "On an emotional level there was much pleasure, I was pleased in a way I can't explain . . . At the time I had an offer to start a soap opera and a film series; in fact, I left a film project. In other words, it was a time of excitement about the purpose of it all [*del porque*]. I wasn't clear why I was doing it; I only knew that I had to do it. It was an opportunity to learn."[7]

Monteforte was working at the Archivo Etnográfico Audiovisual at the time. He remembers being at, but not participating in, the "Antropología y Comunicación" seminar, in 1989. A combination of skepticism and a general "anti-institutional attitude," kept him from taking interest in the transferencia proposal. In fact, Monteforte admits that he had accepted a position coordinating production at the archive, mostly as a way to protect an INI-produced documentary he was editing from "accidents," and earn a little money doing it.[8] When Muñoz asked Monteforte to join Cruz and Gutiérrez on the TMA project team, Muñoz convinced him with the following logic, which became one of the project's principal rationales: "Look, Guillermo, mass media are going to reach [indigenous people] anyway, what we can do is make sure it reaches them in a way they can appropriate it, make it theirs so they can become more than passive beings invaded by all of this stuff."[9] In addition, opposition to the project within the INI in fact fueled the commitment of the project developers, who felt it was a special challenge to prove the erroneousness of INI staff who claimed that teaching indigenous people who lacked literacy how to use video was absurd.[10] Despite the twinge of truth to the assertion that teaching indigenous people to make their own videos was, in effect, teaching themselves out of a livelihood, TMA project developers felt it was more important to "create the potential for the development of indigenous visions of themselves than to make one more ethnographic film."[11]

The term "video indígena" first emerged in this contested institutional context. According to Monteforte, who is the only original member of the project team who has remained closely involved with the development of indigenous video in Mexico, video indígena was "una cosa completamente nuestra" (something completely ours), meaning it was of nonindigenous origin: "We invented it, we who are on this side, wanting indigenous people to do video."[12] The idea itself of indigenous people doing video, or at least taking it seriously as a development tool, was also theirs: "Nor was there a demonstrated necessity on their part for video. They were doing their thing, some were playing with their little cameras, but there were very few people who said: 'Here, let's do something to develop this.' "[13]

Despite the existence of several indigenous media projects underway in other parts of the world during the late 1980s, not to mention the important legacies of revolutionary and anti-imperialist cinema in other parts of Latin America, the creators of the INI's transference program believed they were "discovering something completely new."[14] The only project that served as a precedent for them was also "Mexican"—an independent Super-8 film workshop given to Huave-Ikoods women in the village of San Mateo del Mar, in the Oaxacan isthmus, in 1985. The INI's archive postproduced two documentary films from the workshop and still holds the rights to distribute them: *Tejiendo mar y viento* and *La vida de una familia Ikoods* (1987). Video indígena is an open category and "happens" all over Latin America today, but it has particular roots as a formation and process that are located in a specifically Mexican context, given *carácter nacional* by the INI.

Teaching Video Indígena: TMA National Video Workshops

The transference program was created in Mexico City, at the offices of the INI's archive, but the program was given shape by the project team through a series of four national video training workshops that took place annually, from 1990 through 1994, at the INI's training center in Tlacolula de Matamoros, in the Central Valley of the state of Oaxaca (only thirty to forty-five minutes from Oaxaca City by road). The workshops lasted six to eight weeks each and covered the basics of preproduction (how to conceive and organize a video), production (basic camera technique, framing, and movement), and editing (how to put images or sequences together to tell a story). And at the end of each workshop, the INI gave each participating organization or community a video production package, which included a camera, tripod, editing station (with two monitors, a playback and record deck, and an edit controller), a set of lights, and an aluminum shelving unit. In the four workshops, a total of eighty-five participants representing thirty-seven different organizations from thirteen different states were trained. Nearly half of those organizations were from the state of Oaxaca (Cremoux 1997).

The INI's delegation from the state of Oaxaca positioned itself early to play a central role in the program's development. The largest INI state delegation, representing the largest indigenous population in the country, the Oaxacan delegation had a reputation within the institution for being belligerent toward central authority and sought to corner valuable resources by hosting TMA workshops.[15] The Oaxacan delegate managed to fully equip and furnish the new training center in Tlacolula using TMA funds, and successfully secured four of the ten trainee spots at the first workshop for Oaxacan organizations.

The formal selection process for the workshops initially entailed mobilizing the INI's national network of state delegations and CCIs to propose candidates for the first workshop, though problems with relying exclusively on the institution's own circuit quickly surfaced. The project team sought to attract members of community organizations rather than individuals, in order to increase the chances that the resources given by the INI (both training and equipment) would not be used for personal gain. But even with this intention in mind, the use of the CCIs as nominating bodies was problematic since many of the trainees who showed up for the workshop were named not for their interest in or potential to benefit from video, but because they were either members of INI "client organizations" who were owed a favor of some kind from the institution, or members of organizations created with funding from the National Solidarity Program (through the Fondos Regionales) and little community representation (Cremoux 1997).

Furthermore, placing the selection process in the hands of regional INI leadership facilitated the exclusion of organizations and communities deemed problematic by the INI. For example, members of Radio y Video Tamix, the media collective I focus on in chapter 4, were intentionally not invited to attend the first workshop, because the INI state delegate feared the institution would be seen as supporting a community known for engaging in land disputes.[16] A related problem with the selection process for the first workshop was that it provided the team with no way to screen out the *becario profesional* or *cursólogo profesional*, folks who go from workshop to workshop as their modus vivendi, according to Cruz and Gutiérrez. Thus, the first workshop made for an odd mix of trainees, but a good source of anecdotes, as Monteforte described to me in an interview:

> On one hand, you had the son of a cattle-owning *cacique* [local boss] from the Yucatán who wasn't even indigenous, and on the

other hand, you had participants like Don Procopio, a Tepehuano elder from Nayarit with limited command of the Spanish language. Don Procopio seemed to be confused by the whole idea of video production. It wasn't until the fourth or fifth day of the workshop that we finally realized that Don Procopio thought he had been sent to attend a workshop about pig husbandry and simply did not understand what we were doing with all these cameras![17]

On the flip side, two Oaxacan men who later became "stars" of the INI program were not on the original list of participants, but were practically forced to attend at the last minute after two of the candidates the Oaxacan delegate had insisted so much upon didn't show.[18]

After the first workshop, the TMA implemented an application process that included interviews in Mexico City. Delegations and CCIs were still enlisted to spread the word about the program, but an open call would potentially solicit participation from organizations outside the INI's purview. Additionally, the application and interview process gave the team a chance to select representatives from organizations with proven track records or at least with some clear idea of a video project (instead of, say, animal husbandry). The new protocol also gave the team the opportunity to take an applicant's age and gender into consideration.

The eight-week workshops inherently posed a problem of time commitment for older people serving official cargos (positions of authority) within their communities and for women who were in charge of feeding their households, cared for young children, and faced gender biases.[19] For different reasons, youth presented other problems. Though young people were generally very taken by the medium, their levels of maturity and follow-though compromised the project on a long-term basis, according to Cruz. On the other hand, younger trainees held the potential of becoming video instructors who would one day replace the original project team, which, according to Cruz, was an important goal of the team. Thus, the team set age parameters above fifteen and below fifty years of age for trainees. From the beginning, the team insisted on including female trainees, and sought to incorporate a female graduate into the teaching team for subsequent workshops, according to Cruz, but this goal was only partially met. Of the eighty-five participants trained in the national workshops, less than 20 percent were women.[20]

These considerations accompanied specific institutional guidelines that prohibited the TMA development team from working with political organizations. Only productive and cultural organizations were invited to participate, "because INI followed Salinista policy: we were not to work with political organizations . . . This was made explicit" (Gutiérrez, quoted in Cremoux 1997, 75). And within these parameters, institutional guidelines true to Solidarity program's emphasis on "profitable and recuperative" projects steered them toward a preference for productive organizations over cultural ones, because it was believed that productive organizations would be able to offer at least minimal resources for video production (Cremoux 1997, 75). For the most part, this theory did not prove true. In 2000, of the surviving production units formed during the national workshops held from 1990 to 1994, the majority were funded by individuals who paid for expenses out of pocket (mostly from teaching salaries) or obtained some kind of grant specifically for video production. Of the selection criteria mentioned—age, gender, clear vision for video, type of organization, and community representation—the last was of most importance to the project team. If the organizations that received the equipment and whose members were trained did not have solid relationships in their communities, then TMA, in Cruz's words, would be akin to "arrando en el mar" (tilling in the ocean). While seeds from the program did take root in communities, the project nevertheless confronted an ocean of unexpected obstacles in home communities.

The workshops were not only the main activity of the first phase of the project, but served as a learning and testing ground for the development of the idea of video indígena itself (much as the CCIs in the INI's development were considered "pilot projects" in the 1950s). The team's teaching methodology evolved on the job, in a self-consciously intuitive manner. Cruz calls their method "maravillosamente intuitivo" (marvelously intuitive). The team divided their work in a way that came "naturally" to each member's strengths and individual skills, an organizational pattern that Monteforte would later recreate in the production collective Ojo de Agua Comunicación S.C. (chapter 3). Gutiérrez made constant and conscious attempts to overtly shape the teams' visions of video indígena by taking prolific notes and working out their emerging ideas on paper (a role he played later at the Communications Forum of the EZLN's Foro Nacional in 1996). Monteforte, an accomplished film editor, took charge of the postproduction section of the workshop. And Cruz, the only member of the team with any actual teaching experience, was the principal video instructor. In his own opinion, Cruz was the best candidate for this position, which implied more sustained contact with the trainees, because he has the most "ethnic" looks of the three, something that he thought would grant him more potential success as an instructor. He considers himself "closer to indigenous people in terms of color, language, vocabulary and general appearance."[21]

Their approach to teaching indigenous video involved teaching technical aspects of production and editing as well as fostering a critical perspective about media more generally. The technical aspects involved quite a bit of translation and demystification. The team perceived a pervasive feeling that video production was simply beyond the reach of many trainees, and it didn't help that everything was in English. Cruz proposed that all the technical terms, such as "play" and "record," be translated into indigenous languages, in order to erase the cultural imposition (imperialism) of English, but that proposal was never rigorously attempted. A handful of terms, however, were consistently translated into Spanish—like "*balance de blanco*," for "white balance," and "*grabar*," for "record," while others, like "pause," "iris," and "focus," either did not need translation or were used in English (as were "zoom" and "play"). In particular, the term "*videoasta*" (videomaker) presented imperialist dilemmas to the team, and they searched for more "organic" titles like "*creador de imágenes*" (creator of images). At the root of their concern was the recognition that the project was potentially creating individual artists, modeled after themselves, despite (or even against) their interests in community solidarity: "Before there can be a community videomaker or 'creator of images' there has to be an expressed need. A community needs to first recognize that it lacks a videomaker and then dedicate the effort and social recognition to develop one."[22] If this need is produced or imposed, Cruz argued, they run the risk not only of uselessly tilling the ocean, but also of creating *seres desvinculados* (disconnected beings).

In this first part of their approach, the team felt they had a relatively high success rate. Cruz recalled only two encounters where people had difficulty learning the equipment itself, and in both cases there were obvious intervening obstacles. The first was an elderly Cora man who spoke little Spanish and, like Don Procopio, had signed up for the workshop without realizing that it was about video. His lack of interest and general frustration inhibited the learning process. The second case was a Mixtec traditional healer who simply did not see the value in video and was very concerned about being away from her patients. It was not until the second week of the workshop that Cruz realized she had extremely impaired eyesight—a limitation, Cruz reasoned, that did not affect her own work as a healer who uses touch and spiritual intervention more than sight. After she was fitted with prescription eyeglasses, she finished the course with enthusiasm.

The second part of their approach in the workshop, which consisted of a kind of crash course in media literacy, was less successful. Many workshop evenings were spent screening classics in Mexican cinema, in an attempt to create the basis of a critical approach to stereotypical representations of Indian people in mainstream media. But, Monteforte observed, "they can see a film that is completely insulting to Indian people and enjoy it."[23] Any emergent critical understanding of stereotyping in mass media was even harder to apply to their own work. In this, Cruz says, "we really failed; we were never able to achieve it." Cruz believes that cultural inhibitions related to "offending" or "hurting" one another are responsible for this lack of openly critical discourse, but the project team may have undermined their intentions to foster a critical attitude toward media in part by introducing video as transparent, an "electronic mirror," rather than as a medium in which everything from framing to editing involves making active choices.

Underlying the group's "marvelously intuitive" teaching methodology was a commitment effort to facilitate the creation of an "indigenous visual language" or to at least provide the conditions for it to emerge.[24] Pragmatically this commitment translated into an attempt to refrain from imposing Western stylistic conventions in order to let the trainees' own visions or visual language surface. Team members continually questioned themselves about whether they were, in effect, reproducing a particular, Western way of looking at the world. Both Cruz and Monteforte agreed, however, that this constant questioning resulted in bewilderment among trainees, rather than a clearing of the aesthetic decks. As Cruz put it, "We realized that we were generating profound confusion, because for the students to have the teachers say 'this is how this works, but don't do it that way' . . . 'Do it or not? What in the devil are you teaching me?'"[25] Cruz remembered an anecdote about a Mixtec student who returned drunk from a weekend of R & R and confronted the trainers, saying, "Don't tell us lies because we're not stupid [*pendejos*]. Why don't you just tell us clearly what we are supposed to do?"[26] Following this frank, if inebriated, breakthrough, the team decided to follow a more conventional teaching plan—more along the lines of what and how they had been taught—with the hope that later, in the analysis and critique of the work, they would be able to foster the beginnings of a *propuesta indígena* (indigenous proposal).

Cruz hoped an indigenous visual proposal would emerge right away: "We thought that that was going to be the first step, but decided, in the end, that it was going to be taken later." Indeed, despite their best intentions, many trainees produced versions of cliché television formats (including on-camera interviewers and heavy-handed voice-overs). Monteforte remembers being enraged by this and even accusing his students of "copying." On the other hand, he also remembers being totally floored by beautiful abstract images a young man taped during the first workshop. A surprising, elegant mix of natural textures —wood, *zacate*, tree bark, sky, and a close-up of ants—turned out to be a result of not having figured out how to zoom out. Years later, Monteforte is still not sure what an indigenous proposal is or might be: "The difference between a complete error and something we can call experimental vanguard is totally in your head, no?"[27]

Some of the team members' frustration with the reluctant emergence of a "propuesta indígena" or the preponderance of mainstream, commercial media conventions needs to be situated in terms of the general "mediascape," as Arjun Appadurai (2000) would call it, in which trainees are enmeshed.[28] In other words, how do they experience audiovisual technology in their everyday lives? While I was not familiar with all the communities the trainees in the 1994 TMA video workshop called home, I did visit several, either during that particular trip to Mexico or on other occasions. In many indigenous communities throughout southern Mexico, you awake to a mix of roosters crowing and radios tuned to popular music stations. The INI's broad system of indigenous radios is also part of the mix providing music, local news, and a variety of announcements, often in indigenous languages. Loudspeakers call individuals to the phone both or make announcements about community visitors, meetings, or obligations, such as *tequio*, or "communal labor." Televisions are also present, though certainly not in every home, and are most notable in the afternoons and evenings, as the day winds down and that familiar blue glow emits from windows. Inside people's homes, photographs of important family events—baptisms, graduations, weddings, and community ceremonies and fiestas—are common and displayed prominently and with care in the collective, more formal areas of the home that often include a television set, delivering mostly commercial programming.[29]

Within this mediascape, dominated by commercial television, the TMA project developers inserted their preference for the documentary genre and relied on the idea of video as an "electronic mirror," as a way of translating the technology to first-time users who had had little to no interaction with production technology. It is worth reiterating that TMA project developers all came from documentary film backgrounds, and the institutional setting of the project—the Archivo Etnográfico Audiovisual, the INI's documentary production facility—prefigured video indígena as documentary. Moreover, the documentary—like testimonial literature, "a form advanced in large measure by *indígenas* who are increasingly speaking up for themselves rather than being the passive subjects described by non-indigenous writers" (Kearney and Varese 1995)—is closely associated with an imperative to set the historical record straight by revealing the long-ignored realities of marginalized peoples' lives. For these reasons, the documentary was "naturally" taught as the genre of video indígena and remains the prevalent format for most indigenous media productions in Mexico today.[30]

Two pragmatic issues reinforced the trainers' tendency to teach documentary over fiction: the possibility of shooting alone, or at least without relying on the kind of crew and talent needed for fiction, and the need of many organizations to have a simple record (or document) of their activities.[31] But on a deeper level, the project team developed the whole idea of video indígena around the idiom of the electronic mirror, a transparent window to the "real" world. The notion of the electronic mirror was intended to neutralize the video-capturing devices, render them nonthreatening, like a mirror on a wall. In the hands of indigenous people, the video camera could capture the real world, which is the opposite of the world of lies represented in mass media. Mass media present a world in which indigenous peoples do not see themselves reflected, as the Mixtec videomaker Emigdio Julián Caballero asserts in his statement entitled "La T.V. no es realidad" (1994). In other words, as the TMA (quite literally) invested in the possibility for indigenous peoples to represent themselves, the project granted video the "truth" of the real. Video indígena hinged on a presumed direct and unmediated relationship with the nonfilmic world, and curiously it is precisely this approach that complicated the project developers' efforts to develop a critical, deconstructionist approach to media generally, potentially limiting their ability to foster a "propuesta indígena."

The limitations of the real are apparent in a story Cruz told me about a discussion with the Mixe leader Floriberto Díaz. Cruz recalled that Díaz did not accept video's ability to represent reality. For Díaz, Mixe reality exceeds what the camera can capture, because in addition to the surface level, there is the root level (underground) and the sky. If all these levels are not represented, Mixe reality is incomplete.[32] Cruz discussed this exchange as a moment in which he realized the limitations of the ways they had been teaching video indígena. Rather than propose to Díaz ways that root and sky levels could be represented on video, Cruz accepted the shortcomings of their "intuitive" methods. Another community leader, Crisanto Manzano, a Zapotec man from Tanetze de Zaragoza who participated in the first TMA workshop, in 1990, and of all the trainees, the one who had probably made the most of his skills and the medium in general, resisted the video at first. Defending his preference not to attend the workshop to a friend, Manzano said, "I don't know how to do video . . . I haven't ever even had a photographic camera in my hands, much less a video camera . . . And then joking, I said, 'I am old, I'm not "video"'—because in Zapotec 'video' means child—why am I going to learn to be make 'video' if I already know how to make 'video'?" (Manzano, quoted in L. C. Smith 2005, 166; my translation). But at the urging of his wife, who is a teacher and progressive figure in his life, he did take the workshop and quickly got it: "I realized that you can transmit your sentiments, what you have inside, here in your heart and mind. That is how I started to work with this video, no? And since then I realize that, yes, you can do many things with video, transmit messages, sentiments, happiness, no? Everything, everything you want to, through this medium of sound and image" (Manzano, quoted in L. C. Smith 2005, 167; my translation).

Beyond methodological experiments or limitations of the real, investing in the transparency of video underpins the notion that video in the hands of indigenous people is an *herramienta* (a tool) with which indigenous people can see themselves unmediated by others. Forged into such a tool, video provides a way for strengthening indigenous identities and cultures. Had the instructors invested more time in teaching how video, as an artistic and creative medium, could be used to express the reality Díaz describes and the sentiments Manzano affirms, they may have seen the beginning of a propuesta indígena or a "different visual language," despite the impossibility of such a thing being singular. But teaching video as a transparent medium belies the inherent manipulation and creativity of the person or people behind the lens, let alone those in the editing suite. Documentaries don't lie, but once you learn the craft—how video is assembled and all the choices that go into its making—you can also deconstruct visual languages and visual statements, and discern how biases are represented, especially by those who participate in the continued denial of full indigenous rights by depicting indigenous subjects as either backward, stuck in the past, or passive. The TMA team did attempt to teach media literacy and critical approaches to media reception, but not surprisingly this lesson took much longer to sink in than, say, how to press the bright red "rec" button.

By the fourth and last TMA workshop, in the spring of 1994, the original project team had ruptured and Muñoz and Warman had left the INI in what Monteforte describes as an "institutional drama." The disruption of the TMA project, however, was just a ripple compared to the shockwaves rocking the country after the EZLN, on the first day of the same year, declared war on the Mexican government and the ruling PRI party began assassinating its and the country's leadership.[33] The TMA was given a new director, Cesar Ramirez, an anthropologist and photographer who was hired from within INI ranks. Ramirez had a previous friendship with Monteforte and convinced him to stay on, and Monteforte in turn convinced Cruz, who had left the project early in 1994, to return to teach the last workshop. According to Cruz, the INI had become a *caja de crystal* (crystal box), fragile and empty, a box no one dared touch after the EZLN launched its rebellion. Radio stations sponsored by the INI, one of which was captured by the EZLN in its first offensive, were brought under direct control by the state as the INI installed technology to remotely cut the signal at each station, leading Cruz and others to think that the video program would soon follow. But despite the rebellion, assassinations, acrimonious departures, and ruptures, along with severe budget cuts, the TMA survived 1994.

The next section of this chapter serves as a visual reprieve, featuring direct quotes from the CVI's teaching manual, *Taller introductorio de video indígena,* and a series of photographs I and the instructors took during a video workshop held at El Pípila, Oaxaca, a multiethnic indigenous community in the isthmus of Oaxaca that only gained rights over its land (in the form of an *ejido*) in the late 1970s, after decades of government negotiations and violent struggle with a private mestizo landowner. The center conducted hundreds of three to four day video workshops from 1994 to 2000, but the El Pípila workshop was one of the only workshops given specifically for women during that period. This workshop was for the women's caucus of the Peasant and Indigenous Union of the Northern Zone of the Isthmus (UCIZONI), considered to this day one of the "bright spots" in regional indigenous movements by experts (Stephen, paraphrasing Díaz Polanco 2009, 132).

A *Taller Introductorio de Video Indígena*, Oaxaca, Mexico

When you learn to work with video, you begin to understand some basic elements that permit us to capture and manipulate images and sounds that communicate our ideas with clarity. We hope these pages will serve to help us remember some of the concepts and techniques discussed during the introductory course that we give at the Centro de Video Indígena, Oaxaca (CVI 1996) (see figure 2.1).

FIGURE 2.1. Learning to focus. The CVI's *Taller introductorio de video indígena*, El Pípila, Oaxaca. Photo: Juan José García, 1999.

It is very important to clarify that this is an introductory course to learn how to make video indígena. This is a course that teaches some elements that those of us who are not indigenous use when we make video, so that indigenous videomakers will modify them according to their own vision, realities and expressive needs. (CVI 1996) (see figure 2.2)

FIGURE 2.2. Heading out for a video exercise while members of the community prepare dishes for lunch. The CVI's *Taller introductorio de video indígena*, El Pípila, Oaxaca. Photo: Sergio Julián Caballero, 1999.

If the original cultures of the American continent are different than those of European and mestizo origin, then the manner of expressing themselves with images and sounds does not have to be the same. The task that indigenous videomakers have is to determine how this form of communication can serve to strengthen their own pueblos, building upon their own modes of aural and visual communication, such as language, traditional stories, music, symbols, landscapes and figures that appear on textiles and crafts. (CVI 1996) (see figure 2.3)

FIGURE 2.3. El Pípila's municipal building. The CVI's *Taller introductorio de video indígena*, El Pípila, Oaxaca. Photo: Erica Cusi Wortham.

Rules and definitions exist to be defied, questioned and finally broken when necessary. In order to define a video of indigenous pueblos, this process is of utmost importance. (CVI 1996) (see figure 2.4)

FIGURE 2.4. Discussing the final exercise, edited in-camera. The CVI's *Taller introductorio de video indígena*, El Pípila, Oaxaca. Photo: Erica Cusi Wortham.

What is written here can be considered as a starting point so that one day indigenous videomakers can write their own manual that proposes elements and concepts that will result in a truly indigenous video. (CVI 1996) (see figure 2.5)

FIGURE 2.5. Shooting titles. The CVI's *Taller introductorio de video indígena,* El Pípila, Oaxaca. Photo: Erica Cusi Wortham.

TMA Phase Two: Centro de Video Indígena

Rather than part of a clearly articulated plan, the second phase of the TMA was conceived as a kind of repository of unfinished business, a place to pursue what remained beyond the reach of the national workshops. Guided by an imperative to secure the rootedness of the TMA in the face of institutional insecurity and significant community-based challenges to video indígena (having mostly to do with limited resources), the team sought ways to provide continuity for the project and secure the viability and future of the project, independent of the state. Project continuity was addressed through the creation of the Centro de Video Indígena in Oaxaca City, in 1994.

Much like the INI's expansion phase, 1971–88, discussed in the previous chapter, the second phase of the TMA was characterized by "national" ambitions that exceeded the capacities of the program staff

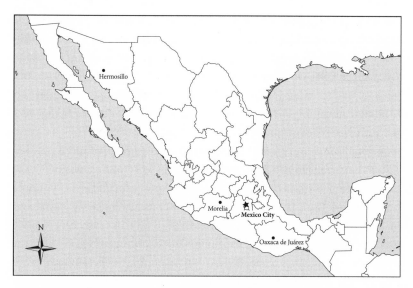

MAP 2.1. Map of Centros de Video Indígena © Daniel Dalet, d-maps.com.

and sacrificed quality in favor of quantifiable results: the number of production packets distributed, courses given, and indigenous communities involved (Cremoux 1997, 76). Cruz recalls that the national goal of the project was to have roughly one hundred video production units in place throughout the country, or two units per ethnic group (using the INI's official count of fifty-six, though now the CDI claims there are sixty).[34] Thirty-seven indigenous production units were created during the four national workshops, and while the INI did not donate equipment to indigenous organizations since the last workshop, in 1994, many more indigenous organizations and individuals received video training through the INI's network of CVIs.

After 1994, the INI established three additional CVIs—the second in Morelia, Michoacán (opened in 1998), the third in Hermosillo, Sonora (in 1999), and the fourth and most likely last CVI in Mérida, Yucatán (in 2000) (see map 2.1). Under the CDI, the Indigenous Video Centers have continued to operate but are less focused on training and community participation than in the early INI years.

The TMA project team was less concerned with infrastructural expansion than with cultivating the seeds they planted at the workshops. There was a general recognition among them that without follow-up community visits, video indígena might not take root at all. Cruz remembered that the team proposed an annual TMA work plan to the INI that involved regular community visits of at least a week in duration, visits in which video instructors (whether members of the original project team or trainees turned instructors) would address problems related to videomaking in communities. While such an ambitious plan was never fully implemented, some community visits did take place. "Our expectations were unfortunately very high," Cruz admitted. "The vast majority of the equipment was being profoundly underutilized" in the communities. Despite the enthusiasm many of the trainees demonstrated during the workshops (especially the younger ones), video took second place to their community obligations and responsibilities once they returned home. In fact, in many cases, video was an "absurd proposition for their families, even sometimes for the organizations that sponsored their participation in the workshops."[35] Cruz added: "Our first reading of this was profoundly disconcerting; it was very painful. We felt that we were not capable of making this happen quickly enough for it to root itself and have products immediately. Afterwards we consoled ourselves a bit by understanding that we were thinking about utopian youths living in ideal conditions, and the reality was that each indigenous community was far from ideal." Cruz's consolation amounts to a frustrating array of adversities for indigenous people trying to grow the seeds the TMA team planted once in their home communities.

The most common adversity was a chronic lack of resources. As Juan José García said, "It's one thing to train someone how to use a camera and editing equipment, but quite another to assist someone [from] poor communities, where video is not considered a productive activity. . . . Because video . . . is not like the irrigation project or the rabbit breeding project or the cultivation of tomatoes, [people say] 'We're going to let it wait for a bit; there's not very much interest [from the community]; it doesn't matter right now; it's not urgent.' So the equipment is shelved and eventually damaged."[36] Most videomakers at the time were also heads of families, community authorities, or had agricultural or domestic responsibilities that left little time for video production. And a lack of community interest—or, as I discuss in chapter 4, outright community opposition—provided more incentives to shelve video indígena than to make it happen. As for the TMA program, a lack of funding and no solid distribution plan left the community video-production units with little to no means of looking beyond the community for support, though some videomakers did receive international production grants that significantly boosted their chances of producing finished programs.

An underlying issue challenging video indígena even further is that "there is not a clear idea about what communications media are," according to García. He explained, "Videomakers leave the workshops convinced of the usefulness of video, that it presents an opportunity for them to be heard, but if they don't have clear, defined projects. . . . They say they are going to use video to rescue the culture of their community, but they aren't specific, and without a plan, they are not going to get the support of their community leadership who controls the financing."[37] These two related obstacles to video indígena—a lack of a clear understanding about the project itself and a lack of financing —were addressed over time by CVI staff. The specific problem of turning an understanding of the "usefulness of video" into a video program that "rescues culture" was addressed by the productions of individual mediamakers, according to García, but those productions were a result of careful and dedicated work of CVI staff.

The imperative to root communications media in terms of the community's needs also highlights the importance of grounding emerging videomakers, lest they remain "disoriented beings," as Cruz worried might happen. García characterized the videomaker's trajectory (most are men) in his community as going from *la malinche* to *líder*, from a traitor dealing with the enemy to being a community leader.[38] In other words, a lack of understanding about the project affects not only the technical aspects of making a video that rescues culture, but how to get the community to support making video in the first place. In the process, individual videomakers must locate themselves as videomakers in their communities by proving the usefulness of video. They must achieve its embeddedness.

Financing video indígena needs to be understood on both those levels, as well. The cost of tape stock, electricity, equipment repair, and travel forced the more ambitious videomakers to seek outside funding for their projects. Oaxaca-based indigenous videomakers have successfully competed for a number of production grants from national (state and federal) and international foundations.[39] However, funding in and of itself does not secure the viability of video indígena; on the contrary, in some cases, outside funding has made the whole enterprise much more challenging, especially for mediamakers working within their communities, where grants to individuals can strain the redistributive system and fuel an already healthy breeding ground for jealousy. Outside funding lends videomakers a needed source of motivation, moral and financial support, but can also estrange them from the very communities they aim to represent and strengthen.[40]

Another general concern of the TMA project team, related to the project's long-term viability, was distribution. Cruz observed, "Part of the original plan that we insisted on a lot was, yes, that they produce work about indigenous people and for them as well, but we also—I came to think that they are part of a world and that world is first a region, then a state, then the country and then the whole world— insisted there had to be a development towards the creation of distribution and exhibition possibilities."[41] But distribution was not incorporated alongside production as a priority for the TMA, which raises the following question. If the TMA project was founded in part to fulfill Mexico's constitutional directive to "represent Mexico's pluricultural composition," to whom were these videomakers representing Mexico's pluriculturalism without a viable system for getting their work screened? The INI's system of radio stations were a broadcast-based project, but no counterpart was ever established or envisioned for video, as far as I could tell, despite the Mexican government's close relationship with commercial television and the existence of a least one public television channel that regularly programmed "cultural" content. Instead, distribution was relegated to the TMA's catchall second phase. As media professionals accustomed to the imperative of distribution for success, the TMA project team discussed distribution as a possible solution to the issue of financing video indígena. It is important to note that in most cases TMA staff use the Spanish word *difusión* for "distribution," which carries a bit of the "diffusion" the word implies. Less direct or deliberate than distribution, difusión is about getting the word out, about putting video indígena on the map, so to speak, through exhibition. It was not about selling tapes. Difusión has mainly taken place through festivals and noncommercial exhibition circuits in local, regional, national, as well as transnational contexts, and while some attempts have been made to show video indígena on mainstream television in Mexico, the constraints of quality and duration have at times been rejected as impositions antithetical to the goals of the project.[42] Once they became independent from the state, however, indigenous videomakers who form part of the Ojo de Agua media collective have gotten get their work on Mexican television, mostly through an educational series funded by the Ministry of Education.

It is precisely these kinds of challenges to the TMA that have fueled some of the project's critics. Jaime Martínez Luna, the Zapotec anthropologist and renowned songwriter who has written extensively about the notion of comunalidad, believes that the only worthwhile aspect of the TMA is the fact that some of people working with the project are very committed to indigenous struggles and, he admits, "some support is better than none at all." "But that is the only redeemable aspect of the project, because it functioned like any other government agency, with projects pulled from their sleeves, elaborated into written proposals, and taken to the communities when the people don't really need them and obviously don't give them much attention."[43]

The concrete step taken in the TMA's second phase, intended to address the concerns of community acceptance and distribution, was the creation of the Centro de Video Indígena in Oaxaca City, in May of 1994. The idea for a video center first emerged in 1992. According to Monteforte, he and Muñoz arrived at the idea almost simultaneously, as a way to sustain the genuine enthusiasm of so many TMA trainees. They also envisioned the CVI as a way to provide some access to videomaking for indigenous people who had cameras but did not participate in the INI workshops. In 1993 there was a flood of money from the Solidarity program into the TMA, and Monteforte was asked to put together a CVI proposal and figure out how to spend $200,000 in fifteen days. Monteforte remembered starting the proposal, but ultimately decided to wait; he didn't feel right about spending so much money without taking the time to carefully think things through. He submitted the project to the INI the next year and it was approved (after Muñoz had left the INI) just months before the EZLN declared war against the Mexican government.

When the CVI first opened, it was tucked behind a row of eucalyptus trees in an upper- and middle-class residential section of Oaxaca City, located several miles north of the city's historic colonial center, known as La Cascada. It was housed in a two-story concrete structure that had originally been built as a four-bedroom, two-bathroom home, complete with a full kitchen and an outdoor patio that was overrun by a prolific, leafy avocado tree. The brown exterior belied the vivid interior. The walls were alive with a deeply saturated blue paint and an elegant display of framed INI photographs from the video archive's collection. A dormitory crammed with bunk beds and lockers shared the lower level with an expansive den and dining room that served as the center's general meeting and eating space. Upstairs, in the four rooms of the former home were the center's office, two VHS editing suites, and the center's "online" suite, which featured Beta SP decks and a computer-driven postproduction program called "Videomachine." The Macintosh computer that ran Videomachine was the center's only computer and was in constant demand. Three large closets upstairs stored the center's lending equipment—a fairly robust assortment of VHS and Hi-8 cameras, tripods, a few lights, cables, and batteries—and the video collection. The center's video collection, which García once described as the center's "backbone," consisted of approximately five hundred catalogued titles. The CVI's staff and its constituency regularly checked out equipment and titles from the collection.

In the wake of the national workshops, the CVI offered a kind of continuing education for videomakers, with basic production and editing skills as well as introductory workshops for beginners. Cruz recalls that the center was originally envisioned as "school"—on par with Oaxaca's famous painters' school—that would not only provide continuous movement to the TMA project but would also launch videomakers' careers.[44] In addition to training, the CVI had become an important postproduction facility, where videomakers came to transform the rough edits done in their communities into polished programs with titles, effects, and often subtitles (in English or Spanish, or sometimes both, depending on the intended audiences). For many years, the center coordinated the participation of indigenous videomakers from all over Mexico, in video festivals far beyond Oaxaca.

Guillermo Monteforte was the CVI director from 1994 to 1997. Monteforte's committed, 24–7 personal working style, combined with his healthy anti-institutional attitude and a chronic lack of resources, formed the CVI's "NGO" identity. The sumptuous budget Monteforte was originally offered in 1993 went into refashioning the La Cascada home into a video center, but the INI's "consumerist policy" left no funds for an operating budget. According to Monteforte, TMA director Cesar Ramirez "spent loads of money on the promotion and press for the inauguration. He put a lot of effort into the exterior façade of the project without thinking about how the interior should be," meaning the staff. The CVI was inaugurated in May of 1994 without an operating budget in place and just months before Mexico headed into a major economic recession and currency devaluation that severely crippled the INI's budget. The result of this unfortunate timing was that the CVI, under Monteforte, learned to operate with very little money. Monteforte recalled the absurdity of the center's first year: "There was a lot of money, but not one cent for gasoline. In other words, you could buy things, like a truck, but you couldn't use them. There was no money for salaries, for operating costs."[45] Monteforte paid the staff from his own pocket during much of the year, dipping into award money he received for one of the INI's last major documentaries, *Pidiendo Vida* (Monteforte 1992).

The staff at the center consisted of three people: Monteforte, an administrator, and a technical assistant. Each was inexperienced at his or her respective jobs, recalled Monteforte, including himself—he had directed videos, but not video centers like the CVI. There was Yolanda, "the administrator who had never worked as an administrator before or even secretary, nothing. Even receiving a phone call was chaotic."[46] And there was Sergio Julián Caballero, who "had worked in the fields in the north, but found it hard to commit at first and to learn how to work efficiently."[47] Caballero's first days at the CVI are illustrative of how the center initially took shape.

He left San Antonio Huitepec, his highland Mixtec community, for the CVI, on the advice of his *paisano*, Emigdio Julián Caballero, a TMA "graduate" and rising video indígena star at the time. Emigdio assured Caballero there was a job opening. Caballero went to the CVI and met Monteforte almost by accident after waiting for hours in front of the locked building. The CVI needed a twenty-four-hour watchman because the equipment was arriving soon and there was no security system in place. Caballero accepted the position without asking questions or even returning to Huitepec, and soon found himself virtually locked up in an empty building with no electricity. He lived two entire months this way, looking after more than a dozen shiny new boxes of video equipment, using candles to see at night and venturing only to the corner store to buy cheese and tortillas, and for some human contact. "I was educated in my community that if you are given a job to do, you stick to it and carry it out to the end."[48] Two weeks into his new job, when his money ran out, Caballero dared ask Monteforte about getting paid. Monteforte gave him 450 pesos, literally from his own pocket, until he managed to establish a monthly salary of 500 pesos.

"The CVI developed in fits and starts in this way," recalled Monteforte. But the center's *linea política*, or "political line," was developing in a steady manner, very personal to Monteforte and very much linked to the emerging Zapatista movement and struggles for indigenous self-determination. "Video wasn't seen so much as a threat to state power," but Monteforte admits he pushed it in that direction. One of the first things he did as director of the new CVI was to participate in a highly politicized regional meeting convened after the murder of a community organizer in the Zapotec Sierra Norte region of Oaxaca. This meeting was an opportunity to announce the opening of the CVI and was where Monteforte first promoted the idea of *comunicación de lucha* (social struggle media). "I think that it was at that meeting that I situated the CVI as something not totally institutional," Monteforte remembered. "We have tried from the beginning to maintain an informal atmosphere, much less bureaucratized . . . and people are surprised to learn it is part of INI. It looks more like an NGO."[49] García, the CVI's second and last director before the INI was transformed into the CDI, recounts how during a recent visit from a Canadian minister, the CVI appeared on a list of NGOs when "it [was] clearly not an NGO; it [was] a federal institution."[50] Nevertheless, the center is "totally different, much freer, with all the possibilities of what an institution in public service should do: serve the needs of the community or society, and not the other way around, employing society to be at the service of the institution, which is normally what happens in Mexico."[51]

García met Monteforte in 1992, when the TMA project team did a brief video-production workshop at the INI's new radio station, XEGLO Radio Guelatao, "La voz de la Sierra" (The voice of the mountains), in a small but prominent Zapotec community, Guelatao de Juárez. Named after the nineteenth-century Mexican president Benito Juárez, Mexico's famous "native son" and principal author of the constitution of 1857, Guelatao is known as an important regional center within the indigenous autonomy movement, in large part because the organization Fundación Comunalidad A.C. and its founder, Jaime Luna, are there. García grew up in Guelatao, though he spent his early childhood at an INI boarding school and does not speak much Zapoteco. He had been involved with the community's radio station initiative well before it became a reality under the INI's auspices. He became an experienced videomaker during the early 1990s, when, as member of Fundación Comunalidad, he produced a series of videos about natural resources in his region for the environmental summit in Rio de Janeiro. García also produced a short-lived television series called *Revista de la Sierra* (Magazine of the mountains), which aired on Oaxaca state television, Canal 9.

By 1997 García was one of the most experienced indigenous producers in the state and his close affiliation with Monteforte and the INI's radio station positioned him as one of the only viable candidates to take on the directorship of the CVI once Monteforte decided to step down. He was named director in 1997. Following closely in Monteforte's footsteps, García claims the center has been able to "transcend the institutional shadow" of the INI and defends the CVI's "independent" stance by citing the TMA's mandate—to facilitate indigenous appropriation of communication tools. "The real protagonists are the people in the indigenous communities," García insists, and as an employee of the INI he "supports, encourages, assists indigenous productions without taking credit for them."[52] Under García's and Monteforte's leadership, the CVI did not censor indigenous productions, though Monteforte did acknowledge some degree of "self-censorship."

In many ways, the center was able to maintain the independent stance of a nongovernmental organization because of the liminal way the transference program was situated within the INI, without a formal position within the institutional structure. The CVI reported directly to the TMA headquarters at the video archive in Mexico City, circumventing the authority of the INI's state delegation in Oaxaca City. The center depended on the will and effectiveness of a few individuals (TMA directors) who lobbied within the INI for the center's budget; its staff and directors managed to trade a lack of institutional security for a degree of autonomy that was crucial in the development of the CVI and how it shaped video indígena more broadly. But the fact that the center's staff and directors have had to carve out their autonomy at all, as García points out, belied the project's commitment to transference. Indeed, transferring the CVI was envisioned as an integral part of its establishment. According to Cruz, the project's developers expected to see it given over to an indigenous organization within its first year of operation. Instead, the center came under tighter control by the INI, starting in 1997, when the CVI was repositioned administratively under the state delegation.

In 1999, while I was conducting an informal interview with an INI anthropologist at the state delegation in Oaxaca City, an assistant peeked into her office to ask what was the final decision about the CVI's collection: was it going remain at the center to be transferred to the delegation? The CVI's very "backbone," as García described the collection, was possibly going to be transferred back to the INI, without ever having been actually transferred to indigenous control. The anthropologist (who wished to remain anonymous) explained to the assistant that while no decision had been reached, she wanted the collection to remain at the CVI, out of respect for García and the center's broad constituency of indigenous organizations that used the collection. Today the bulk of the archive, the collection of video programs amassed during the 1990s, is housed in the Oaxaca delegation of the CDI, in Oaxaca City. The CVI is there, too, but Monteforte, García, and Caballero left the INI one by one to form a new media organization—an actual NGO—in 1998, called Ojo de Agua Comunicacíon. Ojo de Agua emerged as a logical sequel to the CVI, considering its founding staff's overt support for indigenous self-determination and the government's obvious retreat from the idea of transference that originally underwrote the INI's program when it was invented in the late 1980s.

Looking at how video indígena was actually taught on the ground allows us to see the emergence of an entangled media form devoted to social change. A somewhat abstracted or removed interest in aesthetic possibilities, in what "an" indigenous visual language would look like, was replaced by a more engaged interest in fostering a form of media communication that supported or expressed a social and political postura. This move necessitated a shift away from government sponsorship, and nearly two decades later, a shift away from the indigenous label.

Independent of government sponsorship, the Ojo de Agua today focuses more on production than training, though it continues to be a clearinghouse (with a large collection of its own) offering vital support to indigenous videomakers in the region and beyond. In the most recent edition of Ojo de Agua's *Plan Rector* (work plan), for 2010–12, the organization details plans to start a formal study program or training center for indigenous media (Ojo de Agua 2010). This program would be widely discussed among their constituents and advisers, but Monteforte, the principal author of the organization's work plans, envisions it as a "complete program, structured and eclectic, technical and conceptual, politically committed without losing personal quality" (Ojo de Agua 2010, 24). Such a school would leave the electronic mirror far behind, replacing an "intuitive methodology" with a robust and vetted proposal "from below" for indigenous media production, a proposal drawn from wealth of experiences teaching video as "comunicación de lucha" to hundreds of indigenous individuals and organizations.

PART 2

Indigenous Media Organizations in Oaxaca

THREE

Regional Dimensions

Video Indígena beyond State Sponsorship

Communication founds culture. In it we recognize ourselves as
subjects and discover the necessity of the Other, the mirror of
ourselves. In this reflection and in the discourse that emerges
from it we find our place in the cosmos, we construct our identity. The problem is that we have been produced in a foreign
design, imposed from power and its vision of the world. The
place that we find ourselves in is not ours; it is the place of exclusion that power assigns us. Exclusion and power have been the
method and foundation of communications media.

Ojo de Agua Comunicación S.A. (Ojo de Agua 2000, 1)

The initiatives that predated or emerged from the transference program of the Instituto Nacional Indigenista (INI) attempted to move
video indígena outside the sphere of government sponsorship, and
they complicate and ground video indígena as a social process, filling
the social space of media production with yet more actors, activists,
and a diversity of perspectives from which to understand what is at
stake for indigenous people. The INI's national (and nationalistic)
scope is moderated, on the ground, by situated actors and activists
responding to regional demands and priorities from, in this case, the
Sierra Norte of Oaxaca. In the process, the notion of a "comunicación
de lucha" (where "lucha" means social struggle) empowered by the
redemptive project captured in the quote above, pushes video indígena to become self-sufficient. Communication is grounded as a fundamental aspect of culture, a basic right that has been withheld from
indigenous people. Video indígena returns to indigenous peoples the
tools to construct their own identity, according to their own design,
and yet, a decade after getting out from under government control,

video indígena, as a category, has lost some of its currency. As Juan José García discussed recently in a phone interview, video indígena "has gradually settled into history; it had its moment."[1] Today Ojo de Agua defines itself as an "NGO with eleven years of experience turning communications media, principally radio and video, into useful tools for the strengthening of indigenous *pueblos*" (Ojo de Agua, 2011, 5). They support *comunicación alternativa* (not video indígena per se) "because [they] want to contribute to the free expression of indigenous peoples" and distance themselves from the neoindigenist practices of the CDI (ibid.). The video indígena that Guillermo Monteforte and others invented during their time with the INI appears to have stayed within those confines, while comunicación alternativa thrives independently, resisting previous categorization but still working for indigenous peoples.

Three indigenous organizations in Oaxaca that turned to media production in the late 1980s and early 1990s collectively articulate the process of disentangling their initatives from government sponsorship: the community-based, nongovernmental group Fundación Comunalidad A.C., which spent nearly two decades trying to launch a regional radio project that eventually came under the INI's prevue; K-Xhon Video-Cine Zapoteca, an urban-based, independent organization that claims to have inspired the INI's Transferencia de Medios Audiovisuales (TMA) program; and the production organization Ojo de Agua Comunicación S.C., which grew directly out of the INI's TMA program and the Centro de Video Indígena (CVI). Narratives of these indigenous organizations demonstrate how indigenous activists choose communications media—radio, video, and low-power television—in their efforts to consolidate regional solidarity, an important step in recovering community values and building notions of autonomy. Not surprisingly, the INI played a role in the development of these organizations, if in different ways.

The region I envisioned before I started my field research encompassed the entire state of Oaxaca, but I quickly realized that becoming familiar with indigenous organizations across the state would require a team of field researchers and a considerably longer research period. For example, apart from attending the video workshop in El Pípila, which is located in the Oaxacan isthmus of Tehuantepec and a short visit with Teofila Palafox, the Ikoods-Huave videomaker who was trained in the Super-8 film workshop the INI sponsored in 1985, I was

MAP 3.1. Sierra Norte and Cajonos regions, Oaxaca © Daniel Dalet, d-maps.com.

not able to do sustained field research in this region of the state. A world unto itself, the Oaxacan isthmus is particularly known for the municipality of Juchitán and the leftist Zapotec peasant coalition the Worker-Peasant-Student Coalition of Tehuantepec (COCEI), which stands out in recent Mexican history for electing the first opposition municipal government (Campbell, Binford, Bartolomé, and Barabas 1993). Far from the warm, sandy winds of the isthmus, I focused on Oaxaca's northeastern Sierra Norte, where the dense terrain of social organizations rivals the *nudo*, or "knot," of mountains that characterize the state's topography (see map 3.1).[2]

The net I cast to gather the organizations discussed in this chapter was guided by a desire to contrast the INI's overdetermined way of "inventing" video indígena, but also to look at how an organization created under INI's auspices was able to reinvent itself, free from state sponsorship.[3] Fundación Comunalidad, and in particular its director, Jaime Martínez Luna, is the intellectual author of notions of community and indigenous autonomy that are pervasive among members of Ojo de Agua. Fundación Comunalidad is also intimately tied to INI's indigenous radio stations in Guelatao, Oaxaca. The story of that organization's struggle to establish a radio station adds a contrasting dimension to understanding state-sponsored media, by revealing differences in the way the state perceives radio and video. Members of K-Xhon claim to have inspired the idea of "un video indio," conceived of by the INI's director Arturo Warman, and position their organization squarely in opposition to the INI's program and state sponsorship more generally. Ojo de Agua, whose members were trained in video production and indigenous solidarity during the 1990s, at the CVI in Oaxaca, continues to be one of the most vital indigenous media organizations in Mexico today.

The sociologist Jorge Hernández Díaz and the anthropologist Benjamin Maldonado, who both live and work in Oaxaca City, have compiled comprehensive descriptions and analyses of Oaxaca's ethnic organizations.[4] The impressive number of social organizations *de lucha* (who support social change) can be understood in part by noting the relative need the state's population has for support from nongovernmental organizations. Oaxaca, like Chiapas, continues to be at the top of most major poverty indices. Maldonado identifies two types of organizations within the indigenous movement in Oaxaca. The first type are small community-based groups composed of a "few men and women who seek to construct collective alternatives to face crises within, not beyond, their community" (Maldonado 1998). These organizations generally cohere around productive projects and pursue the democratization of community politics in the face of *caciques* (local bosses). The second type consists of broader intercommunity groupings of municipal authorities that usually form in the process of negotiations with state and federal government agencies (Maldonado 1998, 369). This second type of organization tends to appear in regions with long trajectories of defending local autonomy and self-government, such as the Sierra Norte, a region active in Oaxaca's earlier declarations of sovereignty from Mexico (1914–1920) (Stephen 2002, 230).

Hernández Díaz situates Oaxaca's indigenous organizations historically, as part of a broader class-based social movement of the 1970s. Disenchanted with a homogenizing, classist ideology that did not consider cultural specificity, sectors of the movement reorganized around notions of ethnicity in the 1980s. Fundación Comunalidad and K-Xhon have roots in this reorganizing phase, what Hernández Díaz calls the "second generation" of indigenous organizations. And within the second generation, organizations from the Sierra Norte played a pioneering role in regional consolidation, according to Hernández Díaz.

Members of Fundación Comunalidad and K-Xhon cut their political teeth through direct participation in organizations of the Sierra Norte.

In 1982 indigenous activists from the Sierra Norte drafted a document that, according to Maldonado, "acquired national relevance" (Sarmiento and Mejía 1987). The document, called "The Struggle of the Autonomous Pueblos," expresses clear demands and proposals for the indigenous self-development of the region and invites other sectors of society to form alliances with the activists. The document also includes a critical revision of local history that repositions Benito Juárez—Mexico's famous "native son" was a Zapotec from the Sierra Norte—as an *autóctono renegado* (indigenous traitor) for his liberal reforms, which undermined communal principles of land tenure, leading to the renaming of the mountainous region as the "Sierra Juárez."[5] After this initial and unprecedented regional collaboration, the organizations suffered rifts and concentrated their efforts in smaller sections or "microregions" of the sierra.[6]

Fundación Comunalidad A.C. • Guelatao de Juárez is a small highland Zapotec community of 544, in the district of Ixtlán de Juárez, with a big claim to history. It is the birthplace of Mexico's only indigenous president, Benito Juárez, whose administration transformed the Mexican economic landscape in the nineteenth century with penetrating liberal reforms. The extensive neoclassical monument marking Juárez's birthplace wraps around the southern edge of a curious little lake whose extinct population of fish used to help feed the community. Fundación Comunalidad A.C., which is known simply as Comunalidad, is located on the corner of a short, paved street just steps from the monument to Juárez. At the other end of the same street is the INI's radio station, XEGLO Radio Guelatao, "La voz de la sierra" (The voice of the mountains). Comunalidad was a training ground for several Ojo de Agua members (Tonatiuah Díaz, Francisco Luna, Clara Morales, and Juan José García, in particular) and was one of the most prominent indigenous "voices" of the Oaxacan sierras.[7]

Comunalidad's story is about consolidating regional solidarity through the use of communications media. Its director and founding figure, Jaime Martínez Luna, is a prolific and recognized Zapotec intellectual and a nationally acclaimed musician, as well as a trained anthropologist with a degree from the Universidad Autónoma de México,

Mexico City. Martínez Luna's musical group, Trova Serrana, formed the basis of Comunalidad in the early 1980s. Indeed, more than half of the organization's office is dedicated to their recording studio and audio mastering system, and the group is widely known in the Sierra Norte, and Oaxaca generally, through their original songs—many sung in Zapotec—about life as a serrano. Underwriting the group's musical style and use of content that culturally resonates within the region is an understanding and articulation of community that is based on Juan José Rendón's four-part concept of community—territory, communal authority, tequio (communal labor), and the fiesta (Rendón 2003).

Martínez Luna dates his interest in communications media back to childhood curiosities about Superman and how comics are produced. After university training, Martínez Luna's curiosity was transformed into a more critical awareness of mass media and their the impact in the community: "Commercial media that foment the opening of consumer markets with the introduction of foreign elements into the community has been both my starting and end point."[8] But it was his involvement and leadership in a regional social movement, the Organization in Defense of Natural Resources and Social Development of the Sierra Juárez (ODRENASIJ) to wrest control over the forest of the sierra from logging and paper companies, that launched his career as a cultural activist. With extensive government concessions, multinational companies had unlimited access to natural resources located in indigenous territories of the sierra.

Martínez Luna first saw regional communications media as a way to "inform people about the richness of their lands, their territory, and the wide range of alternatives that could be designed to protect them." Of equal concern at the time was finding a way to deter out-migration from the region. It was very clear to Martínez Luna that migration was being directly stimulated by mass media. In the late 1970s, during discussions with teachers from his home community, Guelatao de Juárez (Martínez Luna was hired to teach ethnographic research methods to students there), the need for a radio station was identified, along with the imperative of regional communicability. Martínez Luna remembers asking, "If radio or television transmitters are private property, run by people that are putting them to commercial use, why the hell can't we do it?" The original proposal for a Guelatao-based radio station developed in this context, but the idea was refined by a team of communications graduates (the first generation of communications graduates from Mexico's Autonomous University) whom Martínez Luna encountered somewhat by chance during an ODRENASIJ meeting in the mid-1980s. He arranged for the team to live in Guelatao, with all expenses paid by the organization and the community, as they did research throughout the region and developed the proposal for the radio station.

The proposal was submitted to various government agencies, including the National Radio and Television Commission and the INI, but it got no support. "INI was in the process of building Radio Tlapan and other stations around the country at the time—[stations] that were not being solicited. Here was one being solicited by twenty-six organized indigenous communities, and they didn't pay attention to us," recalls Martínez Luna. He approached the INI several more times, as the institution continued to be the most viable route available to secure funding and infrastructure, but it was not until 1988, when, with help from a friend in the Salinas administration and a significant amount of research and petitions gathered from the sierra to demonstrate the need and potential coverage for the station, that the INI approved the radio project.

In March of 1990, with 5,000 watts *de potencia*, Radio XEGLO went on the air from Guelatao's municipal building. By November of that same year, the new station building was complete. At the time, it did not matter to Martínez Luna that the station belonged to the INI, even after nearly two decades of nurturing the project at the community level, through annually rotating municipal governments. "Like Zapata said about land. A radio station doesn't answer to its owner, but to its operator," said Martínez Luna. Francisco Luna, a member of Comunalidad from the neighboring village of Ixtlán de Juárez, recalls: "When we went on the air, each one of us had our programs and a well-defined area of work. We were well trained. When we went on the air from the new building, we even had new programming and a new image. From that year, from 1990 through 1994, our work went really well; everything was looking up. We even displaced commercial stations of the region that the population preferred before we came along!"[9] The station's success in the region was easily confirmed by hundreds of pieces of written correspondence that arrived at the station. The origin of the correspondence also gave the station personnel a good idea of their coverage, a radius of about 80 kilometers as the crow flies, which included Zapotec, Chinantec, and highland Mixe communities.

The station implemented many outreach strategies (outlined in Comunalidad's original proposal) that the INI later institutionalized (or, according to Martínez Luna, "stole") for its radio program, such as the use of community advisory councils made up of community authorities, community correspondents whose job was to assure community representation within the radio station, and community-based Radio Production Centers (CPR) that produced multilingual, diversified programming from throughout the region. The station selected the content delivered from the field with an interest in maintaining "harmony" among its constituent communities, careful to censure programs or news that might pit one community against another (for example, in agrarian disputes). An important indicator of the success of the station—and radio's location as a community project—is that in many cases community radio correspondents were folded into the system of community cargos (community obligations), making radio producing a part of rotating those cargos.

In accordance with Comunalidad's proposal, Radio XEGLO was set up with video equipment from the beginning. During the first years of operation, Martínez Luna recalls that there was a bit of tension over whether the group would give priority to video or radio production, and while the immediacy of radio won out over video, members of the station staff were very interested in "the little camera" and the idea of being able to separate and join images. One of those staff members was Juan José García, who had been involved with Comunalidad as a percussionist for Trova Serrana. García was born in 1970 and grew up in Guelatao until his family relocated to a town near Oaxaca City when he was fifteen, where García studied internal combustion engines at a technical high school (L. C. Smith 2005, 169). His real interest had always been in music, and he spent most of his free time traveling as a roadie with Trova Serrana. By 1989 García had traded engines for drums, studying percussion in Oaxaca City while holding down a couple of part-time jobs (one as a broadcast and recording technician for a semi-commercial radio station). In 1990, García joined the band. After a tour in the Yucatán with Trova, García returned to Guelatao with the band and became involved with the radio station.

In 1991, Monteforte and other instructors from the INI's TMA team gave a video production workshop at the radio station, which allowed the group's interest in "the little camera" to flourish and the group to establish a series of social relations between Comunalidad and TMA, which continued through the 1990s. A Cree contact in Canada secured the group's first outside financing for video production, and by 1992 Comunalidad had produced four programs on the sierra's natural resources (forest, culture, traditional medicine, and coffee), to be screened at the conference on sustainable development in Rio de Janeiro. Martínez Luna sees this experience as formative in the development of individuals who are now in leadership positions as indigenous videomakers in Oaxaca.

The enthusiasm and sense of possibility that characterized the radio station's first years abruptly ended in 1994, as the INI exerted tighter control over its radio stations, following the Zapatista rebellion. As Luna recalls, "we became involved in that whole thing, and started transmitting information as it came in," but eventually the government pressured them not to transmit messages related to "the conflict." Broadcasting in Zapotec, Chinantec, or Mixe gave the station personnel some room to evade government pressure, but local "ears" were paid to report on the station's programming content. By the end of the year, the INI installed cut-off boxes at all its stations allowing the signals to be cut remotely from the INI's offices in Mexico City. The station was taken off the air a number of times, and XEGLO's Zapotec director, Aldo Gonzalez, who became involved with the Zapatista movement as an adviser to the Ejército Zapatista de Liberación Nacional (EZLN), was eventually forced to resign. Luna was poised to be selected as the station's new director, but the INI decided to give the station to a nonindigenous "outsider," chosen from the INI's state delegation in Oaxaca City. Luna left the radio station, but García stayed on to keep up the work they had done. Comunalidad petitioned the INI to transfer the radio station to indigenous control—a demand specifically stated in the San Andrés Accords—but their request fell on deaf ears. Turning to video, Comunalidad produced a video called *Breaking the Silence*, which includes an interview with the new station director, who defined the station as an "entertainment medium"—not exactly what Comunalidad had in mind.

Shortly after the INI tightened the reins, Comunalidad was invited to do a regular program for the state television station, Canal 9. Using the four programs they made for the conference in Rio, the group launched a weekly magazine show called *Revista de la sierra* (Magazine of the Mountains). The effort lasted just over six months, as the group found it difficult to sustain the demanding production schedule and was frustrated by the station's limited signal strength, which did not reach over the mountains to most Sierra Norte communities. However, a convergence of a more fortunate kind opened new possibilities for Comunalidad members who, as Martínez Luna recalls, now considered themselves television producers.

Alfonso Cervantes, a television and satellite engineer, was trying to set up a transmitter to receive a satellite signal for his mother's home community, Jaltianguis, a Mixtec village in the sierra, adjacent to Guelatao. Frustrated with the lack of financing and major logistical obstacles (such as the lack of accessible roads and insufficient electricity), the engineer sought the advice of the nearby XEGLO station staff. "The only question we had for him," recalls Martinez Luna, "was, if you can bring the signal down with the transmitter, can't you also send one out?" "Of course! You can send whatever you want!" was Cervantes's response. Cervantes joined Comunalidad for a period, and together the group turned their energies to creating television programming. They chose only the "best elements" from commercial television— "news from Channel 3, movies from Channel 12, cartoons from Channel 5"—and combined their own videos to create a "really nice program that people really liked," recalled Martínez Luna.

They were on the air from 1994 through 1997, and joined efforts with Canal 9 to install a retransmitter in the sierra, which would potentially increase their own coverage in the region. Comunalidad secured a place in a community for their antenna, but the station preferred to transmit from an uninhabited hilltop close to Guelatao, where TV Azteca, a commercial network based in Mexico City, had an antenna that was in disuse because of a dispute with Televisa, the mega media conglomerate. The station agreed to let Canal 9 use its antenna, but in the process of the negotiations Azteca resolved its conflict with Televisa and also went on the air. This was the death of their *canalito*, or "little channel." With twenty thousand watts of transmitting power, TV Azteca's signal, which used the same frequency as Comunalidad's canalito, knocked their twenty-watt signal off the air. "It was a question of zeros," Martínez Luna said. Though short-lived, the group's intensified work with video and television, and in particular the regional coverage it provided, precipitated a more reflexive period for Comunalidad. According to Martínez Luna, "We had converted the region into a potential for its own education. That is to say, the conscious potential to produce . . . fundamental values of community life, which for us is a huge, huge step."

Martínez Luna recounted this story to me on a cool evening in Comunalidad's offices in Guelatao, while Cervantes and a couple of assistants were on a nearby hilltop, testing Comunalidad's new fifty-watt transmitter. Whereas the previous transmitter carried their canalito to eight communities, this time they hoped to reach twenty-one communities, or a radius of approximately fifteen kilometers. Martínez Luna estimated at the time that there were at least ten television sets per community, though he knew of several cases in which families had more than one, even three, per home.[10] Signal confirmations were called in from several communities that had previously been out of range, blocked by a mountain or canyon. This new transmitter, specially designed by Cervantes himself, sent both FM radio and television signals (though not simultaneously). Comunalidad's plan was to send out radio programming in the morning and television programming in the afternoon.

Comunalidad didn't have a name for the station yet, but they had very clear objectives for community participation. With a concrete and relatively limited number of communities involved as receivers, they hoped to integrate a cohesive group of representatives from each community that would meet regularly in Guelatao to decide on programming. Martínez Luna observed, "It's a smaller but much more participatory project in which the signal [content] is designed by the communities through their direct representation." His philosophy was to aggressively counter the homogenizing effect of commercial television by creating programming through community consensus. He was aware that consensus may have meant accepting certain commercial programs, especially music, that people liked—evidence of "victimization by market logic," in his view—but he was confident a middle ground could be reached. The new television initiative was a pilot project that the producers hoped would one day form part of a regional network of community television stations throughout Oaxaca's Sierra Norte, linking up with other independent community television initiatives in the region.[11] Establishing regional radio and television links among communities embodied the group's main objective, to revalorize community values and to find solutions to the region's problems, with deep, intracommunity participation.

A regional network of community television stations and local production units would have circumvented state control of XEGLO and flown in the face of what the Mixe leader Adelfo Regino Montes calls "the policy of the state to foment localism": "It is not in the interest of the state that we be interrelated and in communication."[12] Regino Montes was involved in making the solicitation to the INI to transfer Radio Guelatao to indigenous control in 1997. The INI director Carlos Tello flatly denied the possibility of transference, saying that "radio stations were a matter of national security and could not be in the hands of the pueblos."[13] Low-power television transmitters under twenty watts can operate legally in Mexico without licenses. Comunalidad was clearly pushing the limits with a fifty-watt radio and television transmitter, but Martínez Luna was not concerned. Given the systematic way their communities have been ignored by the government, their presence on the airwaves of the Sierra Norte should remain sufficiently under the state's radar.

A decade later, community radio stations have proliferated in Oaxaca and the sierra, especially after the popular movement of 2006 in Oaxaca City made radio and access to mass media a central part of their protest strategy. Community television, on the other hand, has not proliferated, according to García.[14] The relative costs of producing original programming, and changes made to the federal communications laws for radio and television under the Fox administration (known as the "Televisa Law"), which reduced the airwaves available for public or community use, has put many low-power television projects beyond the reach of indigenous communities. Comunalidad, too, has not been able to sustain regular television programming as they wished, despite their efforts, though XEGLO is still on the air. The media scholar Antoni Castells-Talens writes against current trends in discourse proffered by government representatives, grassroots communicators, and academics who claim that "indigenist" radio is "ni indígena, ni comunitaria" (neither indigenous nor communitarian) (2011). In his analysis of the CDI's network of indigenist radio stations, he insists that when you look at how the stations work at the level of practice and community participation it is not easy to cast them off as pure state enterprises. Comunalidad's experience with the state and media production tells a similar story of entangled enterprises. Even though the state holds the purse strings and can cut the signal, indigenous radio stations with clear social and political mandates based in notions of community participation have served a vital function in connecting and consolidating regions.

K-Xhon had a different position regarding government participation, one of absolute nonengagement. Of the constitutional reforms to the Oaxacan constitution that moved to recognize indigenous forms of self-government (usos y costumbres) at the municipal level and legitimize collective labor, celebrated (though not without constructive criticism) by most as "progressive" and responsive to the indigenous autonomy movement in Mexico, the K-Xhon collective declared that what activists had "accomplished with their efforts is that the state and its ideologues fine tuned their programs to—once and for all!— integrate us into Mexican-ness" (Topil 1994, 6). Not surprisingly, K-Xhon's run-ins with the INI over media production in the late 1980s were not entangled as much as accusatory. Given the relatively INI-friendly social circles I was running in during my field research in Oaxaca, members of the K-Xhon collective were also not so easy to find.

K-Xhon Video-Cine Zapoteca • Physically locating the K-Xhon Video-Cine Zapoteca collective was a bit of a challenge. I had heard about the member Marta Colmenares for years prior to full-time research, mostly from Native American mediamakers and enthusiasts in New York who had met her at indigenous film and video festivals in the late 1980s, but in Oaxaca, her home base, she was hard to find. At first it seemed strange to me that video indígena folks at the CVI, who knew of her, did not make any overt attempts to include her or the collective in their activities, but once I had the good fortune of meeting Marta's partner and cofounding member of the collective, Alvaro Vásquez, I began to see the borderlines separating video indígena and video-cine Zapoteca.

Milling about the courtyard of the Hotel Colonial with Monteforte during an a break in the "Atención al Migrante" conference, a slender man with a sculpted face and a long ponytail approached Monteforte somewhat reluctantly, his hands shoved deep into the front pockets of his Levis. "¿Tú eres Monteforte?," Vásquez ventured by way of introduction. Monteforte knew who Vásquez was, too, but the two men had never met, and Vásquez was not shy about admitting that Monteforte's relationship with the INI precluded, until recently, any common ground between them. Vásquez had heard from a variety of sources that Monteforte was now "on the outside" and enjoyed much respect from indigenous people. Realizing that I had found the elusive collective, I took advantage of their encounter to ask for Vásquez's phone number.

After several phones calls to the number Vásquez gave me, I was able to confirm an interview with Vásquez and Colmenares at their home in the Volcanes district of Oaxaca City. The collective had suffered from uneven membership since their first days, in the early 1980s, and they had not made a video since 1992 (though Colmenares included a short animation her then thirteen-year-old son made in 1999, on the collective's list of productions), but they were still close friends and seemed eager to return to their more dynamic days as they shared their story with me. I met with core members of the group on two separate and lengthy occasions: Marta Colmenares, Alvaro Vásquez, Inocencio Mena (who relayed my phone messages), and Fernando Hernández Mata. This section offers a brief account (taken from the interviews) of their formation as a regional organization and focuses on how they turned to video and developed what they call their own "aesthetic."

The collective's journey to video—one they characterize using the popular fable of the donkey that learned to play the flute (to underscore their success with video as kind of unexpected miracle)—includes brief but problematic encounters with the INI and other government initiatives that were formative in the collective's fiercely independent position. While the collective is no longer active, these encounters further our understanding of video indígena by offering different, oppositional vantage points from which to situate the emergence of the INI's TMA program, this time from a different microregion of the Zapotec sierra, known as the Cajonos (southwest of Guelatao).

K-Xhon was the media-producing subgroup of a regional organization known as the Asamblea de Autoridades Zapotecos y Chinantecos de la Sierra (AZACHIS, the Assembly of Authorities of the Zapotecs and Chinantecs of the Sierra). K-Xhon is best known for their newsletter, *El topil*. Unlike Fundación Comunalidad, K-Xhon is not a legally constituted organization, hence no "A.C." or "S.A." suffix to its name. It would almost be against their resolute antigovernment position to seek an official stamp of approval or legitimacy for their organization. In 1996 the EZLN invited the staff of *El topil* to the Foro Nacional, to participate as advisers at the "Access to Communications Media" roundtable. In a letter to the EZLN, *El topil* explains why it was forced to decline the invitation: "Our absence is due to the fact that we are so independent that we didn't have the resources to attend, plus the daily community tasks and responsibilities have us really busy" (Maldonado 1999). The group often used the lack of financing as a measure of their independence. In addition to lacking resources and having a full schedule of community obligations, however, they also avowedly lacked a communications proposal, because they "don't negotiate with their culture" (ibid.). I am not sure I ever got to the bottom of that statement, but I imagine it had mostly to do with not wanting to systematize something that others could then coopt, as their experience with the INI suggests, but it may also have to do with "their way of seeing," which they described as whimsical, "without any intent to manipulate the image"[15] (Vázquez 2000).

In the same letter to the EZLN, the group takes an opportunity to position their own views on autonomy: "To this day, we are not subject to any government agency, not for lack of opportunity to be so, nor for purism, simply because we want to prove that we are capable, as Zapotec people, to use media that are pertinent to the development of our own culture. Many Zapotecos and non-Zapotecos, among them Mexicans, understand us and share and collaborate with us in this project in order to accomplish this immense task of doing things with our own efforts, shaking-off paternalistic education however *neosolidaria* it might be [referring to Salinas's Solidarity program]" (Topil 1993).

Each of the members I interviewed discussed their participation in the collective as part of personal returning or relocating experiences. Their idea from the beginning was very clearly about learning from their communities, returning to reintegrate themselves rather than impose what they had learned while they were away, living in cities.[16] Mena recalled the pull of the fiesta:

> What characterizes us as individuals is that we were professionals or students, and in my case who love the sierra. We loved to go back, no matter what the conditions. In the fiestas you arrived walking, even when we were adolescents. I got there walking when I was 12

or 13 years old; it took me 4–5 hours to get to my village fiesta because that is what we had, we were from there, we love the food, to dance to the *jarabes*, talk with the people. I loved being with my people. I remember with tenderness the old ladies, the children, and the whole atmosphere of the fiesta.

But Mena reflected that they initially returned to their communities with the wrong attitudes. Educated in Oaxaca City as a teacher in the Normal System, he was sent back to his region as a professional. "I was trained like teachers were, with the sentiment of an apostle, a person who sacrifices for the development and well-being of the pueblos, that we were the ones that were going to bring these people out from their backwardness. That's what I believed at the time, that they were backward and screwed [*jodidos*]! And I had to work hard to shake off those ways."[17]

Colmenares left her community as a young girl and ended up studying dentistry in Mexico City. She always had a clear idea that she was going to improve health issues in her home community and once she finished her studies in Mexico City, she met other people with similar interests and decided to return to Oaxaca City. She first returned to the Cajonos region in the late 1970s as a social worker employed by missionaries. She did tooth extractions, cleanings, and promoted dental hygiene.

Vásquez also left his community at a very young age to be educated in the city. He remembered that at the time, being educated outside your community was seen as the best way of getting ahead—to "stop being who they were"—though he recognized that this "progressive" attitude was built on the internalized experiences of a previous generation being forced to leave their communities. Vásquez's father, who was municipal president in his home community during President Cárdenas's administration, received an "invitation" to send two kids from the community to a government boarding school. He announced the invitation, and the community responded, "If you want to obey the government, send your own kids!" When Vásquez left his community, at the age of seven, being schooled in the cities was already a generalized criterion for "preparing oneself" (to get ahead, presumably). He was in college in Mexico City studying civil engineering when "1968 happened," the massacre of student and civilian protesters at the hands of the Mexican military in Tlateloco Plaza, in

Mexico City. He remembers being scared when he first saw pictures of Che Guevara, but once he realized many of his fellow students were sons and daughters of working-class parents, he joined a fairly organized movement of student brigades.

All three members of the collective see their work in their home region as a kind of self-imposed "reeducation" that forced them to reevaluate leftist ideologies in terms of what people in their communities were actually living: "It was like an initiation period in which we questioned all the proposals we had, all our forms of organization."[18] This reeducation taught them to take on education itself as a vehicle for assimilation and creating cycles of dependency—"when the government starts coming into their communities and teaches them how to ask for help." In Vásquez's view state education teaches individualism, which directly clashes with community values: "We notice that when a *paisano* [compatriot] studies, that is, goes to school, that is when he is more beholden to the Constitution and less to the law of the pueblo. Some defend their choice not to participate in communal work by citing the Constitution's Article 123 that says all work must be remunerated. Some bring a permission slip signed by the Social Security Administration that excuses them from work, and others say they only have one boss, the one that pays them" (Vázquez, interview). As an organization, AZACHIS sought to provide community-based alternatives to government dependency and to elevate community values in the face of what they saw as atomizing liberal ideologies and notions of progress imparted through state programs.

One of the group's first projects, to build a community dining hall in a Cajonos village, was first and foremost a productive project with an economic rationale—"the dining room idea was about making some money in the community." Built with tequio labor and paid for in large measure by migrants' remittances, the dining hall began as a participatory endeavor involving most sectors of the village but ended up staying in the hands of the family that had put up the land on which the dining hall was built. After two years of hard work "the whole effort went down the drain." The group decided to analyze the failure of this and so many other projects and called a series of regional meetings to discuss the issue. What emerged from these regional meetings was an imperative to foment regional solidarity to combat prevalent divisive tendencies. "Our most significant contribution would be in connecting people, in fomenting regional solidarity," Vásquez said. But still the group's idea was very economically driven: "We didn't see the cultural thing as something to develop because we simply lived it." After a few more meetings, they formalized as a regional committee in the early 1980s that would represent Sierra Norte communities in negotiations with the government.

During that time, the federal government was promoting its Conasupo program, a rural subsidy program that relied on a series of regional warehouses and local stores. Their first commission as a committee was to organize a broad petition that demanded of the government one of the region's most hard-fought resources: roads. "How could the Conasupo distribution system work in the region if there are no passable roads?" they reasoned. The group amassed the petition and solicited a meeting with the governor of Oaxaca in 1980. They were granted a meeting, but "were barely even noticed" by the governor, said Vásquez. Thus, it was in the halls of the state capitol building in Oaxaca City, freshly rebuffed by the governor, that the community authorities from various corners of the Sierra Norte region decided to hold regional assembly meetings. Members of the K-Xhon collective I interviewed committed themselves to serve as the "Exterior Relations Committee" of what would be called two years later, the Asamblea de Autoridades Zapotecas y Chinantecas de la Sierra, or AZACHIS.

The regional assembly meetings required a tremendous organizing effort, considering how difficult it was to get from community to community in the sierra, without proper roads or transportation, one of the main reasons they were organizing in the first place. The few roads that were in place at the time were *brechas* (unimproved dirt roads), and it would take residents up to twelve hours to reach some communities, and even longer during the rainy season, when dirt roads would get washed out. However, as exhausting as the meetings were, they represented an important period of growth and consolidation for the group, especially because the meetings put the group in touch with important leaders and elders from the region, who were able to round out their reeducation. Connecting people from different pueblos who had not had overt contact with each other for years was tremendously rewarding for the group: "People at the meetings started extending their knowledge of their own region. What appeared to them to be really far away—another world, like it seemed to us the first times we went!—formed the basis of a knowledge about the Zapotec region that reached beyond the neighboring community."[19] A significant factor motivating the regional meeting was the desire to encourage community leaders to move beyond the divisiveness caused by rampant agrarian disputes in the region (which Vásquez attributes to the state's long history of a "divide and conquer" strategy for controlling indigenous and peasant communities).

Even before the group consolidated into the Exterior Relations Committee, they realized the need for a medium to circulate information to people in the communities. Their first intent in the late 1970s was "Newsletter No. 1," when they were calling themselves Gatch Tuz, which roughly means, "we are united" in Cajonos Zapoteco. This *boletincillo*, or "little bulletin," a one-page, hand-written, hand-delivered mimeographed page (with room to spare—they "didn't have a lot to say"), was the beginning of *El topil*, the Spanish-language newsletter the group is widely recognized for today.[20] To complement their newsletter—and address its limited accessibility to monolingual Zapotec speakers—the group turned to visual media.

Their use of visual media evolved from photomurals to video. They began with a mural of photos mounted on a hinged, wooden triptych that they folded and carried on their backs from community to community. Still images of the region (forests, people, and communities) were mixed with photographs from meetings and text that gave updates on how the road question was going, or excerpts from an interview with the governor. Before they turned to video, the group animated their still photos in audiovisual shows that combined slides with taped music and narration. The group used video for the first time at the one-year anniversary of the regional assembly. On loan from a colleague in Oaxaca City, "the equipment entailed two suitcases [carrying a Betamax camera and record deck], cables and a generator." Once they incorporated video, they would tape and screen footage the same day in the communities: "People would crack up laughing! They didn't even have television then and for some people it was the first time they had seen electric light."[21] Through the same colleague who loaned the group the equipment, they met a video editor in Mexico City and started to edit their footage into programs.

The group had been taping fiestas and had one or two edited programs when they meet Fernando Hernández Mata. Trained as a painter and musician, Hernández helped formalize the group's commitment to video. His "returning" narrative is about finding AZACHIS, a group he had heard about but was tentative to contact because of a lifetime of being told to maintain distance from his parents' highly conflictive home community, Yalalag. Suffering from what he calls an "identity conflict"—torn between the education he received in his Zapotec-speaking home and at school—Hernández yearned to learn more about the group behind *El topil*. His sociology teacher, who tested his knowledge of Zapotec by making him read from a Zapotec calendar published in 1985 by *El topil*, encouraged him to contact the group. When he finally tracked down Colmenares, she invited him to join them on a trip to the sierra. On that visit, Hernández was dying to use the group's video camera—to test what he had learned about filmmaking in school—but it was not until the he organized a screening of the group's videos in his migrant community of Yalaltecos, in Oaxaca City, that the group invited him to do video.

The group recalls with humor that after the screening Hernández said, "I think your work would be better if you used a script." With Hernández on board in 1984, they began to use the name K-Xhon Video Cine Zapoteca. By this time the group had upgraded to VHS video equipment, thanks to the generosity of their paisanos in Los Angeles. As their video work began to circulate in migrant communities in California, video cameras proliferated in communities in their home region. Community people "saw that it wasn't just the foreigners who use these magical instruments, but people just like [them]." The rare video camera quickly multiplied into two or three and then ten to fifteen—"even children [were] using them!" This explosion of home movie making is partly responsible for leading the group to differentiate how they used video. In general, community people wanted to see the entire fiesta on tape, which implied three to four days of non-stop taping, something that was beyond the capabilities (and interest) of K-Xhon.

What they describe as "their own way of seeing" was developed on the fly, by not limiting themselves to certain conventions but taping in a whimsical manner. "We put the camera wherever we felt like it. We'd get inside a corral, on top of its fence, under it or to the side, whatever we felt like doing in that moment. 'I like this!' and we'd tape it, period. Those are the kinds of things that started marking, we still say it, our own way of seeing," explained Vásquez. Reflecting on their style, he continued, "perhaps it was not having technical cinematographic training that permitted us to totally develop our own language . . . without intentions, in the sense that we did not have intentions as artists, as directors. We were not working for the masses or for the critics, or for awards, not even for expression; we were just having fun, totally committed without any intent to manipulate the image. Our only intention was for people to see it. Plus, the people know us, we couldn't do it any other way."[22]

Though I do not consider it my job to evaluate the basis of their claim to their own way of seeing, their earliest video, *Danza de los coloquios* (1989), a twenty-minute documentary about the annual fiesta in the Zapotec community San Juan Yaée, gives some indication of what they mean by not having "intentions to manipulate the image." The program is based on a rather unremarkable sequence of the fiesta —philharmonic bands, dances, fireworks—the loose camera work and lack of direct interviews or voice-over lend an unpretentious quality to the tape. It is not that the camera seems "not perceivable," which is another way they describe what their way of seeing looks like, but that the camera work is less than deliberate.[23]

Over ten years after the group began their work with video, they dedicated most of the fiftieth issue of *El topil* (1993) to defending their status as "pioneers in América: Indians and the use of video technology" (Topil 1993). The reason behind the defense is a familiar story of government cooptation that shapes the group's antigovernment bent. According to the group, it is their success with video that "left them open to be preyed upon by government agencies" (ibid.). They back up their claim to success with references from two independent videomakers based in Mexico City and a radio producer based in San Francisco, but they also received international festival awards for their production *Danza Azteca* in 1987.[24] Cooptation by the "government machine" happened twice during that same year; in both instances, anthropologists were the connection between the group and the government agencies.

At the International Congress of Applied Anthropology, in Mexico City, in 1987, an informal meeting took place among some of Mexico's leading anthropologists, among them Arturo Warman, Salomón Nahmad, and Gerardo Gárfias. K-Xhon Video Cine Zapoteca was invited to the meeting to show their work, and according to the collective, the person who showed the most interest and positively reviewed their work was none other than Warman, whom they describe as a "combative" researcher turned government *funcionario*, noting his long career as an appointed member of government. Of this encounter, K-Xhon writes, "We believe—though we hope we are wrong—that this experience affected him, because when he arrived at INI he immediately put these media in the hands of indigenista organizations" (Topil 1993, 2). By "indigenista," he meant organizations working with or within indigenous communities who enjoy the INI stamp of approval.

K-Xhon claims they also "inspired" a second government initiative with video that was put into practice on a state level. During the administration of Oaxaca by the PRI governor Heladio Ramirez, who is generally praised for having been instrumental in opening the door to state constitutional reform to recognize indigenous forms of self-government, Gárfias implemented the government's Casas del Pueblo program. As modestly funded community cultural centers, Casas del Pubelo were designed to be spaces for community cultural projects where dance, arts, and crafts could flourish. Gárfias's innovation with the casas program was the addition of video equipment, and K-Xhon members believe this innovation was directly a result of Gárfias's exposure to K-Xhon's videos at the meeting in Mexico City.

The collective's assessment of their cooptation is structural: "In the end we offer free information to government agencies and intellectuals, which serves their interests to make programs that justify their existence as organisms that 'serve' indigenous peoples" (Topil 1993, 3). Just as K-Xhon claims to have created their own way of seeing "without intending to," they write: "Without meaning to we have been turned into informers of our own oppressors. We've given them material and information with which to strengthen their institutions and turn this information around on us, increasing their control over us. Faced with this dilemma, we are committed to writing and publishing this little magazine, which like it or not, will continue to be used by those who, at all costs, will find a way to exploit us be it culturally, intellectually or economically" (ibid.). While I was not able to confirm K-Xhon's claims to have inspired the creation of the INI's TMA program—Muñoz denied any knowledge of the group—K-Xhon's own history with media as well as their antigovernment discourse offers a different vantage point from which to view the INI program. As in Comunalidad's story with the radio station, government sponsorship of indigenous media must be positioned in relation to indigenous struggles to build regional solidarity and find solutions to regional issues, such as road building and the uncontrolled exploitation of natural resources by outside interests, which in turn reinforce community values and indigenous agency. From K-Xhon's perspective, the government is a menace seeking to corrupt, usurp, and co-opt, whereas Comunalidad and the members of Ojo de Agua position themselves in entangled relationships with the government, producing indigenous media that circumvents and, to some extent, reinvents the government's stance toward indigenous peoples doing in practice what the government often only promises to do.

Disentangling Video Indígena from Government Sponsorship: Ojo de Agua Comunicación S.C.

Ojo de Agua Comunicación S.C., an urban-based media collective with indigenous and nonindigenous members, was established in 1998 in the face of the INI's increasing reluctance to transfer the CVI to indigenous control.[25] The emergence of Ojo de Agua can be discussed in terms of the limits of the INI's project of transference, this partial and incomplete policy to shift resources and decision making to indigenous control, but also in terms of the Zapatista movement and the imperatives the movement placed at the center of the indigenous autonomy movement. The comunicación de lucha approach that Monteforte forged at the CVI could fully flourish at Ojo de Agua, but disentangling video indígena from government sponsorship was a protracted process. What happened along the way, as former TMA leaders shook off their dependency on government sponsorship, is that video indígena per se lost some of its currency. More than two decades after having participated directly in the "invention" of video indígena, members of the Ojo de Agua collective use a more open category to describe their work, more akin to alternative media, work that still services indigenous communities and their struggles without the insistence on the indigenous label.

The shift to independence—from the INI's CVI to Ojo de Aqua—happened gradually. García took the helm of the CVI in 1997, after Monteforte stepped down. During the first months of his tenure, the center went from having a direct relationship with INI headquarters in Mexico City to being under the state delegation's control. After this repositioning, the CVI's budget was parceled out, bit by bit, by the delegation, and García lobbied hard to raise the salaries of CVI staff. In 1998 there was some promise that they would receive raises, but after many months of negotiating the delegation announced, in November of that year, that not only would there be no raises, CVI staff would also not be paid the back salaries they were owed. Making matters worse, the state delegation announced that they would no longer reimburse the CVI for per diem expenses. This last announcement severely crippled the CVI, as it had survived economically by covering a range of operating expenses with per diem funds, including staff salaries.[26]

Caballero, who under Monteforte's tutelage went from being the CVI's night watchman to its principal on-line editor, recalled several immediate consequences of the CVI's shift to state-level control. "We were told to work only until four in the afternoon, when CVI has always been a 24-hour place. An eight to four hour work day is just not enough to advance on a video project, you need more time."[27] The intense, around-the-clock editing style Monteforte instituted at the CVI was being dismantled by the INI with claims of fiscal constrictions, but CVI staff felt that the INI was motivated by more than budget cuts. "The people at the Institute don't understand; they don't even come to see what we are doing or to evaluate our situation. Since I have been here the INI delegate has never come here to see what we might be lacking or to see how we work," Caballero insisted. The distance the CVI intentionally put between itself and the INI—essential to its characterization as a nongovernmental organization—was being played out against the CVI.

Caballero admitted that they never insisted that the delegate come visit the CVI, either, but he also thought the delegation was getting back at the CVI for never having made a production for the delegation, something that would have clearly violated the CVI's mandate to work exclusively for indigenous organizations and communities. "We have always respected what has been said from the beginning, that you have to support indigenous community organizations only. We have never made programs for the Institute, so they have put a rock in our way: 'If you don't want to help us, well, here goes this!' "[28] As for their salaries, Caballero reflected that as employees of the CVI they were complicit because they had never put their foot down, threatened to stop working. "We have to insist they come to see what we do," Caballero suggested, but for García (his boss), the CVI's "independence" was more important. "So that's how we are working," Caballero said. "The post-production unit is down because a head broke in the record deck; the editing station is about to break, too, but we keep working because we can't deny the people coming from far away who say, 'We want to edit.'

There is no way we can say no. That's how we are working now, without the same enthusiasm as before, to give everything you have for the benefit of the CVI."[29]

The potential motive behind the INI's increased control over the CVI was, not surprisingly, political. García learned in 1999 that the institution was conducting an extensive survey of its CCIs (regional coordination centers) to determine what "kind" of organizations the CCIs were working with. The CVI in Oaxaca, a state long ruled by the PRI, had no party-affiliated organizations within its network. In fact, the CVI worked almost exclusively with social protest organizations that either had no political party affiliations or were affiliated at the time with the Partido Revolucionaro Democratico (PRD), one of the leading opposition parties that for a time played an active role in the opposition or "parallel" government backed by the EZLN, in Chiapas. Under García's leadership, the CVI took advantage where it could of the INI's retreating support.

For example, in 1998, during the EZLN's Consulta Nacional, a national referendum on the "Recognition of Indigenous Peoples and an End to the War of Extermination," which was organized with significant participation from prodemocracy civil organizations throughout the country, the CVI was unofficial host to more than a dozen of the 1,000 Zapatista delegates, who traveled to Oaxaca to promote the vote. The delegates canvassed the entire country, collecting over three million votes in support of the demilitarization of Chiapas and the original version of the Peace Accords, which was signed in 1996 (not President Zedillo's watered-down version submitted to congress earlier in 1998). The thought of CVI dormitories filled with hooded Zapatistas must have certainly increased the INI delegates' frustration with the CVI. García capped his speculation by concluding that as the new millennium began the INI was "trying to wear [them] down." He recalled, "It's the perfect way to finish with something that still has great potential. In other words, you don't just cut if off or remove it or simply cancel it, you let it die and once it's dead you bury it because there is nothing else to do—it even smells bad. So you are actually doing us a favor if you take it at that point. It's as if first they handicap you, take away your skills, and then once you have no purpose, they cancel it. That might be what is happening."[30] As the CVI was brought further into line with the INI's political agenda, Ojo de Agua gained momentum, but leaving the physical space of the CVI, the ample house-turned-media-center in La Cascada, took a good year. During that time the two organizations functioned in a parallel manner, or in Monteforte's words, "walked along very similar paths," at least until the CDI reinvented the CVI under the "neoindigenista" purview of the state delegation (Castells-Talens 2010, 87).

During the first months of 1999, a beckoning flute riff that served as background music for the video promoting the Consulta Nacional dominated the aural space of both the CVI and the office of Ojo de Agua, emanating nonstop from editing and postproduction suites as Tonatiuh Díaz, an Ojo de Agua member, was putting the tape together. The prevalence of the music in both spaces underscored the blended, entangled relations of the organizations, one a federal institution, the other a production collective serving indigenous organizations de lucha. On any given day, members moved fluidly from one office to the other, a short journey that implied going just a few blocks up or down one of Oaxaca City's main north-south arteries, Avenue Porfirio Díaz (named after Mexico's nineteenth-century dictator, an Oaxaca native). The activities and resources of one organization supplemented the limitations of the other. Not only were the lists of each organization's personnel almost identical (though Ojo de Agua had members the CVI did not), their "similar path" was rooted in the same origins. As García said, "To not recognize the origin of [Ojo de Agua] would be like, I don't know, like not recognizing your own mother." The origin he refers to is, of course, the TMA and the INI, but to follow García's metaphoric language, as the off-spring matured they rebelled, wanting nothing to do with their progenitor.

Nevertheless, García's "wearing down" analysis seems correct. As I finished up an extended stay in Oaxaca in the spring of 2000, unofficial reports were coming from Mexico City that the new TMA director was on his way to Oaxaca to "shut down the CVI." Shutting down the CVI amounted to the protracted process I have described, with the concrete separation taking place after 2000, when the INI itself was transformed into the CDI and the Oaxaca CVI was physically moved to the state delegation building. The CVI's "backbone"—the video collection —was "transferred" during the process to the CDI delegation, as well, though Ojo de Agua maintains its own substantial *videoteca*, made up of much of the same material the CDI has in its archive. In retrospect, most of the TMA leadership in Oaxaca, as well as members of the original project team, anticipated problems with the INI and sought to secure the survival of video indígena in the absence of government support. The organization of Mexican videomakers known as OMVIAC was one such attempt, but was ultimately a failed one, based on a phantom national constituency of indigenous videomakers. Ojo de Agua, on the other hand, was in many ways already up and running; they just had to secure resources of their own.

While TMA leadership in Mexico City denied that the INI was strangling the center in Oaxaca, in 2000, the INI delegate in Oaxaca City placed the onus of transferencia on indigenous people, citing the lack of a multiethnic indigenous organization that could effectively manage and share the resource across the state and region (on the INI's map the Oaxacan CVI also serviced the states of Veracruz and Puebla). Ojo de Agua was the only viable candidate to receive the CVI. They had (and have) solid relationships and a strong track record with indigenous organizations across and beyond the state, but the organization's ethnic composition, which includes nonindigenous, even non-Mexican individuals, to say nothing of the members' politics, eliminated Ojo de Agua from any serious consideration (not that they would have wanted to be tethered by the strings the INI would have surely attached to the deal). In the organization's 2010–2012 Working Plan, Monteforte (its principal author) explains: "As some of the key actors in the TMA program, we understood that in order to truly accompany and strengthen processes of indigenous communication with audiovisual media, we had to act outside government spheres. This was one of the principal reasons Ojo de Agua Comunicación emerged" (Ojo de Agua 2011, 13).

"Transferencia," in this context, looks more a myth of bureaucratic perpetuity than a policy or program. In Luna's words: "[The INI] will never, never give over [the CVI]. It's too bad, but I think we have to recognize that if TMA lasts for thirty years, the promise of transference will last for thirty years."[31] There is also the legacy of dependency at play here, engendered over years of clientelism, which Monteforte mentioned as an obstacle of transference: "People in communities really appreciate the CVI, especially being able to have a place to [eat and sleep] while they are in Oaxaca, but they appreciate it in part because they don't have the burden of its expenses—who would want something transferred to them if INI is paying for it?"[32] Whether a matter of clientelism or frank incommensurability between costs and resources, the burden of expenses is, indeed, significant and has been a problematic aspect of indigenous media projects everywhere. Video technology has been relatively inexpensive since the 1980s, but the constituency video indígena serves is not relatively wealthy, but by and large very poor. Additionally, video indígena, as the INI conceived of it, entails more than a recording device (sent, as is frequently the case, by a migrant family member living north of the border); it involves editing equipment and computers and the training to produce polished programs. Without some kind of outside support, video indígena is rarely a viable enterprise, and to complicate matters more, outside funding can also be a source of additional challenges for community-based indigenous videomakers.

The limits of transference, both practical and political, also return us to the problematic issues inherit in the category "indígena" and by extension, video indígena. As García said early on, while video indígena may not exist, "video Zapoteco" or "video Juan José" are real possibilities. The INI's argument that no multiethnic organization exists to inherit the CVI was based on this impossible idea of an indígena that is somehow not positioned culturally, politically, and geographically in specific ways. As with transferencia, the institution reifies notions that underwrite its purposefulness, while resisting positive change in favor of the constituency it is supposed to serve. Members of Ojo de Agua virtually dropped "video indígena" from their vocabulary, replacing it with "comunicación alternativa" (as their earlier title "COMAL," which stands for Comunicación Alternativa, suggests), in part because they have broadened the scope of organizations "de lucha," with whom they work, especially since the crisis in 2006, but also because the term "video indígena" is to a degree positioned itself, within an uncomfortable legacy of government sponsorship.

Today Ojo de Agua has six active members, most of whom have been with the organization since the INI days in the late 1990s. They consolidated as a group as time and energy permitted. Many had other jobs and responsibilities in Oaxaca City as well as cargos, unpaid community service jobs that lasted one to three years, in their home communities. While the depth of the dedication they showed was often belied by their disorganization during their first years—a frustrating mix of qualities largely imparted by the personal styles of Monteforte, the group's first *coordinador general*, and García, who pushes the limits of even the most exaggerated stereotype of "Mexican time." The 24–7 working style Monteforte promoted (by example) at the CVI was in full force at Ojo de Agua and has only been attenuated to the extent that members have more sane relationships between work and family. One member, known as "Cheve," described working and learning at the CVI as a lot like doing tequio, mandatory communal labor so important to life in indigenous communities in Oaxaca (L. C. Smith 2005, 196).

The group's genealogical tree has three principal branches, which grew from the Zapotec collective Fundación Comunalidad, in Guelatao de Juárez; university communications departments based in Mexico City; and, of course, the CVI in Oaxaca City. In addition to Monteforte, García, and Caballero, the members Ojo de Agua include Tonatiuh Díaz, or "Tona," a communications graduate from Universidad Autónoma de México—Xochilmilco (UAM-X), in Mexico City, who did his "social service" with Fundación Comunalidad; Clara Morales, the daughter of a well-known community organizer from the Tuxtepec region of Oaxaca, and Juan José's former wife (they met and fell in love during an overlapping stint with Trova Serrana in Guelatao); Ceberino Hipólito, or "Cheve," a CVI-trained Zapotec videomaker from Santa Ana de Valle, in Oaxaca's Central Valley; and Roberto Olivares, also a communications grad and independent video producer from Mexico City. A seventh member, Francisco Luna, a Zapotec colleague of García's from Ixtlán de Juárez, who was a video and radio producer at the INI's XEGLO radio station, in Guelatao, left Ojo de Agua in 1995 to work for a regional environmental organization called Grupo Mesófilo A.C. Finally, another former member, Bruno Varela, continues to be an important influence in the ongoing development of indigenous media in Mexico and beyond. A classmate of Tona's at UAM-X, Bruno left the university setting looking for a more hands-on way to learn video production and ended up spending an extended stint at the CVI as a volunteer. Bruno has his own media organization, Arancatorce, which fosters a more experimental approach to videomaking. As García himself observes, Ojo de Agua existed long before they formalized the organization. Most of its members have collaborated since 1994, when the CVI was first established and several of them had worked together since 1990—García, Luna, Tona, and Clara at Fundación Comunalidad and XEGLO, and García and Monteforte at the TMA video workshop given at XEGLO. Olivares was also in Oaxaca in the early 1990s, working at the state television station—"a sort of public television station with commercials" (L. C. Smith 2005, 208)—producing a series called

Compartiendo ideas (Sharing ideas), a talk show about alternative solutions to community issues (for example, ecological "dry" toilets).

The group's biggest challenge has always been to maintain self-sufficiency to the degree that members can work full-time at Ojo de Agua, but the group disagreed somewhat about how to get there during the early years. In the interest of economic self-sufficiency, Ojo de Agua regularly takes on institutional (rather than community) productions, something most members could refuse to do when they worked at the CVI. Olivares first met members of Ojo de Agua when he hired them to crew for a series of television programs funded by Mexico's National Institute for Art and History (INAH), programs about how the INAH was working to restore historically significant buildings in Oaxaca, following a strong earthquake in 1999. When Olivares joined the group, he offered them full access to his production equipment and office, allowing Ojo de Aqua to fully wean itself from using the CVI's equipment. Along with his production equipment came a more entrepreneurial vision; Olivares saw a clear need to capitalize first and undertake community projects second, once the group achieved economic stability. García initially feared that they would become just another production house and lose sight of their "deep social commitment." Like García, Monteforte worried that prioritizing profit would steer them to "become just another business making videos for whomever." And of Olivares's business mindset, Monteforte remarked, "It doesn't enter his head that we can make a video without charging." But after more than ten years of producing together, Olivares has since learned to produce tequio-style, balancing volunteer hours with paid work, and Ojo de Aqua has a learned to balance making videos for money and working pro bono for communities.

The list of communities, community-based organizations, funding institutions, government agencies, television outfits, and the individual mediamakers with whom Ojo de Agua has coproduced video programs is as impressive as their list of awards and festival screenings.[33] For most of the collective's eleven-year history, members have divided the work according to each individual's expertise, be it editing or camera work, and they maintain a teaching environment, so everyone constantly learns and improves. A brief description of a few videos gives the picture.

During my extended time in Oaxaca, most members of Ojo de

Agua had a personal production of some kind underway and assisted with collective projects such as training workshops or community-solicited productions as needed. For example, Cheve, who was first exposed to audiovisual communications media at XEGLO when he was sent as a translator of Central Valley Zapotec, was deeply involved in a video program based in his home community of Santa Ana del Valle, a program about their community museum.[34] Alternating from Oaxaca City to Santa Ana on the weekends, Cheve worked with members of Santa Ana's Community Museum Committee to envision a video program that would "entice visitors to Santa Ana, and ideally, contribute to the pueblo's economy" (L. C. Smith 2005, 198). He used CVI equipment to gather footage and edited the program, *Shan dany* (1999), at the CVI, under Monteforte's and Caballero's guidance. The program screened at CLACPI's fourth festival in Gualtemala and at the First People's Festival, in Montreal, but did not make much of an impact at home. Nevertheless, *Shan dany* is an example of a video program created at the request of an indigenous community and tells an intricate story of how this Zapotec pueblo actively seeks alternative, community-vetted and approved sources of economic sustenance. It also demonstrates how the value of the video program on the international stage matters little to the relative value of the video program in the home community, a global-local disconnect that is common in indigenous media.

From 2002 to 2005, Ojo de Agua produced a twenty-five-part television series called *Pueblos de México*, which was financed by Mexico's Ministry of Education and broadcast nationally through state television stations, the satellite-based education program EDUSAT, and commercial and cultural channels with public funding (Canal 22 and Canal 11). Each program is twelve minutes long and covers different aspects of various indigenous and afroindigenous peoples in the states of Oaxaca, Guerrero, Puebla, Yucatán, Veracruz, Chiapas, Tabasco, and San Luis Potosí. The programs do not present ethnographic portraits of each indigenous group, but rather situate them in the present, engaged in actively sustaining their communities, whether it be through music, dance, pottery, environmental conservation and reforestation, traditional medicine and agriculture, or the links between cosmovisión and territory. Olivares and Monteforte directed the majority of the programs, though several director credits go to Tona and Caballero.[35] Two of the series programs, *Unidos venceremos/*

United We Will Overcome (2003) and *Nuestra tierra no se vende/Our Land Is Not for Sale* (2003), were especially celebrated in the international festival circuit with screenings at CLACPI's seventh festival, in Santiago, Chile; Geografías Suaves, in Mérida, Yucatan; Terres en Vue, in Montreal; the Latin American Environmental Film Festival, in New Orleans; and the twelfth Native American Film and Video Festival, in New York City.

Nuestra tierra no se vende/Our Land Is Not for Sale (2003) is preceded by the snazzy, quick-paced introduction to the television series *Pueblos de México*. A professional voice-over narration presents the "pueblo" of this program, the Nahuatl pueblo in the state of Guerrero. Using state of the art graphics, the program zooms into Guerrero on the map of Mexico. "We speak Nahuatl" the voice-over continues. "We number 137 million in Mexico and 140,000 in Guerrero." Switching to location-interview voice-over, the program shows images of a beautiful river valley, the Upper Balsas River valley surrounded by green, rolling hills. Women paint pottery well known in Mexican craft markets, further situating this region of indigenous Mexico. The voice-over explains that the Nahua of this region have organized to oppose the construction of a hydroelectric dam, called San Juan Tetelcingo, that would flood twenty-two communities. An elder in a tight head-and-shoulders interview says, "It breaks my heart." Much of the struggle this region organized to stall the dam project is depicted through *amate* paper drawings, another well-known and well-commercialized indigenous Mexican craft. Brightly painted, the amate work shows a crowd of people holding signs reading, "Viva Zapata! Viva Mexico! Viva Guerrero" and "No a la Presa San Juan Tetelcingo!" (see figure 3.1). From a meeting of townspeople, we learn that the government agreed in 1992 to suspend the dam project, but the community recently learned that it was alive again. "What are we going to do?" asks the leader. "Mobilize again, march again?" The group responds with a definite yes, and the program shifts back to amate drawings such as the one depicting the march to Mexico City.

This time we see men and women painting the drawings. One elderly woman affirms that they know the government won't take care of them if they are relocated. Another asks, "How we will care for our dead, how could we possibly take our dead with them if they leave?" The community leader explains how it works, why they won't give up the fight: "When we are born our umbilical cords are buried here

FIGURE 3.1. Amate drawing used in *Nuestra tierra no se vende/Our Land Is Not for Sale* (2005, 12 min.) by Ojo de Agua Comunicación. Courtesy of Ojo de Agua.

where we live. When we grow, the land provides for us and when we die we return to her." The videomakers include an important aspect of what the community is doing in response to the government's lack of consideration for their well-being. "Development is not a dam," one man says. They have started a bilingual school to teach their children how to read and write in Nahuatl and have set up a temporary school in front of the governor's palace in Chilpanzingo, to demonstrate their resolve. *Nuestra tierra no se vende* is slick and to the point, just right for television, but it is smart. The videomakers make frequent use of familiar visual idioms—indigenous crafts—to tell a story of indigenous determination to preserve their way of life in the face of direct conflict with government development proposals. This portrait of the Nahuatl pueblo of Guerrero is not just about their crafts, their customs, their dress, and language, it is about their resistance, something television shows about indigenous peoples in Mexico rarely show.

While working with a television format can have frustrating constraints (mostly of time), these programs satisfy Ojo de Agua's imperative to reach the general public in Mexico with substantive alternatives to the "erroneous, stereotyped and racist visions of indigenous peoples that vary from romantic and mystical to disrespectful and full of hate" (Ojo de Agua 2009, 6). Ojo de Agua's vision statement frames communication as a fundamental part of culture that has been extorted from indigenous peoples through centuries of conquest, colony, and assimilationist state policies. Quoted on the opening page of this chapter, their statement continues:

> When communication recuperates the meaning that has been torn from [our culture], we are in a position to find our place, to find ourselves again. Our project is aimed at indigenous peoples of Oaxaca, Mexico and starts from the idea that by recuperating the original and shared [*solidario*] meaning of communication, we construct through media a historical discourse of our own as well as an ethical and aesthetically dignified representation. Ojo de Agua, a collective of alternative communicators, some of whom are indigenous, proposes to recuperate visions of the world that communications mass media have denied.
>
> . . . This project proposes to apply training, production and distribution of video and Internet for different indigenous communities and organizations in the state of Oaxaca, making its impact reach not only Oaxacan communities but also other regions of Mexico and various other countries. (Ojo de Agua 2001, 4)

Their current work plan, which covers 2010 through 2012, emphasizes video and radio production; whereas the Internet is barely mentioned. In 2000 the Internet was a space to be conquered. Ojo de Agua felt an urgency then to have a presence on the World Wide Web and to offer basic computer training to communities who were gaining access to the Internet for the first time.[36] The shift to radio production is in response to increasing demands for autonomous community radio stations, following the 2006 crisis. The teacher's union's radio station, Radio Plantón (Radio Sit-in) has played an important role in organizing and informing teachers during sit-ins, which are annual events in Oaxaca City. In the context of state and local police's attempted forced removal of the teachers' protest, and the popular movement that rapidly organized to defend the teachers (as well as a host of other organizations that had joined the struggle), Radio Plantón became the "tactical lifeline" of the movement while at the same time being directly targeted by state police (Stephen 2011, 1). When Radio Plantón's equipment was destroyed, on June 14, 2006, Radio Universidad was used to regroup protesters in order to confront the poorly trained state and local police. The protesters prevailed that day.

Additionally, the takeover of the Corporación Oaxaqueña de Radio y Televisión (COR-TV), the state-owned radio and television station, by a group of female protesters, with many teachers and indigenous individuals among them, helped to position radio as the primary voice of direct political action and social protest.[37] García, who was on hand at COR-TV to assist the women with the broadcasting technology during the protest, commented to me that there seems to be a growing sense in many communities that there is a need for a radio station, in order to stay connected and informed should another crisis occur.

In the meantime, however, communicators at some of the new community radio stations are programming without serious guidelines, and Ojo de Agua is preparing to offer some workshops to provide some guidance. On their website, the collective addresses the new urgency for radio:

> [Following] the current effervescence for the use of radio as part of social mobilizations, [that are] constantly repressed by state and federal governments, [we find ourselves] at a juncture in which we wish to apply our experience in working with community media from a perspective of autonomy. For this reason we are developing training programs which strengthen the social responsibility of the community-based communicators to the transformation of their communities and regions. We believe that this way we can contribute to the formation of a more critical societies that are better connected to each other—better mobilized, we would say—in their search of a better life.
>
> Many initiatives in the city and especially in indigenous regions of Oaxaca try to break the media fence, which the government and private interests use to create the false illusion that nothing is going on here. That way popular discontent is criminalized, the violation of human rights goes unpunished and civil society's initiatives are discredited. Community radios are marvelous tools for supporting the everyday transformation we are seeking. However, there is a need to create spaces for creative and technical training that can replace commercial production conventions that commercial and state media impose on us.[38]

The indigenous media school the collective proposes to begin planning for in the coming years would offer a systematized training program for indigenous communicators. The increasing proliferation of video cameras, community radio, and the Internet, the possibility of broadcasting, webcasting, and using social media technology to reach broad audiences, sparks Ojo de Agua's sense of accountability to nurture the seeds they have so actively sought to plant.

In 2000, the Zaptatista rebellion was very much the overarching framework for positioning Ojo de Agua's broader project of supporting indigenous autonomy and self-determination. In 1999, García, clearly speaking for the group as a whole, told me, "We don't feel outside of the process [of the Zapatista movement] or like add-ons, rather we are an integral part of the process and have been for a long time." Several Ojo de Agua members have worked as video instructors in the Chiapas Media Project and served as advisers to the EZLN. Ten years later, Zapatismo continues to be an important referent for their work, but the movement born out of the 2006 crisis in Oaxaca proper seems to have reframed Ojo de Agua's mission, as is evident by their shift in vision statements, toward a more inclusive or open application of rights, access to information, and the means for authoring it.

Fundación Comunalidad A.C., K-Xhon Video-Cine Zapoteca, and Ojo de Agua Comunicación S. C. turned to communications media for similar reasons. The first two positioned themselves to consolidate regional solidarity after decades of state-sanctioned divisionism. Their communities demanded resources, respect, and roads, and both Comunalidad and K-Xhon used visual media, song (XEGLO, Trova Serrana), and the written word (Martínez Luna's writings and *El topil*) to unite their microregion, known as the Sierra Norte, in order to better defend themselves against misguided government programs and commercial interests seeking access to their forests and mineral deposits. Both organizations had to deal in one way or another with the INI, one of the state agencies with the biggest presence in rural indigenous Mexico. Comunalidad hounded the INI to establish a radio station in Guelatao, so that they could broaden their own presence through the region and mobilize people to protect their culture and way of life, their comunalidad. Members of K-Xhon turned their back on the INI, seeking to distance themselves from an institution that stole their ideas and didn't give them credit. Ojo de Agua, on the other hand, credits the INI as their "mother," as García put it, but the "comunicación de lucha" that Monteforte, García, and the others produced in spite of their progenitor was clearly shaped by the social struggles for regional solidarity and indigenous autonomy in the Sierra Norte and elsewhere. The significant antigovernment undercurrents evident in the indigenous video program since the early TMA days, when the INI was teaching video indígena in national workshops, were given new purposefulness as the perceived and urgent needs to create the means for indigenous video to exist without government sponsorship became an imperative that was impossible to ignore once the EZLN launched its rebellion and "all things political changed" (Stephen 2002, 229).

FOUR

Dilemmas in Making Culture Visible

Achieving Community Embeddedness in

Tamazulapam del Espíritu Santo, Mixe

The notion of being socially embedded is considered one of the distinguishing features of indigenous media (Ginsburg 1991; Córdova and Salazar 2008)—the mediamaker positioned such that the representation offered is from the "inside looking in," free from the othering lenses and filters that nonindigenous outsiders cannot easily cast off. Nonetheless, there are dilemmas present in making culture visible because embeddedness cannot always be taken for granted; rather, in the context of Radio y Video Tamix (Tamix), embeddedness had to be achieved. A look at the RVT offers a rich and complex case study of how video indígena, as taught through the Transferencia de Medios Audiovisuales (TMA) workshops sponsored by the Instituto Nacional Indigenista (INI), fares in a community setting. The RVT members who were trained through the TMA participated in the workshops when notions of *comunicación de lucha* (where "lucha" means social struggle) were not yet solidified, and the "intuitive methodologies" used by TMA instructors were easily adapted to meet a different set of intuitive methodologies that responded to the particular interests of the group's members. However, what TMA instructors failed to teach —how to achieve sustainability, navigate community power relations, and secure community representativity—was worked out, for better or for worse, in the everyday life of the community.

I chose to do extended research in Espíritu Santo Tamazulapam, Mixe, mostly because of their television project, TV Tamix, and because the Mixe were known for cultural resistance and political autonomy. I was first introduced to the media collective at a screening of their work in 1993 in Mexico City and was very taken by their story. By the time I entered "the field," however, I realized I had chosen to focus on an organization that was approaching the end of a prolific ten-year run. Ironically, the success of the collective that landed them state sponsorship, a full video production package, and significant foreign, state, and national funding for production and travel to festivals, added up to a kind of capital that fostered jealousy and suspicion among community members, disturbing community-based relationships of power and eventually serving to dismantle the organization. A description a of the Mixe territory, woven from the published ethnographic record of the region and my own field notes, foregrounds a detailed history of Radio y Video Tamix and offers some ethnographic depth to the strategies the group uses to embed their video production.

Having learned video production through the INI's TMA project, which did not carefully delimit what or how newly trained videomakers were to work once in their home communities, members of the Tamix collective put the new technology to use through a communication proposal developed along idiosyncratic lines. An idiosyncratic approach is not inherently problematic; in the field of media for social change, positioned somewhere between art and activism, visionary proposals are not uncommon. But Radio y Video Tamix did not set out to make "video Genaro" or "video Rojas" (to pick up Juan José García's discussion about the difficulties in defining what exactly video indígena is); rather, their intention was to "rescue, preserve and promote Mixe Culture through recordings and use of video equipment," as the Radio y Video Tamix brochure from 1992 states. If properly preserved, their vast archive of programs and raw footage will stand the test of time and fulfill their stated intention, but in 1999 and 2000 their proposal clashed with the very notions of community solidarity the collective was trying to represent—such as tequio (communal labor). Meanwhile, the leaders of Radio y Video Tamix articulated a form of working they called "televisión sin reglas" (television without rules), which was a catch-all kind of phrase designed to keep their work (as well as their technical gaffes) entertaining and stimulating, rather than overly structured. Not exactly comunicación de lucha, televisión sin reglas, the whimsical, unstructured quality of TV Tamix, serves as a pertinent reminder that even in one of the more politically autonomous indigenous regions in Mexico, making culture visible is not a linear process. Securing access to communications media is, indeed, an achievement, as is its embeddedness. How the media is put to work depends heavily on the particular and idiosyncratic dynamics of a situated group of individuals.

Mixe Territory: Situated Autonomy

I met Genaro Rojas, one of the founding members of Radio y Video Tamix, for the first time in 1993, during an anthropology conference in Mexico City. Five years later, my first visit to Tamazulapam was guided by his careful instructions. He, his wife, Etél, and youngest daughter, Itzia, greeted me in Oaxaca City a week before going to Tamazulapam, known as "Tama" for short. I took a cab to their apartment in a new subdivision demarcated with a fancy, pink archway and empty streets prepped for future homes in the sprawling outskirts of the city. While Etél prepared the first of many excellent meals she was to offer me, Genaro and I booted up a laptop computer and tested the printer I had brought him (at his request) from the United States. All systems were go, so we taxied with bellies full of *chicharrón en salsa roja* (pork rind in red sauce) back to the center of town, where we walked along the cobblestone streets of the city's main *zócalo* (plaza), had an ice cream, and then carefully counted our steps to the bus terminals that service the Mixe region. There were two options, as Genaro and Etél explained, the Tama bus, which makes only two runs a day between Oaxaca and Tama, and the Santa Maria Tlahuitoltepec buses that make hourly runs throughout the day, between Oaxaca and Tlahuitoltepec, the town just beyond Tama. Given the *estado de guerra* (state of war) between Tamazulapam and Tlahuitoltepec, over a protracted land dispute, I was to take the Tama bus even though it was smaller, ran more infrequently, and was not always as clean as the others; they insisted. Despite my best attempt to follow their instructions, the Tama bus was not running on the day of my first trip to the sierra, so I went down the street to the Tlahuitoltepec terminal and purchased a ticket (with a small degree of trepidation): "Tama, por favor."

While the three-hour bus ride from Oaxaca to Tama is nothing like the rugged journey most early Mixe ethnographies describe, it still contains a strong sense of crossing boundaries from the Zapotec dominated valley to the mountainous, remote Mixe sierra (see map 4.1). Once past the town of Mitla, which Etsuko Kuroda called the "center of monopolistic Zapotec merchants who dominate the Mixe region" (1984, 9), the steep climb to the Mixe region begins at a northeastern edge of the valley. Men, women, and children carrying bundles and boxes get off and on the bus at any point along the narrow, two-lane road that winds higher and higher over hills and ridges. They head down barely noticeable footpaths to small ranches perched on terraces or nestled in small valleys. The no-man's-land feel of the journey ends abruptly at San Pedro y San Pablo Ayutla, the first Mixe town. A sign first painted when the road from Mitla to Ayutla was finished, in 1966, claiming Ayutla is "El Puerto Mixe," still hangs above the busy central plaza. As a port of entry, the village is poorly planned to handle the increased traffic of hulking buses and trucks whose skillful drivers respond to the swift hand gestures and staccato whistles of pedestrians in order to maneuver the narrow turns between the church and the market structure. The crawling pace of the traffic crowds the plaza, giving street vendors plenty of time to sell tamales and drinks to passengers.

Once past the market, the trip through Ayutla is quick, a matter of just one kilometer (and at least six *topes*, or "speed bumps") since most of the town extends above and below the paved road. Tama comes into view about ten kilometers or twenty minutes later. Though only a short physical distance separates Ayutla and Tama, the villages are very different. Characterized in most ethnographic studies as examples of "progressive" and "conservative" towns, respectively, they represent different points along the continuum upon which anthropologists once used to plot culture change (Kuroda 1984). When the American ethnographer Ralph Beals set out in 1933 for a three-month field trip to the Mixe country, at Elsie Clews Parsons's urging, to look for "aboriginal survivals," the Mixe were "not only a virtually unknown people but they [inhabited] an almost unknown land" (Beals 1973, 1). The Mixe were, in fact, known—Beals himself quotes from the 1670 journal of a Dominican friar—but they were known "among other people in Oaxaca [for their] bad reputation" (Beals 1973, 12). For Beals, the Mixe's "notorious shyness and distrust of strangers" is a result of their "poverty-stricken culture and forbidding landscape [that] operate to exclude outsiders" (1973, 9). The Mixe sierra is apparently devoid of mineral wealth—the reason, according to Beals, why the Mixe "have been left very much alone in their mountains." But the record clearly shows that whatever shyness or distrust the Mixe demonstrate (characterizations of the Mixe I sometimes heard in dominant Oaxacan society) are also a result of centuries of defending their land and culture from incursions and exploitation by Aztec, Zapotec, Spanish, and Mexican interests.[1]

In a linguistic and demographic analysis of the contemporary Mixe language, Ayuuk, and territory, the linguistic anthropologist Teresa

MAP 4.1. Mixe District, Oaxaca © Daniel Dalet, d-maps.com.

Pardo explains the unusually high tendency toward monolinguism and language retention among the Mixe with familiar facts about isolation and difficulty of access, but she also (thankfully) includes historically rooted practices of cultural resistance: "The strong territorial concentration that they have managed to maintain in addition to a nearly inexistent level of dispersion [and] the achievement of having the majority of their territory recognized as a single district, constitute some of the mechanisms that have decidedly impacted the conservation of the Ayuuk language" (1994, 603). The Mixe are known as the only indigenous group in Mexico to have successfully resisted military conquest by the Spanish (Kuroda 1974), and while Mixe villages architecturally acknowledge their submission to colonial rule—the acceptance of the Catholic Church and the *reducción* that established the plaza system—Mixe territory continues to be the basis for their identity and autonomy. Later studies also discuss the Mixe's situated and historical autonomy. Of the 30 districts in the state of Oaxaca only the Mixe district carries an indigenous name (see map 4.1).

Solomón Nahmad has studied the Mixe for nearly half a century. He did his first fieldwork among the Mixe in 1965 as a young anthropologist employed by the INI to find the most appropriate location for establishing an INI outpost, or Centro Coordinador Indígena (CCI), in the region. The stated objective of his research articulates the INI's applied anthropological approach to the "problema indígena" of the time: "We think it is necessary, thus it is the objective of this study, that the Mixe transcend the small world of their communal and ethnocentric life in order to integrate into the great world of regional, national and historic life so they will be capable of evolving from self-contemplation to participation in national life, from solitude and loneliness of community consciousness and subjective conception of the universe to objective knowledge. This will permit the Mixe to become owners of themselves and achieve their full and true development, along with their compatriots" (1965, 10). Notwithstanding his early espousal of assimilationist policy, Nahmad contributed detailed and systematic knowledge about the Mixe region with his 1965 study and developed a critical approach to indigenismo that culminated in his attempt as the INI director in the 1980s to hand CCIs over to indigenous control (a move that cost him two years in prison). Nahmad is now widely recognized as an active defender of indigenous rights and autonomy in Mexico, lessons learned in large part by coming to terms with Mixe autonomy.

In his edited volume on ethnographic sources about the Mixe, published in 1994, Nahmad openly narrates his struggle as a scholar to move beyond the pervasive currents of homogenization and integration to understanding ethnic identities as precisely oppositional to national projects. Of the Mixe, he writes, "Land is considered the basic factor of identity, given through collective work, communal work and unity of the group; always with the objective of preserving their own autonomy in face of external groups and in the face of the Oaxacan state and the Mexican nation" (1994b, 539). The consolidation of Mixe *municipios* into the Mixe District in 1938—the only district in the Republic of Mexico to have an ethnic title—stands as a unique example of recognized indigenous autonomy. As a result, "this group is eminently a pueblo that has an extraordinary self-sufficiency; its own production of coffee, maize, fruit and artisanry allows it to maintain its own form of biological and social reproduction while it preserves its own [cultural] tradition" (Nahmad 1994b, 540). Moreover, this degree of self-sufficiency positions the Mixe to successfully and selectively appropriate modernity and technology, according to Nahmad (1994b, 541–42), but dilemmas emerge in the process of appropriating video indígena as a community project.

Like Ayutla, Tama *centro* (sitting 1,880 meters above sea level) is cut through the middle by the paved road from Oaxaca valley. And like most rural communities in Oaxaca, the heart of Tama centro contains the municipal building, church, market, and a central plaza that doubles as a basketball court. Adobe bricks and terra cotta tiles are still part of the local architectural vernacular, but cinderblock, concrete, and corrugated tin dominate the textures and styles of built structures in Tama today, just as television antennae and satellite dishes dot the mountain vistas. According to the 2010 census there are 7,362 people living in the municipality of Tamazulapam del Espíritu Santo, which includes seven surrounding ranchos and at least nine other smaller *localidades*.

Highland Mixe have been more studied than their midland and lowland neighbors, and are often made to stand for the Mixe as a whole (even though there is fairly wide conjecture that the Mixe were originally a lowland group), in part because of their proximity to the sacred peak, Zempoaltépetl, a Nahuatl word for "twenty summits" or "twenty heads." The Zempoaltépetl is the highest peak in Oaxaca, soaring some 3,300 meters above sea level. Nahmad refers to the Zempoaltépetl as the "belly of the world for the Mixe" and writes, "There does not exist a religious concept that is not associated with this extraordinary mountain that constitutes a home where the Mixe have sought refuge for freeing themselves from the hostility and aggression of the ethnic groups that surround them" (1994a, 5). The Mixe god, Cong Hoy (also referred to as a mythic or cultural hero) born from an egg, is said to live in the caves of the Zempoaltépetl, where frequent offerings are made to secure the well-being of the Mixe.

A pantheon of nature-based gods is revered among the Mixe, alongside Catholic saints and virgins, in an uncomplicated manner. The Dominican Church settled in the Mixe region early in the sixteenth century and today the Mixe are nominally Catholic (Kuroda 1984, 14), but as Beals himself observed, in 1933, the Mixe ability to "compartmentalize some aspects of their culture" orders Catholic and Mixe ritual into a parallel and complementary, rather than syncretic, relationship. For example, offerings are made to Mixe gods in sacred mountain spots to ensure that Catholic rituals proceed smoothly, a practice that is part of daily life today.

The Japanese ethnographer Etsuko Kuroda picked up some of Beals's concerns with culture change in the early 1970s and published a monograph on the highland Mixe, based on two years of field research that compares Ayutla and Tlahuitoltepec, the two villages that flank Tamazulapam. Kuroda characterizes Ayutla as "changing" and Tlahui as "traditional" and believes that with the "increasing impact of modern Mexican society . . . little time remains for the documentation of highland Mixe society and culture" (1984, 2). Kuroda makes an interesting assessment of Mixe "space consciousness," which is useful for rounding out this introductory description of the Mixe. The primary category in the space consciousness of the Mixe is the municipio, or "municipality," "an endogamous unit where they live within the framework of kinship, the same dialect and the same traditions of ritual" (1984, 11). Each municipio has a centro with a plaza complex (imposed by the Spanish) but is delimited by a series of outlying ranchos that represent a pre-Hispanic settlement pattern. The Mixe I got to know in Tama do still identify with the municipio, as Kuroda acknowledges after her return visit to the Mixe sierra in the late 1980s (1994, 544), but deeper relationships connect people to the ranchos as they delimit lineage and land tenure, thus constituting a spatial category prior to the municipio. Mixe space consciousness also includes the root level and the sky level, as Floriberto Díaz explained to Carlos Cruz during the INI video workshops. Kuroda's characterization of the outside world beyond the municipio as "dangerous" no longer seemed to be true at the beginning of the new millennium. Three decades after the road was opened between Tama and Oaxaca City, and five years after it was paved, Oaxaca City was more like a backyard for many Tama centro residents than a danger zone. In 1999, Genaro estimated that while 2,253 people resided in Tama centro, an equal number were living in Oaxaca City and Mexico City.

The second and third categories are adjacent municipios and the Mixe region, respectively, and the broadest category of space for Mixe, according to Kuroda, is "modern Mexican national culture," which was quickly becoming more and more dominant during the time of her field research, in 1973–74 (1984, 12). National culture first staked its claim in Mixe territory via schools, in the 1930s, in large part due to the efforts of the renowned "socially progressive" Mixe cacique Daniel Martínez (Beals 1973). By the 1970s, however, roads, telephones, and a series of government offices—including the INI's CCI, established as per Nahmad's suggestion in Ayutla—"drastically accelerated social change" in the region (Kuroda 1984, 48). "In the 1970s the two worlds of the Mixe and the *agats* [non-Mixe] stood face to face" (Kuroda 1984, 20).[2]

The record indicates that the Mixe navigated these spatial categories on a regular basis, despite the dangers leaving the municipio may have presented. Tama residents in particular are known for being traveling salesmen who journeyed to the isthmus for salt and other commodities not available in their highland villages. Furthermore, the coffee boom that took off in the 1930s greatly stimulated regional migration. Midland and lowland Mixe areas were perfectly suited for shade-grown coffee and highland Mixe migrated there regularly as day laborers. In 1945, thirty men from Tama and Tlahui went to the United States as part of the federally sponsored *braceros* program (Kuroda 1984, 19), and migration outside the region remained relatively low throughout the century. The 1990 census recorded moderate levels of out migration from the Mixe area—6.7 percent compared to other indigenous regions of the state, such as the Mixtec and Zapotec, with 17.2 percent and 14.9 percent, respectively (Pardo 1994, 575–76). In 1999, when I began my field research, Tama was experiencing its first serious wave of migration to the United States. Coyotes would regularly appear in Tama to round up migrants and their dreams for the long trip to the northern border.

Like most municipalities in Oaxaca (412 out of 570), Tama elects its municipal government outside the official party system by *usos y costumbres*, which relies on the general assembly of *comuneros* (communal landowners), the "supreme authority of the community." The civil-religious hierarchy, which characterizes much social organization throughout Mesoamerica, is usually referred to as the *systema de cargos*, though in Tama, as in other Mixe villages, the term *autoridad* is used to denote an office as well as an officeholder (Kuroda 1984, 57). People elected to hold office in Tama are also called *servidores* (servers); they serve at the will of their community and without pay. Tama's land, like most land in the Mixe region, is held communally. A colonial land title from 1712 grouped Tama and the neighboring villages of Ayutla, Tlahuitoltepec, Tupuxtepec, and Tepantlali into one pueblo— perhaps a colonial expression of the local legend of "Five Brothers," which says the village founders were siblings that "sprang" from the river below Tamazulapam—but the title has generated countless agrarian conflicts as the "brothers" struggle to define and defend their separate territories.[3] Nahmad writes that resolving land conflicts has become a way of life in the region: "Colonial titles as well as modern documents have generated internal strife that has not permitted the emergence of an alliance for their own development" (Nahmad 1994a, 21–22).

While agrarian disputes characterize the region (as well as its uneasy and uneven history of relations with state agencies), tequio (communal work obligations) are the "barometer by which one may estimate communal solidarity and the power and control of the officials over the community" (Kuroda 1984, 141). Not only an important basis of Mixe identity, tequio is considered by many indigenous activists in the broader sierra region of Oaxaca to be a defining aspect of comunalidad (Martínez Luna 1995). Beals, writing in the 1940s, describes "tekio" as "having a firm hold on the Mixe," as if communal labor is a stubborn tradition or an obstacle to development. Beals believes that "the whole tekio system was a post-Spanish introduction" based on two considerations: that "the absence of pyramids or large public works suggests the absence of any communal labor" and that "tekio is an Aztec word" (1954, 31). Whether a product of organized labor shaped over centuries of colonial influence or a survival strategy in "modern times," tequio is nonetheless a defining aspect of indigenous autonomy at the community level, situated in specific histories, relations, and places.

Visualizing Tequio

Tequio came to play a decisive role in my understanding of the challenges to making culture visible in Tama. I arrived in Tama on the eve of the year's first major tequio, to be carried out on recently cleared fields at the heart of the agrarian dispute with Tlahuitoltepec (known as "Tlahui" for short). Though I had been a bit nervous about asking my Tlahui-bound neighbor on the bus to tell me when we got to Tama (it was getting dark), I was able to get off on the right curve and find Genaro's house without problems. It was, after all, not only right in the middle of town, across from the plaza and just off the main road, but also where both the telephones and PA system are located. The *topil* (a community servant occupying the lowest ranking position or cargo which is to maintain order in the community) paused from calling out blaring tequio reminders in Ayuuk over the public announcement system and passed the microphone to the telephone lady so she could call Maestro Genaro Rojas back to his house to greet me. Genaro gave me a tour of his two-story, concrete-block house as his girls eagerly pointed out where I would sleep and put my bags, in a brightly painted room below the phone booths and across from the indoor kitchen, with an ample bed. They slept upstairs with mom and dad in the room next to the telephone office. The room had a 27-inch television, a king-size bed, and rolling rack of clothing that Etél sold as a side business in the telephone office. A small balcony looked past their avocado tree and bougainvillea vine to a cluttered view of rooftops, drying laundry, and television antennas.

Genaro then led me to meet his mother, who lives below with her mother-in-law in a tiny, wooden two-room house whose textures, compared to Genaro's own concrete-block home, speak of an older generation. We talked in front of his mother's open hearth about the media collective, village dynamics, and family. Genaro's mother, Isabel, extended a warm handshake to me. She spoke only Mixe and while she didn't join the conversation much, my introduction to her seemed to affirm Genaro's connection and claim to Mixe identity. His elder daughter, Silvana (who was eleven at the time), practically sitting in my lap, peered into my eyes (confirming, "azul") and asked me about my earrings, my wedding band, my sisters, and why my parents divorced. Several months after our first meeting, Silvana called my home in Oaxaca City, to express her concern that something may have happened to me because a blond character on her mother's favorite soap opera had fallen ill. Fitting, I remember thinking, that while I came to study Mixe self-representation and their local television channel, my physical appearance placed me in the foreign world of white-skinned, melodramatic TV characters that arrived over the airwaves from faraway places, at least in the eyes of little Silvana.[4]

That next morning I was awoken at six in the morning with the bullhorn calling the tequio, and the usual mix of roosters and radios. We had made arrangements the night before for me to accompany Genaro to Rancho Tierra Caliente, a pottery-making village close to the tequio site. Genaro was concerned, given the heightened state of alert between Tama and Tlahui, that the presence of an outsider would cause suspicion, and we agreed that if asked, I was to say I was in town buying pottery, a neutral and relatively familiar role for an outsider to have in the community.[5] As we left Tama centro, winding

FIGURE 4.1. Genaro heading to tequio. Photo: Erica Cusi Wortham.

down narrow footpaths carved between small houses and patios, the smoke of the bonfires at the tequio site was already climbing out of the valley below (see figure 4.1).

People of all ages (though mostly older), carrying rustic tilling tools, stepped onto the path in front of and behind us, until we formed a steady stream flowing single-file to the river below us. The fields were already alive with very organized activity. Rows of people were rhythmically tilling the newly cleared fields, which seemed to stretch as far as the eye could see, and *yuntas* (ox and plow) were skillfully digging furrows where people had already passed. The mix of smells, sounds, and textures—clods of fresh earth; crackling, smoldering debris in massive bonfires; water gurgling around rocks in the riverbed; grunting, sweaty oxen; and the whips and song of the ox men—filled the air with determination. Tama residents were asserting their control over disputed land by working it; if indeed tequio is the barometer by which one may estimate communal solidarity, Tama had it in spades.

Genaro did end up dumping me in Rancho Tierra Caliente while he saw to an organizational duty the municipal authority had assigned him during the tequio. I visited the potters, got an extended tour of their new textile production facility, and waited in the shade of an oak tree for about four hours, before I secured a ride halfway back to Tama.

Just as I was beginning the rest of the climb on foot, Efraín Pérez Rojas, Genaro's cousin and newest member of Radio y Video Tamix, called to me, in English, "Stop!" He had spent the morning video-taping the tequio and was headed to the Rancho Duraznal field house for lunch. He took me along and made my day. The one-room struc-ture, built entirely of fresh wooden planks from trees felled during the field clearing a few months prior, was filled with women busily preparing a meal of *caldo mixe*—a delicious, spicy chicken broth pre-pared with chickens sacrificed that morning in an offering to secure the success of the tequio and field preparation—black bean tamales, and *tepache*, a fermented drink made from corn. Elderly men of the Duraznal lineage, to which the Rojas family belonged, were already well on their way to getting drunk as younger men and women who worked the tequio approached the field house for rest and refueling.[6]

Despite the long wait under the oak tree, the day was a spectacular, sensual introduction to Tama and to the importance of tequio in the community. On the walk back up to Tama, after the delicious caldo Mixe, Efraín and I talked about how his taping had gone. He had gotten some good shots, but he also got flack from people he was photographing for not doing "real work." The defining element of communal solidarity, tequio, was being overtly contrasted, in a nega-tive way, to video work, setting the Radio y Video Tamix collective on a course to prove themselves within their own community.

A History of Radio y Video Tamix: Achieving Embeddedness

Radio y Video Tamix (Tamix) grew out of a community-based cul-tural organization in Tama.[7] Blending culturally specific idioms that exemplify community life with state and federal government dis-courses that position culture as an important factor in the defense of indigenous peoples, Tamix constructed itself as a "community" media project dedicated to making culture visible to the community itself. Their project of reflecting the community back to itself hinges on their belief that seeing and hearing oneself strengthens the community's sense of self as Mixe or Ayuuk—a process of identity formation that resonates directly with how Ojo de Agua articulates the relationship between communication and culture. The process of rendering culture demonstrable through audiovisual media in Tama (a relatively new technology in the community), however, was accompanied by sharp criticism from community members who felt that Tamix's project was not sufficiently transparent to community supervision and did not constitute "real work." In turn, Tamix's producers complained that "people didn't see" what they were trying to accomplish, which was to "preserve and strengthen their culture." What community members didn't "see," however, was on a material level; they didn't see where all the money went.

A brief history of Tamix—drawn from interviews, participant observation, conversations, descriptive brochures made by the organization, as well as from a handful of the group's own writings and proposals—reveals how the organization deployed local and contested notions of culture and "community" to construct itself as a community project. The history of Tamix can be easily organized into three periods. The first period begins in the mid-1980s, when a loosely defined group of young schoolteachers first began to organize cultural events in the village, and goes through 1989, when they formalized into Tama's Casa del Pueblo. The second period, from 1989 through 1995, covers the emergence and consolidation of the group's media initiative, Radio y Video Tamix. The third begins in 1996 and is marked by a significantly increased operating budget, extended conflict and redefinition, and the ascension of the younger members of the organization to positions of control. Several actors in the collective's history will be familiar to the reader from preceding chapters, evidence of Tamix's participation in the development of video indígena. While Tamix ceased doing regular television transmissions after 2000—in addition to challenges from community members and authorities, the television transmitter was in disrepair and efforts to acquire a new one failed—founding members are still active cultural producers in their town and elsewhere, but focus almost exclusively on producing music and radio, instead of video.

The founding members of Tamix are schoolteachers who left their community as young adults to pursue teaching degrees and returned to Tama in 1984, eager to apply fresh ideas and make their mark in the village. As agents of "positive" change in the community, their strategy of choice was to program cultural events as safe, recreational activities for members of the community who, in their minds, appeared to be bored or unengaged.

Initially they organized dances, song and music variety shows, basketball and soccer tournaments, donkey races for children, and even road races for seniors. In the words of one of the group's leaders, Genaro, they wanted to develop cultural activities together "but [they] didn't even talk about [cultural] recuperation or anything, it was a way of life, nothing more, to distract people and [themselves]" (Cremoux 1997). They enjoyed a great following in the village, especially among young people and children, and their popularity and cohesiveness as a group coincided with a state government initiative to establish casas del pueblo, or community cultural centers.[8] The Casa del Pueblo in Tama was installed in the municipal building in 1989 and inaugurated with great fanfare—even the state PRI governor, Heladio Ramirez, attended the ceremony, accompanied by a camera crew from the Oaxaca state television station. In fact, a number of government agencies converged on the casa del pueblo, swiftly bringing the group into a circuit of indigenous, community-based organizations that enjoyed the *visto bueno* (approval) of the government.

The INI expressed particular interest in the new organization. Having recently installed its indigenous radio station—XEGLO, "La voz de la sierra"—one sierra over, in Guelatao de Juárez, representatives of the radio station invited the Casa del Pueblo to become a *centro de producción radiofónico* (CPR, radio production center). As a CPR, Casa del Pueblo was asked to produce radio programs in the highland Mixe language that would be broadcast weekly by the station in Guelatao. In addition, the director of the INI's Archivo Etnográfico Audiovisual, in Mexico City, Alfonso Muñoz, was on hand to celebrate Casa del Pueblo's inauguration. At the time, Muñoz was organizing the conference on anthropology and communications that formed the basis of the INI's video indio initiative (INI 1989).

With modest funds from the Casa del Pueblo program (about 10,000 pesos annually), the organization commissioned elaborate costumes and larger-than-life puppets for dances and supplemented basic audio recording equipment provided by the radio station with sound amplification equipment. In 1990 the group contacted a paisano (compatriot) working in the United States and asked him to bring home a video camera (paid for with Casa del Pueblo funds). Employed as a record-keeping tool, the video camera was enlisted to tape countless hours of their radio production sessions, numerous official visits, fiestas, and all the important activities of the community municipal authorities such as the *cambio de autoridades* (changing of authorities) on January 1 of each year. Genaro remembers they used to tape everything "official" during their first couple of years with the video camera.

Tama's Casa del Pueblo was initially excluded from the INI's national video workshops, despite Muñoz's enthusiasm for the organization, because the INI's Oaxacan delegate wanted to avoid appearing to be taking sides in Tama's ongoing land dispute with neighboring Tlahui. Nevertheless, as the workshop selection process shifted from invitation only to an application process, two members of Tama's Casa del Pueblo were trained in video production at the third TMA workshop, in 1992. By that time, Casa del Pueblo expressed a relatively clear vision of how video fit into their activities and this suited the desire of the TMA project team to maximize the program's longer-term results. The Casa del Pueblo members Aureliano and Victoriano returned to Tama after the workshop, loaded with equipment—an S-VHS camera, semiprofessional record and playback decks, an edit controller, two monitors, a shelving unit, a tripod, cassettes, and a set of lights. The *aparatísimos* (large equipment) were received in the community with a benediction by a priest and a wave of ritual sacrifices, the customary way highland Mixe secure the well-being and productivity of a community project. Meanwhile, silk-screening had been added to the Casa del Pueblo's list of activities, and by the end of 1992 Radio y Video Tamix T-shirts were out, announcing this new facet of the Casa del Pueblo. Tamix's first edited video program, *Ma'ach/Mash* (1995), was taped during this period of the collective's history; the program evidences the novelty of the camera in the community as well as the discursive framing about making culture visible that the collective learned at the INI workshop.

Ma'ach/Mash (1995) • "Ma'ach," or *machucado* in Spanish (which means "mashed" or "crushed"), is the name of a sacred cornmeal dish prepared annually in Tama, on the first day of August, to celebrate the end of the annual period of scarcity (May to August), when the community faces a diminishing supply of maize.[9] *Masa* (corn meal) cooked with bitter greens is mashed and molded into a volcano shape and placed in a searing hot clay pot, which is taken directly from the open fire to the ground where people gather around in a circle. A spicy, boiling tomato sauce is poured over the corn meal, and like most Mixe foods, the dish is eaten with your fingers, by pinching off bits of masa and dipping them into the tomato sauce.

The footage included in *Ma'ach* was shot in 1990—before Tamix had attended the INI workshop—but it was postproduced at the CVI in Oaxaca City, in 1995. As a result, the tape exhibits elements of both moments, when Tama residents considered the camera a novelty in the community and later, when Tamix members enjoyed a relationship with the CVI. The "loud" visual effects used for transitions (wipes) and titles speak to their enthusiasm for the CVI's newly acquired "video machine" postproduction software.

The opening image of *Ma'ach* flies into an empty black frame from the upper left corner, flipping and turning around on itself and growing in size until it takes the center and fills the frame, over a traditional-looking adobe brick structure with a terra cotta tiled roof, as *música típica* (guitar and mandolin) play. The title—"M A ' A C H"—arranged in an arch and centered in the frame, flips into view and the house recedes with a zoom-out that reveals a hillside of Tamazulapam. The music fades and Aureliano's voice and image comes up with a bold wipe effect. He is wearing a wool *gabán* (man's shawl), standing on a hilltop in front of a television antenna, microphone in hand. The Zempoatépetl defines the horizon behind him. In Ayuuk, he says, "Today is the first day of August of 1990. Today, so beautiful, so lovely the day arrived." And as he turns his back on the camera to look down the slope behind him, he continues, "We can see the sun, no clouds, almost no people walking the streets. With anticipation they await the arrival of the month of lacking, as the elders say." A wipe splits the frame in half and reveals two men, one young and one old, carrying loads of firewood harnessed with ropes slung from their foreheads, walking down a narrow, muddy dirt path. Aureliano approaches the elderly man, his microphone stretched an arm's length in front of him: "Good day, sir. Have you already eaten? No. What are you going to eat today? Machucado. Machucado? Yes, today is the first of August. I see you went early to get firewood. Yes. Do you think the machucado is ready? Yes, I'm going to eat when I get home." The old man laughs into the camera with a wide, semi-toothless smile.

An open wooden door of an adobe house introduces the next sequence. Aureliano, still on camera, is inside a dark kitchen, interviewing a woman: "Why are you going to eat machucado? Today is the first of August; that is why we are going to eat machucado." In this sequence, the woman explains how she prepares ma'ach and her narration closely follows the images. At the end of the sequence, a handful of adults and children gather around the clay pot on the ground, sitting on short stools or the floor, and begin to eat. The first pinch of ma'ach is placed on the ground in honor of the earth spirit.

This eight-minute video ends with Aureliano's interviewing a group of adolescent boys in the plaza. "What did you eat today?" he asks each of them. Between giggles and shoves, they take turns responding "ma'ach" or "machucado." One boy, however, obviously enjoys giving the wrong answer, "huevo" (egg). *Ma'ach* has no ending title sequence.

Aureliano was one of the two Tamix members who later received video training in the INI's TMA program. Using an on-camera interviewing style that the collective would later adopt as a standard style in their television broadcasts, Aureliano demonstrates a funny mix of discomfort and timidity with his role as interviewer and his determination to get the interview. The on-camera, microphone-wielding interviewer is exactly the kind of borrowed-from-TV convention that outraged Monteforte at the first TMA workshops. The somewhat awkward and terse responses of the Tama residents accosted by Aureliano for an interview about the day's meal reveal the novelty of Tamix's camera in the community.

The indoor sequence, in contrast, was prearranged with an aunt of a Tamix member and has a more relaxed feeling to it, even though in the interest of capturing the details of ma'ach preparation the cameraman cut off most people's faces. In general the program's tight correlation between image and narration, the superficial nature of the questions and answers, and the way the on-camera interviewer accosts people in the community speak of the collective's incipient relationship with video and the "older" generation of Tamix producers' preference for Ayuuk-language programs about traditional Mixe cultural expressions.

Seen through the lens of *Ma'ach*, it is plain to see how the INI video production workshop transferred more than video production equipment and basic skills for its use. The workshop also transferred the institution's discourse about the role culture plays in the development of indigenous communities and how self-representation through the use of video can strengthen community identity. Whereas in the early days before the creation of the Casa del Pueblo there was no talk of *rescate cultural* (cultural recuperation), as Genaro pointed out, by 1992, when Radio y Video Tamix released its first promotional brochure, the organization described their "primordial" objective this way: "To rescue, preserve and promote Mixe culture through recordings and the use of video equipment, because we know that communication is a medium for strengthening our identity" (Tamix 1992). Tamix members were as quick to appropriate video indígena discursively as they were technologically, demonstrating how video indígena is produced in a dialogic manner, through the encounter between a community organization and an institutional program. The anthropological language of identity and culture, which underwrites the INI's TMA project, directly shapes the way Tamix represents itself to its own community. The organization's brochure firmly located the Casa del Pueblo within and beholden to the community. La Casa del Pueblo is described as "a community cultural center whose maximum authority is the general assembly of landholders" (Tamix 1992). A question remained, however, about how well this discourse resonated with community members and secured the place of media production as a project representative of the community as a whole. While the discourse of making culture visible was not overtly contested, their practice—the absence of consensual decision-making regarding productions, the lack of fiscal transparency, and rotating leadership positions—undermined their place as a community project.

Espacio Sagrado Goes on the Air

On November 28, 1992, something rather unusual happened in Tama. The Saturday outdoor market was winding down, merchants from the valley were packing up and heading home, and Tama residents were settling in to an afternoon at home—women plucked feathers from chickens out back, children enjoyed treats they got at the market, men bathed in the dimming sunshine on their patios. Television sets were tuned in to favorite news, sports, or soap operas when suddenly the signal was interrupted and two very familiar faces appeared on the screen. Clad in headphones and wielding large microphones, Genaro Rojas and Rafael Vargas, primary school teachers from Tamazulapam, sent greetings to the community in Spanish and Ayuuk and announced the new television station: "Canal 12, TV Tamix, de Tamazulapam." Rafael clutched his watch, repeating the day and exact hour, so as to leave no doubt in viewers minds that they were in fact broadcasting live. Initially, no one understood that the signal was actually coming from Tama itself and wondered how those clowns had managed to get themselves into a television studio in Oaxaca or Mexico City. But a young boy who recognized the background on screen—his schoolyard, where a tall antenna and satellite dish had lain abandoned for years— ran down the road to discover the television crew in action. "Estan en la secundaria! Vengan todos!" For the first time in the fifteen or so years since Tama residents started buying television sets television related in direct way to their experience as indigenous people.[10]

The consolidation of Tamix was complete with the "discovery" of the television transmitter. The group's new understanding of video and how signals are transmitted electronically, as well as the significant boost in equipment given to them by the INI, led them to appropriate the abandoned transmitter in the name of the community. Originally installed in Tama as part of a network of rural retransmitting stations for IMEVISION (a state operation that was privatized in 1980s and later bought by TV Azteca, one of Mexico's largest commercial television networks), the transmitter had never even been turned on, until Tamix got their hands on it. The ten-watt transmitter allowed Tamix's station Canal 12 to reach only a limited radius of television viewers (five kilometers at the most), but because its frequency was preset to channel twelve their signal interrupted TV Azteca programming, not only one of the few signals strong enough to reach Tama homes but, to their advantage, one of the most popular sources of soap operas and national news.

In their television programs, Tamix regularly employed the idiom of the tequio to exemplify their position as a community project and adopt the term *espacio sagrado* (sacred space) as their station identi-fication, in order to ground their project as Mixe.[11] The notion of espacio sagrado further identifies Canal 12 as Mixe and lends a degree of seriousness to their otherwise unstructured working style. In Gen-aro's words, "Our motto—every television channel has one—is Sacred Space because making video is very important to life. When you do something you tend to enjoy it and that is a space of importance and respect; we don't want it to be a place of distraction . . . Humans constitute sacred spaces when we do things with respect and respon-sibility, creativity, all the good things, that is what is sacred" (OMVIAC 1994). The Tamix brochure from 1992 lists the names of the members and describes them as "native speakers of Mixe who lend their service voluntarily in a manner considered like communal work and who are currently distributed among the following areas: camera, assistants, sound, lighting, script writing and editing" (Tamix 1992). Their work is voluntary and not paid, just like a tequio, they argue.

The introductory sequences to their television program visually reinforce the importance of the tequio as the defining element of both the community and its representation on tape. Opening pans of their mountainous landscape and shots of monumental tequio activities (such as road-building and field-clearing) accompany all eight verses of the Mexican national anthem, asserting the importance of both community and territory in a national context. The Mixe anthem (which follows) positions the Mixe as sovereign or autonomous within but respectful of the Mexican nation-state, and plays over images of Tamix members recording radio programs and editing video. Mixe autonomy (indexed by their anthem) is visually linked to their use of high-tech equipment, as the possibility of being Mixe (traditional) and using technology (modern) is asserted. The final sequence of the program's introduction is a local song about the lovely women of Tama. Shots of women laboring in fields and preparing food or religious offerings connects the station to one of the most traditionally "traditional" and visual markers of Tama, the women's distinctive *huipil* and *reboso* (hand-woven tops and shawls, respectively). The sequence ends with Tamix's "own" color bars, an example of "Mixenization" or cultural appropriation of a western technology that Tamix producers found particularly clever. SMPTE color bars is a test pattern created by the Society for Motion Picture and Television Engineers (SMPTE) and used as a standard in NTSC video production in North America for measuring and adjusting color alterations. Usually a few seconds of color bars are included at beginning of a video program so adjustments can be made during playback, but are not part of the program itself. Tamix producers enjoyed including their own version of color bars, a still shot of a Tama reboso that is white with red, green, and yellow stripes, within the program itself, self-consciously asserting their cultural domination of the technology with humor.

Between 1993 and 1995, the collective maintained close ties with the INI's TMA program and, in particular, with the newly established CVI in Oaxaca City. Two of Casa del Pueblo's youngest members, Hermenegildo Rojas (Genaro's younger brother) and Carlos Martínez, practically lived at the center from 1994 through 1995. Receiving no salary but getting most of their living expenses paid for thanks to CVI's creative bookkeeping, Hermenegildo and Carlos learned everything they could about postproduction and became video production instructors in their own right. Living in Oaxaca and working at the center also provided more contact with regional and national initiatives emerging from the TMA program and elsewhere, such as an international conference of indigenous videomakers in Tlaxcala, the creation of the short-lived independent association OMVIAC (Tamix was a member organization), and of course the Zapatista rebellion in neighboring Chiapas, which had just gone public in the beginning of 1994.

Carlos became the center's full-time postproduction editor and eventually took a job as a professional video editor for the Desarrollo Integral de la Familia in Oaxaca City, a local branch of Mexico's National System for Integral Family Development. Hermenegildo, on the other hand, returned to Tama in 1996 to begin producing video programs, after successfully competing for two production grants: a grant of 80,000 pesos (approximately $8,000) from the Oaxaca State Fund for Arts and Culture (FOESCA), and an intercultural multimedia grant for $12,000, from the MacArthur and Rockefeller foundations. When Hermenegildo returned to Tama, he paired up with a recently arrived cousin from Veracruz, Efraín Pérez Rojas, who was seeking to reconnect with his maternal village, and together they began to work full-time at Tamix, marking the beginning of a peak in the collective's activity, as well as the beginning of its demise.

Tamix at Its Prime and Its Demise

Up until the organization received the FOESCA and MacArthur and Rockefeller grants, they had survived on modest funds from the Casa del Pueblo budget and a small grant from the Oaxacan Institute for Popular Culture, totaling no more than 10,000 to 20,000 pesos a year. In one year, 1996, their resources had increased almost 200 percent. International recognition and, more importantly, a potential for economic security previously unknown to the organization, provided by the grants, were quickly overshadowed by the community's increasingly conflictive attitude toward them. Accusations of corruption and fiscal secrecy culminated in their forced removal from the municipal building, a move that effectively split the Casa del Pueblo and Tamix into discrete organizations (even though most people in Tama commonly referred to Tamix members, and their new office, as the Casa del Pueblo). Receiving the grants and being banished from the municipal building were not unrelated events, of course; further inquiry and analysis revealed that Tamix's place as a "community" project was never very secure.

The group lost several members during the split, and television transmissions nearly ceased during 1997, but they did not close down entirely. In fact, the conflict provided unexpected opportunities for younger members of the collective, Hermenegildo and Efraín, to assume more active roles. Less vulnerable to community criticism because of their younger age—around eighteen years old, at the time they did not command authority and were therefore able to act with less accountability—Hermenegildo and Efraín effectively kept the collective alive. Unlike the older, founding members of the Casa del Pueblo, who were teachers by profession, they did not have other jobs to turn to or families to support, so they simply had more time to devote to the project. Plus, Hermenegildo and Efraín were trained in audiovisual media production and felt they had "grown up" at Tamix.

Tamix moved their operations to their present location in 1997 and spent much of the grant money renovating the building and outfitting the new studio. Today when you approach Tama on the paved road from Oaxaca City, a broad curve to the left reveals most prominent sign in town: T-V-T-A-M-I-X (see figure 4.2). Announcing itself above the colorful din of signs for Sol, Dos XX, and Superior beer painted on walls around town, TV Tamix physically claims a central position in the community, in bold letters painted on the front of their cinderblock building, which sits directly above the public bathrooms, in the very heart of the village.

The interior walls of the main office are textured in a lively white and blue sponge pattern, and the office is furnished with a wooden armoire, where production equipment is kept, a set of table and chairs, the main editing console, monitors, the television transmitter, a tall rack of decks, and the video archive, which is neatly stored in two custom-made hanging cabinets with glass doors. The second, smaller office has a large utility shelf filled with cables, cassettes, and supplies of various kinds, and a small table with a Power Mac desktop computer. Both offices have windows protected with rather elegant ironwork that face the town and the valley below, allowing easy surveil-

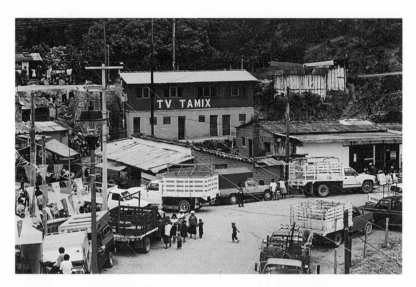

FIGURE 4.2. TV TAMIX, Radio y Video Tamix's television studios, in Tamazulapam del Espíritu Santo, Oaxaca. Photo: Erica Cusi Wortham.

lance of who's coming and going. Finally, there is the studio itself: a narrow room shielded from sunlight, with V-I-D-E-O-T-A-M-I-X spelled out in carefully carved Styrofoam letters across one wall and eight studio lights hanging from the ceiling.

A shift toward video production, instead of television programming, characterized 1997 and a good part of 1998, reflecting both the collective's obligations to the funding institutions and a more careful relationship with the community. Hermenegildo felt that their video programs were directed more toward outside consumption, a direct result of funding obligations, while their television programming was for the community, though they showed their programs on television, for the most part. For FOESCA they produced *Moojk/Maize*, a video about corn and the multiple roles it plays in Mixe life, and *Tun pëk/ Work and Live*, a somewhat experimental piece about the various productive activities of Tama. *Moojk* was selected to screen at the Native American Film and Video Festival, in New York City in 1997, and an invitation was extended to the collective for one member to attend the festival. Genaro, still the main spokesperson for the group, represented the collective in New York.

Moojk/Maize (1996) • When Genaro introduced *Moojk* at the ninth annual Native American Film and Video Festival, in New York City in November of 1997, he explained to the audience gathered that Tamix made the program for their community, that internal consumption was their priority as a collective. Indeed, that was their stated objective, but *Moojk* was clearly made to satisfy outside funders such as FOESCA, as well. Footage for the program was shot in 1995, one of the collective's best years in terms of community approval, as the ending title acknowledges with a mention that the 1995 municipal authority gave their visto bueno (approval) to the project.

Moojk opens with an elegant sequence. The evocative sound of slightly off-key trumpets and a drum beckons over still shots of corn in various settings—green on the stalk, arranged on an altar, in front of the trunk in which the corn goddess is kept—and introduces the multiple roles corn plays in Mixe life. The trumpets fade out to rhythmic pounding, and a slow zoom-out reveals an elderly lady smashing a wooden stick against a bag of dry corncobs (to loosen the kernels off the cob). She sits, dressed in traditional Mixe clothing—a dark blue skirt, wrapped tightly around the hips with a bright red wool sash, a white huipil with modest color stitched around the opening for the head, and the reboso, mostly white, with red, green, and yellow stripes (like "color bars") worn around her head. Her legs neatly tucked under her skirt, she continues to pound the corn as her voice-over comes in: "Before, our corn seed would get infested when March came along. We weren't able to store them until seeding time. These seeds have been stored until now. We clean the corn grains so that they can stay clean." Her name (in Spanish and Ayuuk) flips into the frame as if from behind her head and settles below the English subtitles. Raking through loose corn kernels with her hands, she describes a burning technique they've been using in Tama for three years and how she doesn't like corn treated with pesticides: "My chickens feed from the corn and it isn't good for them." This time, flute and drum music, considered the oldest form of music in the community, comes up over a close-up on her worn hands, as she diligently rubs two cobs together to remove the kernels. The camera follows her to her courtyard and a wipe transitions to the next sequence.

A man in a field explains that at Easter time they make offerings at the sacred mountain spot Cuatro Palos (Four sticks) with the seeds that will be used for sowing. His name zooms into the frame from behind his hat. There are many different varieties of corn in the region. According to elevation, there is yellow mountain corn, white corn, and yellow lowland corn. You can hear Hermenegildo's affirming "um-hums" from behind the camera. He told me he was interested in making the encounter feel more like a conversation than an interview. "Lowland corn and Mountain corn, not the same thing," the man emphasizes with a raised finger as if admonishing Hermenegildo and his generation for not knowing or caring about important differences in kernel size and color.

A wipe and transition to local violin music begins a short montage sequence made up of shots of corn carefully arranged on a variety of alters to the Virgin of Guadalupe and the Mixe Corn Goddess. There is also corn under a saint's coffin in the church. The tape returns to the field where the man begins a discussion of sacred offerings done at Easter, the time of sowing. This sequence follows the preparation of an offering at Cuatro Palos. Several men clean the spring that determines the site; they build an arch of reeds and flowers and prepare the floor with banana leaves. Tamales, potatoes, fruit, eggs, and corn meal are carefully layered before the chickens are sacrificed. Traditional flute and drum music play on the soundtrack. A man explains, "Every person decides how many times to do a ceremony and what to ask for [corn or money]. Some people aren't good farmers because they don't follow tradition; they don't go to the sacred places that nature keeps. The hills and the mountain give life and fertility to human beings. Water as well. They are the main elements that give us life; that's why we go to sacred places to ask for more life. We appeal to the mountains. This way we move forward and live better." A second montage sequence—a mix of close-up and medium shots of dry corn stalks in a field arranged to languid classical violin music (by the Kronos Quartet)—studies the passing of a planting season.

The program returns to the first woman who demonstrates the "burning" process. The trumpets return as she churns kernels boiling in blacked buckets over an open fire, strains the corn in a wicker basket, and lays it out to dry on straw mats on her patio. A close-up focuses in on her expert hands, spreading out the yellow kernels. Another elderly woman in a different exterior location talks about the ways of the grandparents and how young people just don't get it. "Even though we can't read or write, we teach these beliefs. We know our traditions very well." The closing sequence captures men and women dancing with corn stalks to the municipal brass band in a dark, interior space. It is the celebration of the changing of authorities at the New Year, and members of the community are dancing to honor the Corn Goddess. The ending title sequence scrolls over a still image of a wooden plow.

Moojk positions maize as central to the Mixe way of life and touches only the tip of the iceberg of changes in global corn production that are affecting rural communities across Mexico's poorest south. Imported corn—and factory-made tortillas—are increasingly available in Mixe communities and are relatively inexpensive. While government-subsidized corn has been available since the 1970s (starting with the CONASUPO program), commercial corn and tortillas at cheap market prices are a post-NAFTA phenomenon that competes with traditional maize cultivation and thus, as Tamix illustrates with *Moojk*, threatens the very foundation of Mixe culture. Relying on elders who voice concern that younger Mixe generations are forgetting their traditions, this tape is an attempt by Tamix to refocus the community's understanding of corn beyond subsistence, to its importance in Mixe cycles of ritual and connections to sacred, mountain spots that underpin Mixe culture.

Moojk also presents a critique of consumerism and globalization, an aspect of the program that is particularly appealing to outside (international) audiences that look to (local) indigenous cultural practices for critiques of globalization and neoliberalism. But for Genaro and Hermenegildo there is a dilemma in staking out a critical position. Discussing the making of this tape, they asked rhetorically if it is their place to raise issues that the community itself does not explicitly perceive as a problem. If a family's maize supply is insufficient to cover a year of consumption, and if commercial corn and tortillas are cheap, what is the problem? The problem—of continued dependency on outside resources and the potential loss of cultural traditions—is obvious, to Genaro and Hermenegildo, especially in the context of post-1992 constitutional reforms that allow comuneros to sell communal property. But it also reveals a deeper issue for them: in their opinion the community did not have enough of a *conciencia de lucha* (awareness of social struggle). From my perspective, this dilemma is directly related to how video indígena was taught, or more specifically, how it was not taught.

As videomakers cum community activists, their training did not include much instruction on how to vet programs or build community consensus, perhaps in part because indigenous communities generally have such processes (the *asamblea*, or "community assembly") well entrenched in their social organization. Introducing an unfamiliar technology like video production requires more than the notion of the electronic mirror, though the reflexive process is an important aspect of the collective's work. Sharing the production process with members of the community, educating them about how a video is made, explaining the resources that are needed, as well as the technical process itself, are as important as fostering a critical perspective on media they already consume. Furthermore, to ensure community participation and support, the task of choosing subject matter, a matter that reflects collective decision making, would seem a prerequisite to raising an awareness of social struggle.

Toward the end of 1998, Tamix went back on the air with a new television program called *Hoy en la comunidad* (Today in the community), about community affairs, with a focus on children and funded in part by a grant from the Oaxacan Institute for Youth. Efraín's personal initiative, *Hoy en la comunidad* is "an open space for all community members interested in speaking and reflecting about events that occur in the development of [their] Ayuuk people" (Tamix 2000). As a result of this new program and the work he had done in the community's primary school, Tamix had a growing "third generation" of young videomakers, mostly boys ages eight to ten years old, who showed both promise and enthusiasm in 1999 and 2000.

Striking differences in style and tone from earlier program introductions reflect deeper disagreements between the collective's young and founding generations about what constitutes appropriate programming and the role of media in the community. Shots of tequio work are still employed in the introductory sequence to *Hoy en la comunidad*, but pulsing rock music rather than anthems or traditional song accompany the images. These programs were about what was happening in the village, such as a visit from Alcoholics Anonymous representatives.[12] In an effort to solicit interest in an informational meeting for the AA visit, Hermenegildo and Efraín edited an sequence introducing a live discussion with the regional AA leader. The sequence, called "Mareados con la chela" (Dizzy from beer), opens with a fictionalized drinking session and shots (both real and dramatized) of passed-out community members strewn about town after the annual fiesta, shots intercut with image after image of commercial beer signs. Languid classical violin music dramatizes the tragedy of alcoholism in Tama. While the collective missed an opportunity to hear from women residents about the impact of alcoholism in their lives, they visually reframe socially accepted drunkenness as sad and pathetic.

Efraín, who is largely responsible for establishing the look and feel of *Hoy en la comunidad*, grew up in the state of Veracruz and is half Mixe and half Tononac. He does not speak Mixe, but affirms his Ayuuk identity through his mother's lineage and as an active, committed participant in community affairs. Genaro disagreed with what the younger generation considered appropriate cultural and indigenous material for their television programs. Indigenous videos that are primarily in Spanish cannot be considered indigenous, according to Genaro, and he objected to Efraín's programs on the basis that they were conducted in Spanish and did not emphasize traditional cultural aspects of the Ayuuk people. Both Hermenegildo and Efraín thought their television programming should be current, about what's going on in the community, and *Hoy en la comunidad* clearly expresses this objective. From the perspective of the younger generation, they were living in a time of change and transformation, and they thought Genaro's definition of indigenous culture was too rigid and exclusive. In their opinion, their best show was an afternoon of music and interviews with the rock band Ruina Jade, based in Mexico City.[13]

Tamix's younger generation was clearly more comfortable with changing notions of indigenous identity than the older generation. Hermenegildo believed traditional cultural programming was boring to younger people and wanted their television station to appeal across generations. For him and his cousin, there were no inherent inconsistencies between preferring rock music and being Mixe, much as the Mixe anthem played over images of video production technology asserted in earlier program introductions. He also felt that people had pressing issues on their minds that the group could address. For example, he identified serious economic issues having to do with increasing consumerism that exacerbated the community's dependence on products from the city and was driving more and more people to migrate to the United States. Even cilantro, as he pointed out, one of the most basic herbs in Mexican cooking, was coming from Oaxaca City, when it could have been grown locally. Hermenegildo wanted to promote economic self-sustainability and environmental awareness, so that local and natural resources, as well as knowledge about them, were not lost. His expectations for the collective resonated with frequent criticism from members of the community who felt that Tamix could do more to address concrete problems in the community, problems having to do with health, the abuse of women, and increasing drug usage among Tama youth.

On the other hand, according to Genaro, "video is an artistic, creative medium for expressing your crazy ideas [*locuras*]," and Tamix is akin to a circus: "People come to see what's new." Indeed, Tamix began as a pastime for Genaro, something fun, innovative, and creative to do in town. One of his favorite on-air antics was to pretend, as he switched cameras in the studio, that Tamix had an announcer in a remote location, whose signal was being sent to the studio via satellite. On another occasion, Genaro spent two entire days doing solo transmissions with a camera aimed at the plaza, narrating all kinds of locuras over images of the village's rather uneventful comings and goings, such as announcing that a famous French folk singer has just arrived in Tama as he zoomed the camera in on a man getting off the bus from Oaxaca City.

When Tamix first went on the air, there was an overarching concern for technical matters—just getting the signal out or switching from a live transmission to a prerecorded program—and they programmed without vetted guidelines. Genaro justified his lack of concern with content guidelines with what he felt was the imperative to *animar* (motivate people). Unlike the K-Xhon collective, Tamix does not define "their own way of seeing" in terms of having fun or being free of pretensions. In fact, they never discussed their work in such terms. What mattered to Genaro was not "so much what you say, but that you say it in a way that wakes people up."[14]

Genaro and Hermenegildo's divergent approaches point to some of the problems Tamix had in becoming a credible community media organization. Returning to the notion of communal work, or tequio, illuminates some of the deeper contradictions that have challenged the group. During one of the field clearing days of tequio in the area in conflict with Tlahui in 1999, Tamix was asked by the municipal council to tape the community working. Despite this nod of legitimization from town authorities, Hermenegildo and Efraín were continually told by comuneros working in the fields that day to put the camera down and pick up a hoe, in other words, to do "real" work. Not only one of the most important symbols of collective, community life—as

Tamix reinforces in their television programs—tequio is also obligatory and taken very seriously in Tama. A comunero who does not attend the tequio is subject to a fine or a day in prison. Videotaping, in the eyes of many comuneros, was not considered legitimate community work and therefore did not constitute an adequate exemption. Holding a camera on your shoulder, or worse, in your palm, was also not considered real work, in a physical sense. The real work of maize cultivation, on the other hand, is deeply connected to their sense of being Mixe.[15]

Genaro often asserted that video and community television should be incorporated into the civil cargo system of the community or be required community service, as is participation in the municipal philharmonic band. This way the nature of their activities would be clear to the community, and Tamix would potentially be assured fiscal and human resources. Additionally, if the community media program were normalized as a cargo, then not being compensated economically for their work would also be justified, since all cargos are voluntary. Currently, younger folks trained at Tamix often give it up because the future earning potential seems grim, and on the same note, veteran Tamix members feel the time they invest training individuals is wasted when trainees leave in search of more viable economic pursuits. Genaro's suggestion would address one community member's concern about the unusual continuity of Tamix's staff.[16] As that woman explained, the community was used to the idea of yearly rotating cargos. The fact that the same faces have been associated with Tamix from the beginning fuels the community's suspicion that the collective is, in fact, a front for personal gain in terms of cultural, political, and economic capital.

Accusations of personal gain and profiteering can be understood on another level, too. Even Efraín once said that the problem with Tamix "se llama Genaro Rojas" (is called Genaro Rojas). In other words, the group has become so closely associated with this man and his personal conflicts in the community that it is impossible for them to be perceived independently of him, a conflict that also hampers the potential "neutrality" he and Hermenegildo feel media should represent. Genaro has local enemies, left over from a conflict between bilingual, indígena schoolteachers and those in his camp, the *normales*. Trained under different systems and supportive of different curricula, they fought vigorously over control of Tama's primary school in 1994. Genaro has also been accused of appropriating Tama's first telephone line and turning it into a business for personal profit. But Efraín and Genaro share another dimension of the personalized conflict, their family name. Vicilio Rojas, their grandfather, was a dominant force in the community in the 1930s and 1940s, and, as Genaro did in the teachers' dispute, he gained many enemies. For many years, grandfather Rojas was the only person in Tama who spoke and wrote Spanish, and thus controlled all the important recordkeeping—analogous to video's role today—and heavily influenced the community's external affairs. He served as Tama's municipal secretary for approximately forty years, according to Genaro. The Rojas's problematic family legacy further exacerbated Tamix's problems, given their monopoly of the collective's roster.

Most ethnographies of the highland Mixe region do not fail to mention two domineering Mixe caciques, Daniel Martínez and Luis Rodríguez, from Ayutla and Zacatepec, respectively, but make no note of Mr. Rojas, from Tama, who was their contemporary. Curiously, however, there are striking similarities in the cacique profile. Martínez, known as "the Colonel," was, as was Mr. Rojas, "probably one of the few Mixe who spoke Spanish and had a technique for dealing with the problems of the outside world," and "the telephone system was the next step in the extension of the Colonel's influence" (Beals 1973, 35). Kuroda discusses similar processes in her monograph on Ayutla and Tlahui, in which storekeepers and schoolteachers were skipping steps along the traditional path to positions of authority because of their ease with Spanish and the world outside: "The municipal secretaries tend to be chosen from among young bilingual Mixe such as teachers and the *promotores* of INI" (1984, 70). These folks constitute the "new elite," according to Kuroda, an assessment Genaro reinforced when he described life in Tama today as the "época de los maestros" (the era of the teachers). In this era, Genaro says, teachers have supplanted traditional authority from elders, who have remained close to the land; and teachers often dominate the communal assembly meetings. Individual positioning made the group's claims to community representivity highly problematic. In addition, using an idiom of collective work and community identity, such as the tequio, while not incorporating community-based decision making into the collective's operative strategies, further undermined the position the group strove to assert. But the range of problems Tamix experienced in its own community can also be understood as difficulties in their project of making culture visible to the community itself.

Specifically, members of Tamix (young and old generations alike) seemed to agree that video and television function as an "electronic mirror" (a term inherited from the TMA) and they produced media "para que la gente se vea" (so people can see themselves). Showing Ayuuk videos to their own community, rather than to outside audiences, is an explicit priority of the collective, and their motivation is to stimulate critical thinking and reflective processes within their community. Like one's reflection in a mirror, video is a reflexive space, according to Hermenegildo: "When you speak you don't hear yourself until someone says what you've said back to you." That is how Tamix members described their priority, to show the community back to itself. Genaro believed that "an image can make you more human because you will recognize many things and that will benefit the community." For him, seeing oneself opens the door to dialogue: "If they see a program about themselves, they will see that a problem is either bad or good, but you are giving an opportunity for discussion. That is what is needed: material that will open dialogue" (quoted in Cremoux 1997, 134). Aspects of this unstructured, reflexive approach to media continued to thrive, even as the younger producers began to take their work more seriously, but the early days of "puro relajo" (pure fun) had turned into a more self-consciously developed style that they called *televisión sin reglas* or "television without rules." Loose production schedules and flexible content guidelines prevailed, allowing them to be spontaneous and respond to the community's sense of time and what was important in the moment.[17]

In general, members of the community agreed that Tamix's objective was about being a mirror for the community, and the community members liked to see themselves. Canal 12 functioned like a *recuerdo* (memory) for many, and older folks particularly appreciated their programs in the Mixe language, and one lucky day I was able to see this firsthand. Hanging out at my new *compadres'* house after attending Tama's secondary school graduation ceremony, I had the good fortune of being surprised by an unexpected Tamix broadcast.[18] Mauro, a tentative teenager at the time who was among Tamix's third generation, came rushing from the kitchen in the back of the Dominguez residence into the main living-dining and television-watching room. "Channel 12 is on the air!" We tuned in, as did most other households, I later found out, to Canal 12's broadcast of a primary school graduation taped three years prior. Doubled over in laughter, Mauro, his siblings, and their friends poked and chided one another as they identified their younger selves and friends on TV, marching up to the podium to receive their diplomas. About ten minutes into the broadcast, the Dominguez home was so full of children that I went with Nayeli (Mauro's sister and my teenage "godchild") into one of their two bedrooms to watch the transmission on their second television. The unexpected nature of the broadcast seemed to add to the enthusiasm among the audience assembled. Tamix's television without rules on this day took the form of television without prescheduled programming.

Tamix knew that community members young and old appreciated these kinds of broadcasts, which is one reason they saw their television station as more for the community—who outside Tama would be interested in the school graduation? But Tamix members speculated that the community had trouble accepting how Tamix worked, because they didn't see the work (or resources) that go into a production. Unlike working a day of tequio, recording a video tape doesn't leave a furrow for planting corn or a pile of mixed concrete for building the new community market structure. Even though what Tamix recorded was often broadcast on Canal 12, the production process remained opaque and therefore suspect to most community members. In the words of another veteran Tamix member, Vicente Antuñez, people didn't value what members did, because "they [didn't] see culture" as they might have seen the construction of a house. People know what it takes in labor and money to build a house, to make it sturdy and beautiful, he explains, but they can't see where the money for a video production goes. Representing culture on video remained a tricky enterprise for the Tamix because what the people also wanted to see was where the money went.

Hermenegildo compared making video to baking bread: "Video isn't like making bread, where the product is visible and everyone buys it." With video they often had to become "invisible" by leaving the community to tape, postproduce, or screen. "It's not self-evident, so it is suspect," he added. The funds they received from outside sources were not "visible" to the community, further complicating things. Accordingly, Tamix's video production was criticized more than their television programs, because people knew that their videos were built with images of the community—that belonged to the community—

and they accused the group of commercializing something that was not theirs alone to sell. My compadre, Mr. Dominguez, who was municipal president the year after Tamix was kicked out of the municipality, in 1997 (and was also the only president in Tama's recent history who is not Mixe), was sensitive to Tamix's dilemma. He encouraged his son, Mauro, to participate in the group, because Mauro was expanding his skills, learning how to use the new equipment, but he (as had others) reproached Tamix for not sufficiently informing the community in the general assembly about the group's activities and how they spent the money: "Tamix says they do not receive money from the community, so why should they have to inform? This attitude does them more harm than anything else." Had video indígena been taught as a social project from the beginning, its implementation at the community level may have included more emphasis on transparency and community participation; making culture visible may not have been such a contentious process in Tama.

The year 2000 was to be one of renewed energy and community engagement. Hermenegildo was elected into the municipal council as assistant to the *síndico* (who is responsible for organizing authorities and communal work), and Efraín, who had spent a good part of the previous year as a video instructor for the Chiapas Media Project, decided to reestablish his place in Tama. They elaborated plans to move the station's antenna to a high peak directly above the studio, in order to reach people in neighboring towns, and redesigned the collective's brochure in the first days of the new year. In it they described themselves as a community project: "Community and Communication have the same origin as words. We try, day by day, to speak not only our own language Ayuuk but also an audiovisual language that is respectful to our people and its culture. Tamix is a community organization formed by community members interested in promoting communications with television and radio in our community and among other indigenous peoples of Mexico and the world" (Tamix 2000). But neither the words "tequio" or "espacio sagrado" appear in the brochure from 2000. In fact, it reads more like a professional brochure, listing audio, television, and video services, their equipment, and the archive. Solicitous and inviting community participation, the brochure's back panel, written in snappy TV lingo, reads, "A space for communication for everyone, communicate! If you can, visit us. We're waiting for you." Shortly after returning from a trip to Oaxaca City, with hundreds of copies of their refashioned brochure, Hermenegildo and Efraín found Tamix under sharp attack at the first assembly meeting, with newly installed municipal authorities, accusing the group again of secrecy and fiscal irresponsibility. The municipal president even vowed to shut them down. Their doors were not technically sealed, but Tamix was "under investigation." Despite their reinvention and renewed commitment, Tamix never adequately addressed the community's concern with their lack of fiscal transparency. Asserting themselves as a community project and announcing that their doors are open to visitors was not sufficient in the long run to override the underlying contradictions their working style presented to the community.

Before they were effectively shut down, at the dawn of the new millennium, Tamix producers finished an ambitious video program that had been on the slate since they received the Rockefeller and MacArthur grants, in 1996, *Këdung Ajtk/Serving Our Pueblo* (1999). The grant stipulated that the funds were to be used in one year, and indeed, Tamix did a good job of spending the money on the renovation of their new television studio space and on purchasing some new equipment (including a drum set). But the promised video was not complete until the end of 1999, three years later. Hermenegildo defended his production schedule with the finished product—had he hurried to finish the piece within the year he would not have been able to capture the kinds of community and intercommunity interactions in *Këdung Ajtk*. Community affairs unfold over time (years), and understanding them cannot be restricted to a tight production schedule, according to Hermenegildo, one of the defining aspects of video indígena, in his opinion.

Këdung Ajtk/Serving Our Pueblo (1999) • From the first frame, *Këdung Ajtk* signals a stylistic departure from earlier Tamix videos. A black frame with the video's title centered neatly in white letters starts the program, and Tama's philharmonic band fills the silence. The black dissolves to reveal a man draped in a sash with Mexican colors, standing next to a flag at a wooden podium. He addresses an audience in Ayuuk: "Comuneros, I ask you all—children, grandparents, men and women—to help enrich our pueblo and our children, to help maintain order and respect for the good of our happiness." The newly elected council is lined up in the plaza, each man and woman holding flowers, candles, and a baton symbolizing their authority. Fog encases the mountain peaks in background. "You are informed that the fist communal meeting is scheduled for the tenth of January at two in the afternoon," the man continues. "Thank you for coming to see the acceptance and fulfillment of our service."

The next title appears—*Naax Këdung* (communal servant)—again over black. Accompanied with flute and drum, a line of people walk single-file along a footpath on a hill, first toward the camera and then away from camera, in a seamless edit. Daniel Pérez, the authority in charge of resolving land disputes, known as a *servidor*, standing with people gathered around him, says, "We are here so you can tell us about your disagreement. Last year's solution is very clear; now we just have to negotiate your inconvenience so we can close this case." One of the women gathered responds, "The donkeys were getting killed because the señora was tying her animal on the road, and near the spring. I don't know why she does this—we all need that water." The program cuts to an interview with Pérez that structures the rest of the tape. "That is how we take care of our land and our fields. We visit the comuneros to resolve problems. Displacement, invasions, and bad repartitions among families are a first case, other cases are about guarding the limits between communities." Back to the mountain, a group of men carrying satchels and machetes walk in determined fashion, uphill through a narrow, cleared swath of forest. With their machetes, they whack at weeds and branches that have grown into the border zone.

Another communal servidor is discussing borders between family lots with a group of people. Referring to a piece of paper, he asks the women assembled why they signed the paper if they were not in agreement. "We didn't even participate in the agreement," one responds. "Today," the servidor explains, "we are going to reposition the border markers." But later tempers flare as contradictions arise in their testimonies. "Señora, the problem is that you don't maintain your position. First you say you don't know señora Telésfora and that you've never worked together. Now you reveal that you do!" Back to the interview, Pérez explains that there are several members of the municipal council involved in conflict resolution—*tenientes* and *mayores de vara*—to ensure that fair decisions are reached. Back at the site, men measure out distances with a tape and place a large rock in the ground to mark a border. "Ultimately," Pérez says, "the complex process is based on family trees." The tape transitions from intracommunity conflicts to intercommunity conflicts with a sequence about "lands that have never had an owner." Pérez explains that while it is rare for an intracommunity conflict not to be resolved within the community, there does exist a process for appealing to an external tribunal at the district level.

The second half of *Këdung Ajtk* is about the land conflict between Tama and Tlahui—this is the footage Hermenegildo said was particularly worth waiting for. Large groups of people, clad in all sorts of waterproofing (from yellow slickers to swatches of colored plastic tarp), descend a steep and muddy slope. Working under heavy fog and rain, they clear a wide border that delimits Tama land. In a rustic rancho, the group—it looks like all of Tama—is assembled to hear instructions from the síndico. "All comuneros have to sign the document that is going to be presented at the tribunal next Tuesday." Pérez contextualizes the current conflict between Tama and Tlahui with a brief discussion of the documents dating from 1712, in which five "brother" villages were considered to be the same pueblo, and explains in some detail the process of resolving the conflict through the system of agrarian tribunals.

The tape turns to a triumphant tequio sequence, edited to local guitar and violin music, in which Tama residents build a large concrete *mojonera* (boundary marker) on a high ridge between Tama and Tlahui. In a tremendous display of physical effort and defiance, men of varying ages carry concrete mix, tools, water, and wooden molds up to the ridge to build the five-foot mojonera. After the concrete has set and the molds are removed, they paint white around indented letters that read, "Tama 98." Women serve hundreds of bowls of *caldo* and tortillas, and a heavy stream of people heads down to the fields to continue the tequio. People chop down trees, remove underbrush (which will later be burned) with pickaxes, and the *yunta* churns up the earth while others build field houses with planks cut from freshly felled trees.

Pérez comments on the key role women play as wives of servidores, over images of the activities he describes. The women carry out offerings "according to the principles inherited from [their] grandparents." They contract diviners and corn readers who can foretell the success of the tequio and the planting season. They make offerings to the earth and to the universe. "In this way, the woman supports and encourages the man."

The closing sequence of *Këdung Ajtk* begins with images of people voting with raised hands at a general assembly. Pérez concludes: "The community knows how to make decisions. To fulfill a service means to work for the pueblo. To support with strength and skill, to build and design homes and roads and paths, and for our children, to build learning spaces. To fulfill a service means working without pay." As in *Moojk*, the last moving image is of people dancing to the philharmonic band at the change-of-authorities ceremony. But this time they are outside, at the site of a natural spring where incoming council members ritually bathe to cleanse themselves before becoming servidores.

Hermenegildo is satisfied with *Këdung Ajtk*. He feels he managed to achieve a more developed style of his own. But he was particularly tentative about screening it in Tama. He expressed concern that the community would not be interested in seeing something they know so well, something that permeates their life, but offered in his own defense that for younger people the video would demystify community service and teach them what a servidor in charge of resolving land conflicts actually does: how he talks to people, organizes their labor, and handles outside negotiators. What Hermenegildo was more worried about was criticism, which he says can be harsh and awfully direct in the community.

Conflict is at the heart of this piece, and community service on all levels, from one's participation in the tequio to one's fulfillment of an elected office, is celebrated as essential to community life, just as corn is in *Moojk*, but it is made visible through conflicts and their resolution. *Moojk* contains elements of community divisions and generational disagreements about traditions and their role in contemporary life, but these are told to Tamix crew and constructed as a dialogue in the editing of the piece. *Këdung Ajtk* tackles community conflict on location, capturing disharmonious aspects of community life while it is happening, with the Pérez interview providing structure and historical context.

Këdung Ajtk was screened in Tama at Cine Sapito, a makeshift, short-lived "cinema" that Hermenegildo launched out of the municipal band's practice studio, to make watching movies a more frequent activity in Tama, something he thought would help Tamix succeed and earn a bit of money doing it (tickets were only 2 pesos).[19] It was an "invited" screening organized by Hermenegildo that allowed him to limit the audience, which included Pérez, a handful of teachers, and several Tamix members. Victoriano, who was singled out to receive the new president's wrath at the communal assembly in 2000, introduced *Këdung Ajtk*. The program is about how Tama lives, he explained, "how [the people of Tama] participate. It's directed to the people. [They] aren't shown behind the equipment; people themselves are actors."

After the screening, a teacher congratulated Tamix. "It's clear, and well-taped compared to what I've seen here on TV. You have improved quite a bit. We have the equipment in Tama and now it is working well." Pérez enjoyed the program, too, and even though he knows nothing about what a documentary is supposed to be, he said it should "help motivate people, build solidarity." And Genaro commented that after three years of work "all they have is a twenty-three minute video" (as a way to explain once again how the production process works), but he agreed with Pérez that the program should motivate people. A general discussion ensued about the importance of the tequio and how the tape might help get Mixe migrants to contribute to the community, as the Mixtecos and Zapotecos do. "Everyone should see it," Pérez said. But to my knowledge *Këdung Ajtk* has not been screened for the community in Tama.

Hermenegildo submitted the program to the Native American Film and Video Festival, in New York City, in 2000, but the indigenous panel of festival selectors passed it over without much discussion or interest. As a member of the selection committee, I enjoyed the privilege of keeping it on my "top picks" list until the final rounds of selection meetings, but despite my attempt to contextualize the tape for the rest of the committee, as a unique and important example of indigenous autonomy in action, the other selectors "didn't see it" and found the program hard to follow.

Today most founding members of the Tamix collective remain in Tamazulapam. Hermenegildo is now a father and an active member of the community. He has served several more cargos, but his main occupation is as a music producer for the Banda Regional Mixe. He is sought out in the region as an expert organizer for regional cultural events that feature dance and music and assists communities in the region with the installation of community radio stations. Hermenegildo is also working as a researcher for an ambitious ethnomusicology project that CIESAS-Oaxaca is currently conducting.[20]

Efraín, on the other hand, turned back to Chiapas after the asamblea crisis in 2000, to work with the Chiapas Media Project/Promedios. He headed up their operations in the state of Guerrero for most of the decade, until he decided to go out on his own, in 2009. In 2005, looking back at his time in with Tamix, Efraín felt it was an introduction or "first brush" with how video can be put to use in an indigenous community, whereas it was in Chiapas, working with autonomous Zapatista municipalities, that he "got involved with video one hundred percent" (Rojas Pérez 2005). He described himself at that moment as a "video activist," more than as a videomaker, since most of his work had involved "training people to make video in indigenous communities" (ibid.). Since leaving CMP/Promedios, Efraín has started his own media production organization, Mecapal (which refers to the head strap used across the forehead to carry heavy loads on your back). Mecapal and Efraín are based in Lyon, France, where he lives with his wife and young daughter.[21]

Genaro is still a primary school teacher, working mostly in Tama or nearby communities. My most recent face-to-face visit with him was in 2008. Sitting across a table from me in a café in Oaxaca City, Genaro handed me a copy of a DVD with a designed cover (see figure 4.3). I remember feeling delighted and wondered to myself, "Is Tamix finally back?" But when I read the disk's title I tempered my enthusiasm: *10 años de comunicación comunitaria/10 Years of Community Communication* (2005) was about their history, the past, a testament to their efforts, rather than new material. The *10 Años* program is, in fact, Genaro's personal summary of Radio y Video Tamix. In it he traces three periods demarcated by radio, video, and television, respectively, and juxtaposes funny and humbling blooper scenes that demonstrate both the collective's playful approach (televisión sin reglas) as well as their initial lack of experience, with an outsider's authoritative statement about the media collective (in English) and celebratory footage of the community blessing the television antenna in 1997. The program ends with Genaro sitting in front of a Macintosh computer. He explains the group's demise in terms of technical problems: "We used to have transmitter but it has broken down and can't be repair despite all our efforts. We have to keep struggling to get a transmitter, so we can keep sending images and sound in Ayuuk, our principal instrument for survival." By positioning the group's end in terms of technical difficulties, Genaro is clearly appealing to outsiders for support, glossing over the complexities and dilemmas they have faced, as if a repair or new transmitter would provide a total fix.

FIGURE 4.3. DVD cover art, *10 años de comunicación comunitaria/10 Years of Community Communication* (2005, 10 min.), Radio y Video Tamix.

The experiences of Radio y Video Tamix ground the entangled dimensions of video indígena within the complex politics and social relations of an indigenous community. I arrived in Tama unencumbered by notions of communities as either closed, corporate, or harmonious, but I did not expect to focus my study of Radio y Video Tamix on dilemmas. Like a member of a film festival audience, I took for granted that indigenous videomakers speak with the consensus and approval of their home communities, but after a closer and extended look at community-level dynamics, it became clear that community representativity had to be earned. In other words, embeddedness had to be achieved. Indeed, making culture visible in Tama—Tamix's project of showing their culture in order to defend it—was not unproblematic.

Like other indigenous activists who leave their communities and return with visions for change and preservation, members of Tamix were trying to shake things up in their community. Earlier ethnographers were concerned with the "culture change" forced on communities from the outside, but a study of Tamix reveals self-conscious, overt efforts to achieve social change from the inside. Genaro often said he wanted his people to *despertar* (wake up), to question and criticize, to realize what they have in terms of cultural wealth, much like the Zapotec activists sought to create awareness of comunalidad in their region. His personal approach relied on humor and spontaneity—as when he put deer antlers on the video camera and did prank television transmissions about rock stars getting off the bus in Tama— but once he and other members of the Tamix collective became involved with government programs, their project to have fun and wake people up was refashioned into one about strengthening identity. Identity discourse was taught along with video production in the INI's TMA program, but that in and of itself was not the problem, for local notions of identity are well rooted in long histories of cultural difference among indigenous communities, especially among the Mixe, who secured an unusual level of recognized autonomy more than half a century ago. The root of the problem lay more in the encounter between the demands of video indígena and local power politics; in the emergence of contemporary identity that asserted that it was okay to be Mixe and know how to use a camera better than a pickax; and in the unexpected global-local dislocations that access to international circuits of media exhibition and funding provokes.

Video production is not cheap, and Tamix never failed to broadcast this in their television programs, with images of their relatively heavy endowment of technology. Expectations placed on them by what is basically a redistributive economy were complicated by a healthy and widespread economy of prestige and *envidia* (jealousy). As a result, Tamix sent mixed signals to the community. They wanted to achieve embeddedness in the community—have video production become a cargo, like playing in the band or tequio—but offered little community participation. There is no foolproof way of ensuring community acceptance, and media production surely isn't for everyone; it requires an appetite and the patience for drawing stories out of life's normal chaos. Members of Radio y Video Tamix certainly had this appetite, as well as their community's best interest in mind. But following the economic configuration of video indígena, they relied on funding from outside the community, traveled outside Mexico to international film festivals, and did not readily inform the community about how they spent the money or where they went. Video indígena, as a state-sponsored or state-launched enterprise, did not sufficiently address sustainability or teach or require community consensus-building as a prerequisite for producing media in a community setting. Instead, the INI's video indígena project relied on the presumed good standing of community-based cultural organizations to make media production a valued resource for communities. Nevertheless, when considering Radio y Video Tamix's ten-year run and wealth of footage, Nahmad was correct in assessing that the Mixe would successfully and selectively incorporate modernity and technology. Radio y Video Tamix and TV Tamix remain success stories despite their eventual demise.

PART 3

Points of Comparison

FIVE

Revolutionary Indigenous Media

The Chiapas Media Project/Promedios

Every morning when I check in my inbox I find a fresh announcement from Enlace Zapatista, reminding me that after seventeen years, the Ejército Zapatista de Liberación Nacional (EZLN) is still online, challenging the status quo in Mexico on many simultaneous fronts. Enlace Zapatista is the online face of the EZLN, the indigenous organization that declared war on the Mexican government on January 1, 1994. Though Enlace Zapatista did not go on-line as early as 1994, the EZLN commandeered media outlets (such as INI radio stations) as part of their initial strategy to let Mexico and the world know that they had had enough—"¡Ya Basta!"[1] Through their website they connect daily with the wide public that was drawn into the Zapatista movement in the aftermath of the armed uprising. A typical Enlace Zapatista post recently included a document prepared by the Center for Human Rights Fray Bartolomé de las Casas, in San Cristóbal de las Casas, Chiapas, accusing the Mexican government (through their support of paramilitary organizations) of the disappearance of seventy individuals from communities in the highland region since 1994. Also posted was an invitation to sign a petition to hold the governor of the state of Guerrero to his pledge to suspend the building of a hydroelectric dam that would displace 25,000 people. A detailed economic report prepared by the Centro de Análisis Multidisciplinario graphs and pie-charts the miserable state of minimum wage in Mexico, to show how neoliberal economic policy has, indeed, increased socioeconomic stratification in Mexico, making the superrich, super richer while Mexican laborers work more hours for less pay, all within the wider political-economic context of dwindling remittances from compatriots working outside Mexico. The day's announcements also included a *denuncia pública* (public denouncement) from the inhabitants of Nuevo Juan

MAP 5.1. Area of Zapatista rebel territory, Chiapas © Daniel Dalet, d-maps.com.

del Grijalva, Chiapas, about the unjust persecution and imprisonment of several members of the "rural city." The Zapatista website presents a gamut of strategies the revolutionaries employ to confront constant and violent harassment—otherwise known as "low-intensity warfare" —and the Zapatistas themselves prove their longevity, continued resilience, and resistance every day through their autonomous communities, Juntas de Buen Gobierno (Good Government Councils) and regional community centers, called *Caracoles,* where among other things, there are media centers established and supported by the Chiapas Media Project (CMP) (see map 5.1).

The Chiapas Media Project, known as Promedios in Mexico, a binational (United States-Mexico) nongovernmental organization has provided video and computer equipment and training to members of Zapatista civil communities since 1998. The project's history, training strategies, and current initiatives, present productive contrasts to the entangled history of video indígena in other parts of Mexico, but it is also one of the most vital indigenous media organizations in the hemi-sphere today.[2] The opening title of all CMP programs reads, "Produced by indigenous men and women from the Autonomous Zapatista com-munities in Chiapas."[3]

There are important similarities to the emergence stories of indige-nous media in Oaxaca and Chiapas. The technology and skill set came from outside their communities, delivered by sympathetic profes-sionals and newly minted indigenous videomakers interested in indig-enous self-representation. As in Oaxaca, not all the dilemmas and incommensurabilities of making culture visible are resolved in Chia-pas, as sustaining video production inside its communities still de-pends on funding from outside sources and, as in many places in Mexico, female indigenous videomakers have more hurdles to clear than men do. In addition, the media initiatives in Oaxaca share key human resources with the Chiapas Media Project: Monteforte, García, Caballero, and the Rojas cousins from Tama were all involved in shap-ing the Chiapas Media Project during its first years, from 1998 to 2000, as trainers, advisers, and editors. Given this lineage, it is not surprising that documentary is the norm with the CMP, too. Through this ex-tended encounter, the voices of the Zapotec and Mixe sierras of Oa-xaca that ground principles of indigenous autonomy within a commu-nity-based concept of comunalidad met equally articulate, but perhaps more far-reaching, voices of the Chiapanecan Maya that opted for armed insurrection (and all its consequences) in order to be heard. However, while the two contexts of media production are examples of what Monteforte calls comunicación de lucha, the Chiapas project was conceived from the beginning as revolutionary media, embedded within a well-articulated and structured social and political project, the Zapatista movement. Making culture visible in Chiapas is more overtly political, reflecting what scholars have noted about indigenous identity in eastern regions of Chiapas: "Their identity as people is not tied to speaking an indigenous language, wearing traditional clothes, or even having common territory; it is linked instead to 'a common history and experience of repression'" (Stephen 2002, 116). This common history undergirds the postura (political position or stance) that tie Oaxacan videomakers to broader social projects of autonomy and self-determi-nation, but in Oaxaca indigenous media production is anchored more directly to particular cultural identities. With the Chiapas Media Proj-ect, indigenous media production is anchored to a revolutionary

FIGURE 5.1. "You are in Zapatista territory," from *Caracoles: New Paths of Resistance* (2003, 42 min.). Courtesy of Chiapas Media Project/Promedios.

movement. I want to emphasize two things about the Zapatista movement, what the anthropologist Lynn Stephen calls the "novelty of the EZLN"—"its political organization, strategy and objectives rather than its social base or material conditions" (2002, 29)—and the EZLN's use of media from the outset to get their word out (see figure 5.1). The process of consensual decision making, upon which the EZLN organized their rebellion and the awareness of how media technologies can support the lucha, lent the Chiapas Media Project a preexisting framework for introducing media production in a preapproved manner, as it were, which contrasts sharply with the foregoing narrative of Radio y Video Tamix.

The Zapatista Movement

While the Zapatistas and the wider civil prodemocracy movement they sparked seemed to be at the forefront of President Vicente Fox's campaign at the turn of the millennium, the armed movement has taken second stage to the disastrous and costly "drug war" of the Calderón *sexenio*.[4] Fox promised to solve the Zapatista "problem" in "fifteen minutes," as he heralded a new era of democracy after seventy years of single-party rule. This absurd promise, as well as more poignant ones, such as seeing the San Andrés Peace Accords through congressional approval and demilitarizing Chiapas, was little more than campaign talk. In 2001, responding to President Fox's invitation to dialogue, thousands of Zapatistas marched (again) to Mexico City and spoke before congress to affirm their demands. Sadly, however, the original accords, signed by the Zedillo administration and the EZLN in 1996, were once again emptied of any meaningful content that would allow for real structural change, as congress ended up approving a watered-down version of the accords that omitted key clauses on autonomy and self-determination. As for demilitarization, Fox did reduce the number of military checkpoints in Chiapas, but Calderón's United States-funded war on drugs has further militarized Chiapas, as well as the other highly indigenous southern states of Guerrero and Oaxaca, with serious costs to human rights. The spokesperson of the EZLN, Subcomandante Insurgente Marcos, in a recent communiqué about the "war from above," expressed concern that "the social fabric is being destroyed in almost all of the national territory. The Nation's collective identity is being destroyed and it is being supplanted by another."[5]

The Zapatista movement has its roots in a systematic legacy of disenfranchisement of indigenous peoples' lands and resources that began with the Spanish conquest of Mesoamerica in the sixteenth century and reached a tipping point in the 1980s and early 1990s. The region's history and what led to the Zapatista uprising has been well documented by scholars from various disciplines; I relied principally on Neil Harvey, George Collier, Shannon Speed, Lynn Stephen, John Womack, and Bill Weinberg to construct the brief summary that follows. I met some of the hooded revolutionaries during the first days of January, in 1996. I had scored an invitation to attend the Foro Nacional Indígena, in San Cristóbal de las Casas, as an observer, accompanying my friends and colleagues from Oaxaca, who had been invited directly by the EZLN to serve as advisers on a panel about the role of communications media in the new, democratic Mexico the revolutionaries (together with civil society) were envisioning.[6] Once past the cordons of soldiers and civilians that protected the building in which we talked and listened, and once the fanfare that always accompanied the entrance and exit of members of the Clandestine Revolutionary Indigenous Committee (CCRI) settled down, the discussions were as long and methodical as the objectives were clear. The Zapatistas were interested in learning from their brothers and sisters across the country about their experiences with media, in order to formulate a proposal for access to media production and representation that would be taken into consideration as the EZLN drafted their side of the San Andrés Accords.

What brought the EZLN into existence is the complex and disheartening history of land tenure and land struggle in Chiapas (see map 5.1). In general, the Tzeltal, Tzotzil, Tojolabal, and Ch'ol Maya of Chiapas faired extremely poorly at the hands of the Spaniards and perhaps even worse under independent Mexicans. The *encomiendas*, a grant of Indian labor which often included the land on which the Indians resided, that stripped indigenous people of land and forced them into labor during the colony gave way to early Mexican agrarian laws that opened up land surrounding indigenous communities for privatization (Stephen 2002, 92). The process of "deterritorializing indigenous communities" continued unfettered—but not without protest from members of indigenous communities, in what is known as the Indian Movement of 1867–69—alongside the privatization of land and resources (especially hardwood and coffee) throughout the nineteenth century (Stephen 2002, 96). The third wheel of this process was a system of debt peonage that enslaved most of the indigenous population of the state, beholden to the ladino landowners for access to land. For many indigenous people in Chiapas today, "the time of slavery" is fresh in their memories, whether from personal experiences or recounted through a repertoire of stories of grandmothers and grandfathers who worked ceaselessly for the *patrón*, with scarce time left over to work for their own families.

The Mexican Revolution and early twentieth-century land-reform policies had little immediate impact in Chiapas, although the revolutionary general Emiliano Zapata, who championed landless peasants in their fight for "Tierra y Libertad," left an indelible mark in Chiapas and elsewhere. It was not until the presidency of Lázaro Cárdenas, in 1930, when some number of *ejidos* (large, collective landholdings) were formed from expropriated private ranches and coffee plantations. Beginning in the 1950s, however, most of the land given to indigenous peoples was located in the Lacandon forest region, and each subsequent decade saw the tremendous increase in the number of "colonists" that moved into the region: in 1950 one thousand colonists moved onto Lacandon land, by 1960 there were ten thousand, and by 1990 there were approximately 150,000 (Stephen 2002, 102). Moving from landless indentured peasants to *ejidatarios* on difficult jungle land did not solve the problem of feeding their families, but the process did amount to the deliberate insertion of state power in the region, with divisive effects on growing peasant organizations (Harvey 2005, 148).

Bishop Samuel Ruiz, who is known around the world for his role as mediator in the dialogues between the Mexican government and the EZLN, arrived in Chiapas in 1960 to lead the Catholic diocese in San Cristóbal de las Casas. Shocked by extreme poverty in the region, Ruiz began training activist catechists in San Cristóbal and inside indigenous communities where liberation theology was already popular among Catholics. Ruiz quickly recognized an imperative to "validate indigenous cultures and build on their insights" (Stephen 2005, 114). To him, indigenous people had a wealth of "liberating knowledge" that could pave a way out of poverty and marginalization. In 1974 Ruiz organized the First Indigenous Congress, surnamed "Fray Bartolomé de las Casas," in honor of the colonial priest's 500th birthday. The nominally officious event enjoyed the buen visto of the government and the Chiapanecan establishment, but in hindsight it is considered a landmark event in the development of independent civil-society organizations that openly pressure the government. Ruiz and others promoted wide regional participation in the event by working on the ground, so to speak, through the INI's School for Regional Development, in Chiapas, and grassroots organizations, in a manner that was "decentralized" and centered on "democratized decision-making," a style of consensus-building that characterizes Zapatista decision-making strategies today. The congress was multiethnic, with 1,230 indigenous delegates from 327 different communities, representing the four major Mayan linguistic groups in state. At the congress, a prominent Tzeltal leader, Sebastián Gómez, from San Francisco Altamirano, called for self-defense: "We all have to be the new Bartolomé: we will reach this goal when we are all capable of forming and defending our own organization. Because unity is what gives us power" (Stephen 2002, 118). As Stephen, following others, has stressed, "Self identifying as 'Tzotzil' 'Tzeltal' or 'Ch'ol or Tojolabal' at the First Indigenous Congress was as much a means of identifying oneself as part of a particular shared struggle as of specifying linguistic affiliation" (2002, 117).

In the 1980s, Chiapas came to be seen by Mexico's leadership as a national security issue—the state's economy was poorly developed and its border with Guatemala was unsecure. Guatemalan immigrants fleeing civil war and massacres were flowing into Mexico, along with their experiences with guerrilla activity. Federal development plans for the state, such as the Plan del Sureste of 1983, sought to address economic and social development that stemmed from "isolation" and neglect. A similar plan, Plan Chiapas, funded with a budget of 83 billion pesos, had as its stated goal to "unify the actions of federal and state government to rapidly improve living standards of the chiapanecos and to strengthen the social and cultural integration of the state" (Harvey 2005, 150–51). The development plans addressed problems of isolation by building roads, but the colonization of the forest region continued at a rate that far exceeded any increase in infrastructure. Many of the new ejidos were not connected to towns and cities by roads at all, even while the forest was being rapidly depleted of valuable mahogany trees (ibid.).

President Miguel de la Madrid (1982–88) decided to focus on Chiapas and placed a military man, General Absalón Castellanos Dominguez, as governor of the state. De la Madrid was firmly against further land distribution and sought military solutions for border issues, beginning a long process of militarizing not only the border regions but also areas of land conflict (Harvey 2005, 150). The governor attempted to address land conflict through a new program created in 1984, called the Programa de Rehabilitación Agrario (PRA, Agrarian Rehabilitation Program). The PRA was designed to purchase land that belonged to private owners, land that had been occupied by peasants with unresolved land claims (Harvey 2005, 153). This strategy sparked violent conflicts between independent peasant organizations and the state-affiliated peasant organization, the Confederación Nacional Campesina (CNC, National Peasant Confederation). While they fought over the same lands (with the affiliated CNC, not surprisingly, winning many more ejidos than nonaligned organizations), it was the large landholders who actually profited from the program. The PRA created "opportunities for corruption and personal enrichment," as landowners went as far as to invent land invasions in order to receive payments

(Harvey 2005, 154). Meanwhile, the Castellanos Dominguez government protected large tracts of private land from expropriation by issu-
ing thousands of documents of "nonaffectability," effectively putting at
least 70 percent of land used by cattle ranchers "legally beyond the
reach of agrarian reform" (Harvey 2005, 155).

As Harvey narrates, the plan failed indigenous peasants, leading to
more conflict and the mobilization of peasant organizations that
staged large protests in the state capital of Tuxtla Gutiérrez, and in
Mexico City. In addition, organized peasants built roadblocks, occupied regional installations of PEMEX, Mexico's national oil-producing
machine, and a number of municipal palaces. Despite divisions in
some of the stronger peasant organizations, they also built united
fronts like the Coodinadora de Luchas de Chiapas, which coordinated
hunger strikes in the nation's capital and published denunciations in
the national press, calling for the release of political prisoners and an
end to repression.[7] An urban guerrilla organization, the National Liberation Forces (FLN) was also active in the early 1980s, promoting
armed resolution to the lack of government action in the favor of
landless peasants. The FLN envisioned the formation of the EZLN,
and it is believed that Subcomandante Marcos came out of this group
(Stephen 2002, 152). The stage was set for the EZLN to emerge out of
this perfect storm of century-old discontent, poverty, and marginalization mixed with a mobilized peasantry who was fed up with failed and
corrupt government programs, and, more important, had a sizable
concentration of recently settled indigenous farmers in the central
highland and Lacandon forest regions to draw on. As the EZLN consolidated its leadership, indigenous families sent their husbands,
wives, sons, and daughters to join the ranks of the new secret army.

The EZLN was born on November 17, 1983, out of a meeting of
three indigenous people and three mestizos, Marcos among them.
They formed around the notion of self-defense that Don Gómez articulated at the congress in 1974. Rather than creating a guerrilla movement with a clear revolutionary strategy for taking power, the EZLN
saw the need for a regional network of armed self-defense units to
protect indigenous farmers and their families from violence and harassment as they sought land (Harvey 2005, 165). It was "the impossibility of affecting change through legal channels that led to the decision to take up arms," as Harvey writes, and as the world soon noted,
guns were not the rebels' most powerful weapon. Rather, their use of

media and the Internet turned a "local rebellion into a global event" (Stephen 2002, 175).

Their visibility and following in Mexico and around the world is a critical part of the reason they are still alive today, surviving a low-intensity war through their daily battles for autonomy, instead of having been annihilated by a military operation, as Subcomandante Marcos himself said of what he called "international Zapatismo": "This protection is more effective than the EZLN, the civilian organization or national Zapatismo, because in the logic of Mexican neoliberalism, the international image is an enormous stake" (quoted in Womack 1999, 326).

While the EZLN was consolidating and training its army, from the first meeting in 1983 to 1994, when they "went public," several important events further galvanized their base of support. In 1992, the convergence of history and discontent around the quincentenary "celebration" of the arrival of Christopher Columbus in America resulted is a massive march and demonstration on October 12 in San Cristóbal de las Casas. Members from many peasant organizations, including militants marching in formation, holding bows and arrows, brought down the statue of Diego de Mazariego (the colonial exterminator of Chiapas). This event was believed to be the first public manifestation of the EZLN (Stephen 2002, 139). Indigenous Mayan peasants from northern Chiapas also marched to Mexico City, in what is known as the Marcha X'inch, or "March of the ants."[8] This march and many other mobilizations and demonstrations protested the celebratory mood in which Mexico and the world was honoring the decimation of indigenous ancestry, but indigenous peasants also protested the adopted change to article 27 of the national constitution, which ended land reform.

Back in eastern and northern Chiapas, the leadership of the EZLN gave the order to prepare for war. In 1993 the CCRI was formed and the basic structure of the EZLN was consolidated (though it has changed significantly since 1994). It consisted of three tiers: militants (a trained army of men and women), a reserve militia spread out in communities, and *bases de apoyo* (civil bases of support), made up of civilians who subscribed to Zapatismo and carried out the Zapatista social agenda and supported the army on a material level (Stephen 2002, 142). Within this structure, the community assembly is the most important first-level decision-making organism. Each community elects representatives and delegates to the CCRI, and regional CCRIs each have one delegate (eleven altogether) on the CCRI General Command (CCRI-GC), the highest political authority of the EZLN. Subcomandante Marcos is in charge of the military wing and has a seat on the CCRI-GC.

War finally did come. On January 1, 1994, the day that NAFTA went into effect, the EZLN took over five county seats in Chiapas and two INI radio stations. Thirty-six hours later, the Mexican military responded. The number of casualties claimed ranges from the low hundreds to more than 400. Twelve days into the conflict, the government declared a cease-fire and extended an invitation to the EZLN to negotiate. And after seventeen years of attempted negotiations, there is still no resolution between the revolutionaries and the government. Mexico's leadership continues to look to the market and free trade for economic prosperity, while the Zapatistas, their backs turned to neoliberalism, deny all forms of government aid.

The EZLN's network of grassroots support throughout civil society grew in leaps and bounds the moment the organization went on the air during the armed conflict. The EZLN held the Convención Nacional Democracia in 1994, the first Aguascalientes (named after the revolutionary convention of 1914) to begin a dialogue with civil society at large, which continues today in various modes, including the Frente Zapatista de Liberación Nacional. Subcomandante Marcos has repeatedly called for civil society to make armed action unnecessary "to defeat us." The EZLN began seizing land and declaring "autonomous pluri-ethnic regions" in late 1994 and now include over thirty autonomous municipalities in Zapatista rebel territory. The Mexican government launched a major military offensive against the EZLN in 1995 that failed to capture the organization's leadership, but succeeded in displacing thousands of villagers in the central highland region and laid the foundations for the low-intensity war the government continues to wage against Zapatista villagers to this day.

The Zapatistas' own nonviolent war against neoliberalism, capitalism, globalization, and state control is also waged discursively, through targeted and sustained interactions with civil society, and in particular with resistance organizations of all kinds. Set for by the EZLN's Sixth Declaration from the Lacandon Jungle, in 2005, the organization launched La Otra Campaña (The Other Campaign) during a presidential election year in Mexico, a series of talks and roundtables held through the country with union leaders, indigenous leaders, teachers, youth organizations, gay and lesbian organizations, and environmental activists, in order to consolidate a shared oppositional front. At home, in Chiapas, however, Zapatista base communities have reorganized and consolidated their independent, civilian system of governance around Juntas de Buen Gobierno (Good Government Councils), in direct denial of the *mal gobierno*, a reference to the Mexican government and its continued dismissal of the accords. The juntas are made up of frequently rotating representatives from each of the five zones of Zapatista territory, representing thirty autonomous municipalities. They have wonderful names that envision their future. The council in Roberto Barrios is called the Nueva Semilla Que Va a Producir (New seed that is going to produce). As councils, the juntas monitor projects, community works, and the implementation of laws, resolve conflicts and disputes, and govern using the Zapatista logic of *mandar obedeciendo* (lead by obeying), a principle that turns the logic of the mal gobierno on its head through the daily practice of consensus and power sharing (Speed 2008, 160).

The Chiapas Media Project works directly with Zapatista villagers to bring their stories and everyday struggles to the forefront of a movement that is seen by the world, mostly through their incredibly articulate spokesperson, who achieved international celebrity status early on. The Chiapas Media Project also works within Zapatista communities, outside the prevue of the public, to facilitate their autonomous way of life. The Zapatista movement, however, is not perfectly harmonious and is far from homogeneous (though it may have some homogenizing tendencies, as the author John Womack points out). Furthermore, despite their continued ability to fine-tune their own organization and consolidate their base, they operate in a social and political environment that is still rife with difficult and threatening divisions among rival peasant groups, labor unions, and political parties, not to mention the continued and real threats of military and paramilitary forces that relentlessly rack up human rights violations at the expense of the movement.[9] Given this environment, it remains essential that the Chiapas Media Project, like the Zapatistas themselves, maintains a foot in the world outside Chiapas.

Getting Started: Founding the Chiapas Youth Media Project

I was first introduced to Alexandra Halkin, the founder and for many years the director of the Chiapas Media Project, in Tamazulapam, Oaxaca (of all places). Her urban, don't-mess-with-me swagger may have belied her warm personality, but it definitely suited what I soon learned was her enduring seat on the "inside track." Halkin's casual, confident personality and wealth of great stories offered compelling downtime as we traded knowledge and experiences, in English, over coffee at a family *comedor* (dining hall) in Tama, like two expats resuscitating a sense of home in any part in the world.

Halkin, a native of Chicago, first visited Chiapas in 1995, one year after the Zapatista uprising began. She was working as a documentary producer for Pastors for Peace, an ecumenical foundation, based in the United States, that is part of the Interreligious Foundation for Community Organization. In February of 1995, Pastors for Peace sent the first delegation of international observers to the conflict zone in Chiapas, as well as a humanitarian aid caravan that traveled with the larger "Todos Para Todos" Mexican Solidarity caravan. Halkin was hired to document the caravan. Her partner, Tom Hansen, was then director of Pastors for Peace (he left in 1996, to run the Mexico Solidarity Network). Halkin had been producing independent video for twenty years in Chicago and had "always [been] interested in putting video in the hands of people that can really use it."[10] In Chiapas she found herself surrounded by a movement that was "aware of the media, of the Internet. They were interested in getting access to the equipment so they could use it themselves."[11] As she relates in a recent article, "While the 'external' journalists were 'getting their story,' several people in the community came up to me to ask about my Hi8 camera (where I bought it, how much it cost, etc.), clearly demonstrating an interest in and awareness of this technology and an obvious desire to communicate their message to the outside world" (Halkin 2008, 164–65).

Halkin responded to this interest. She talked at length to Hansen, who had many years of experience in community organizing under his belt and close ties to Zapatista leadership. And before leaving the Altos region of Chiapas, she held discussions with Zapatista authorities and nongovernmental organizations that were in good standing with the revolutionaries about the possibilities of bringing video technology to their communities. But, as she writes in her article, she "really only envisioned a workshop or a series of workshops in one region—[she] never imagined what the project would become" (Halkin 2008, 165).

The project took a while to develop. At first she thought of two different approaches—one was to use standard video-production training, the other to provide mini cameras and hidden mics to people on the front lines who could record human rights violations. International human rights forums would be the target audiences because "it's always the word of the communities against the word of government."[12] As it turns out, the first approach, teaching standard video production and using regular-sized, unconcealed equipment, proved to be an effective means of deterring violence. The very fact of the camera's presence, in some instances, caused military and paramilitary operatives to back down.[13] Once the project developed along this course, the first round of concrete conversations about a media project for the Zapatista civil communities took place with Pastors for Peace, but the organization was not that interested, according to Halkin. "They didn't see the idea; it wasn't right for them. So I started working on, 'How am I going to get the money to do the project?'"[14] Halkin identified a need to have youth involvement, as it seemed an important angle for funding at the time. She contacted a Chicago youth media organization, Street Level Youth Media, to see if they were interested in project. They responded positively and she started writing grant proposals under the youth organization's 501(c)(3) tax-exempt status. She was awarded a number of small grants, but by far the most important one was a $21,000 grant from Fidecomiso para la Cultura, a rather short-lived fund based in the United States and Mexico that was interested in fostering cultural exchanges across borders. Halkin hinged her plan to equip local Zapatista community members with video recording and editing equipment on the idea of a cultural exchange program between mostly Latino youth from the Chicago area and young Zapatista activists in Chiapas, along with young indigenous video trainers from Mexico City and Oaxaca. The cultural exchange would serve as a vehicle to get the word out to people in the United States about the struggle and to improve understanding between the two countries.

As funding was secured, Halkin began putting the team together from within Mexico. Her priority from the beginning was to have mostly Mexican nationals, preferably indigenous ones, involved in the project, in order to "minimize a colonial model" and offset the mounting suspicion in Zapatista communities of foreign organizations that

were descending on the Altos regions to offer support with little follow through.[15] Through her contacts in Mexico City, she met Guillermo Monteforte, who was running the INI's video center in Oaxaca
City at the time. Monteforte became the project's principal adviser for
training, and many of his staff and trainees became involved with the
Chiapas project. Sergio Julián Caballero was one of the first instructors, as were Hermenegildo Rojas and Efraín Pérez Rojas, from Radio
y Video Tamix. Pérez Rojas left Oaxaca for Chiapas in 1999, to become
a full-time employee of the CMP, and was at the helm of the CMP's
initiative in the state of Guerrero, from 2000 to 2009. The final member of the initial team was Francisco (Paco) Vázquez, a Nahua youth
from San Pablo Oztotepec, a community just south of Mexico City.
Vázquez became Halkin's right-hand man, default translator, and
guide to indigenous community protocols as well as government bureaucracy. Halkin writes, "Vázquez helped me navigate the Indigenous
cultures, understand Mexican bureaucracy, and in many ways served
as my protector the numerous times the Mexican military and immigration authorities stopped me at roadblocks and checkpoints" (2008,
167). Vázquez moved permanently to San Cristóbal de las Casas in
1999 and continues to be the project's most steady presence at their
headquarters there.

Vázquez grew up in a community he describes as "indigenous and
peasant" (despite its gigantic urban neighbor), and learned about defending his community and cultural identity early in life. As Vázquez
explained to me recently, "I was born in a Zapatista family," referring to
the original Zapatistas, followers of Emiliano Zapata, the general in the
Mexican Revolution who championed peasant rights to land and
coined the famous phrase "Tierra y libertad" that neo-Zapatistas in-
voke today. Vázquez recalls, "My grandparents were Zapatistas and my
parents were also champions of community processes; my brothers
participated in serious struggles to protect the territory and collective
rights of our community. When I was born, it was all about following
my inherited path of participation. Even if I wouldn't have wanted to, I
was involved in it as a child and this is what allowed me to connect here
[in Chiapas] and understand the way people organize. It is very similar
to what my community practices and practiced since I was a kid."[16]
After high school, Vázquez decided to study graphic art and later photography in Mexico City, at the Universidad Nacional Autónoma de
México and the Escuela Activa de Fotografía, respectively, from 1990 to

1995. He worked as a product photographer for a few years, before returning to his home community to collaborate on a greenhouse project that ended up earning wide recognition as a model for community sustainability. Through the greenhouse project, called Proyecto Vivero Tepetlehualco, Vázquez also won a national youth award for "Protecting the Environment," in 1996.

Vázquez was asked to participate in a small conference of indigenous communicators that Halkin and colleagues from Mexico City's independent film community had organized. What caught her attention about Vázquez was the media component of the Vivero project. He regularly used slide shows and some video and radio to teach community members about environmental sustainability. Vázquez's experiences in his home community and Halkin's incipient vision for a long-term project in Chiapas aligned quickly, despite their limited command of each other's language.

With her team in place, Halkin launched the Chiapas Youth Media Project, three years after her initial visit to Chiapas with Pastors for Peace. The first video-training workshop was planned for January of 1998. It was envisioned as a collaborative workshop with mostly Latino youth from Chicago, young indigenous videomakers from Oaxaca and Mexico City, and indigenous youth from Zapatista civilian communities in Chiapas. Halkin and her team had visited Ejido Morelia the November prior, to discuss the workshop with Zapatista authorities. Ejido Morelia was chosen as the best site for the workshop because it had electricity (albeit ungrounded, which meant the supply would surely be intermittent and unpredictable). Morelia also had an Aguascaliente (turned Caracol in 2003) with ample room for housing visitors and the equipment, and it is not far from San Cristóbal. Through the process of planning the first workshop, the project team met Miguel, a Zapatista authority. Halkin writes, "Through Miguel we began to understand the governing structure of the Zapatista civilian authorities. We found that communication and logistics were much smoother when one person per community [such as Miguel] served as a 'key person'" (2008, 167). Despite the organizational similarities among Zapatista communities, "there [was] no 'cookie-cutter' Zapatista structure" (ibid.), and learning to respect and work with the idiosyncratic differences and dynamics of each community and region helped the project establish a pattern for sustainability on the community level.

Nevertheless, bringing outside students into a politically charged and potentially dangerous environment proved to be very stressful, and in the end, not as important as training and producing with the Zapatista communities themselves. Just weeks before the first workshop was to take place, forty-six Tzotzil civilians, mostly women and children, in the community of Acteal, were murdered in their village church during prayer. Acteal is in the municipality of Chenaló, just two and a half hours north of San Cristóbal de las Casas by road. The Acteal massacre, which was spun by the Mexican government and aligned press as a result of intracommunity violence, was in fact a blatant and horrific act of violence orchestrated by paramilitary groups in order to scare Zapatista communities into abandoning the movement. Members of the Mexican military stood by and did nothing during the massacre. The massacre, indeed, stirred panic in the region—and in the Street Level Youth Media group—but it did not deter people from the movement, or Halkin from the media project. Halkin and her team, however, did have to reorganize as the region became increasingly militarized and foreigners were under increased scrutiny. As Halkin recalled, "When Acteal happened, everything got put on hold. The region was much more militarized. It was super mellow in November—chill, no immigration authorities—but after Acteal, boom!"[17] To boot, Tom Hansen was expelled from Mexico on the first day of the first workshop.

Halkin had prepped the youth from Chicago for a potentially unpredictable experience: "I explained reality of war, that people die and get kidnapped all the time. 'This is a war we are going in to, not a vacation.' It was a cultural exchange, for sure, but more; they were going down there to be involved in unique experience. When Acteal happened, the grownups freaked out."[18] What Halkin wasn't prepared for herself, however, was forging ahead with the workshop after Hansen was expelled. Hansen knew the terrain (figuratively and literally) and language much better than she did at the time. He had left Ejido Morelia to buy food with some participants from the United States as the workshop began, and to deal with a bureaucratic problem that had arisen unexpectedly: one of the youths from Chicago had lost his visa and, unexplainably, his passport did not have an entry stamp—to the immigration officials "it was like he dropped out of the sky," Halkin remembered with some amusement. Immigration officials at the checkpoint entering Ejido Morelia allowed the person to pass, but required that he and three witnesses report to immigration headquarters in San Cristóbal within three days, to give all the necessary information. Once in San Cristóbal, Hansen was apprehended by immigration authorities, interrogated, and expelled from Mexico.

A second United States delegation, which was poised to arrive in Chiapas with much-needed equipment for the project, was concerned and considered backing out. But Halkin—who was "a nervous wreck" and held up in the Fray Bartolomé Center for Human Rights in San Cristóbal during most of this mess, for fear of being apprehended herself—refused to back down. "You guys are coming, you can't back out—that's just what [the government] wants," she insisted. The workshop was cut back from two weeks to eight days, but it was a positive experience for everyone, except perhaps for the "grown-ups," as Halkin called the adult members of the youth delegation, who never let go of their fears and alienated themselves from the experience.[19]

Back in the United States, Halkin and Hansen discussed the workshop and decided the project merited an ongoing commitment. Halkin had always imagined a long-term project—that is how she proposed it to funders—but the trip in 1998 only deepened her commitment to sustainability. She started her own tax-exempt organization later that same year, called the Chiapas Media Project, dropping the youth component, to focus on training and production that directly benefited members of the communities in Chiapas. She went about consolidating an advisory board made up of her existing contacts in Oaxaca, Mexico City, and the United States and continued to organize training workshops with visiting delegations from the United States. The delegations not only helped cover basic operating expenses in Chiapas, but also engendered a loyal following in the United States for the project, which has resulted, in some cases, in direct financial support. Yet, more important, they have helped get the word out about the project and about what is going on in Chiapas through independent media circuits in the United States.

Teaching Revolutionary Media

Halkin's experience as a Western documentary producer and artist inspired a certain curiosity in her about what kind of material Zapatista videomakers would produce, a familiar modernist gaze that Monteforte and instructors in the Transferencia de Medios Audiovisuales (TMA) program brought to the first INI video workshops, but she and her team did not shape the project's objectives with a desire to find or foment an "indigenous visual language." In the summer of 1998, during one of their first training workshops (after the fraught youth workshop earlier that year), Halkin remembered: "Sitting next to Manuel, a local Zapatista authority who had a camera in his hands, when he turned to me and asked, 'Don't we need special government permission to use this equipment? . . . Because all the people who come here always have credentials hanging around their necks, given to them by the government'" (2008, 170). Halkin and the team of instructors saw the need to teach people their rights along with how to use the equipment: "Put simply: the villagers had just as much right as the people with the [press] credentials to tell their story and distribute it as they saw fit" (ibid.). In many ways, perhaps somewhat ironically, as much as the conflict is known around the world and the Zapatista movement is celebrated for their savvy use of media, it is the community people themselves, their stories and experiences, that were consistently underrepresented in the media. And yet, it is the community people who continue to withstand the extreme hardships of low-intensity warfare, they who choose to live the life the movement fights for.

As Halkin told me in 1999, "Everyone comes in there and tells the world what [the Zapatistas] are, but they want the opportunity to say who they are, what they are" for themselves. Efraín Pérez Rojas, who was with the CMP for almost ten years, further explained this point in an interview with a colleague of mine:

> The work being done by indigenous people in Chiapas is not coming to replace the work of outsiders who come into the communities. No, video is like a way of seeing, a point of view. It's like a voice that we need to hear to be able to understand the complex reality faced by indigenous peoples, not only in Chiapas but across the country . . . Most of the videos I've seen that are made by foreigners are about icons: the Subcomandante Marcos, the Zapatista army and its leadership . . . whereas films made by indigenous communities are about everyday people, not hooded, armed fighters, but corn-growing peasants.[20]

The Chiapas Media Project was created to show and strengthen this everyday side of the movement. Early on in the project's development, Halkin and Monteforte saw the need to present a formal proposal and media-training strategy to the Zapatistas. While I was not able to recover the proposal or strategy in an actual document, it was modeled after the training workshops Monteforte and his crew had given or supervised for many years in Oaxaca. Reflecting on the broad differences between workshops in Oaxaca and Chiapas, Monteforte wrote in an e-mail to me in 2011:

> In general, we had two very different kinds of training on our hands in Chiapas and Oaxaca. In Chiapas, especially with Zapatista communities in the beginning stages of the CMP, people in the communities had the boot of repression on their jugular, and at the same time a discourse about the struggle that was much clearer, even if their level of comprehension was not always so clear. This resulted in good things, but it also made the process more difficult. The great thing was that with a clear vision about how the media was going to be used, what they were learning, a more globalized notion of their own reality, and a well-defined community structure, our work had a clearly delineated purpose. The bad thing was that the Zapatista bureaucracy was sometimes much more complicated than the government's, and at times, arbitrary decisions were made. The presence of so many NGOs also compromised the autonomous sentiment that grounded the communities. But it was the structure that allowed us to build a long-term project (thirteen years thus far) with impressive results. This, I think, is not viable in Oaxaca.

Workshop trainees were chosen from the beginning by Zapatista authorities directly and the equipment the CMP brought for their use was distributed regionally; it did not remain in one place or in the hands of one group, as was the case with the INI's project. With the TMA, the institution "transferred" video equipment, and ownership of it, to a particular organization within a given community, entrusting that the organization was positioned to foster interest and participation from the community as a whole. Producing media in Zapatista communities obviously had its challenges, too, but achieving embeddedness was not one of them. Media production was introduced into the Zapatista civil communities on their terms, after in-depth discussions with the authorities, and according to a clear organizational structure and operational strategy. Halkin was pleasantly surprised upon her return for repeat workshops throughout 1999 to find the continued support of the project by community authorities and a diffuse sense of the importance of knowing how to use "the stuff" and of being able to communicate their reality to "the outside world."[21]

Soraida, a Tzeltal woman pictured in her early twenties was one of many women chosen by community authorities to attend video training workshops offered by the CMP (see figure 5.2).[22] The CMP incorporated women according to gender equality norms that were spelled out in the Women's Revolutionary Law, which guided the Zapatista movement's vision for a new Mexico (Stephen 2002, 180). Female participants faced particular challenges, however, as Soraida explained in a conversation we had during a workshop in 1999. Soraida's context for things televisual was not one of gender equality. There was a television in her home community, but it was only for men; she didn't even know where it was located exactly much less what they watched. She remembered,

> When I was nominated [to attend the workshop] they told me that they were going to take care of my husband and cover my expenses. When I got here everything was fine, but at home they were critical. [At home] they said my work was in vain, that I wasn't doing anything because they couldn't see the work. They accused me of coming to have relations with other men, women told me this. I was disappointed, but then I thought if I lose heart and don't go they are going to think that they were right, that it was true. But now that they see [the work] they are going to see that it was a lie, what they were thinking about me . . . They are going to see that we are ready, getting ahead, and they will support us.

Soraida stayed with the project for two years after her initial workshop, before her family got access to land in a different community and relocated. She lost touch with the project but Vázquez remembers her natural intuitiveness with the technology and her eagerness to learn.[23] These character traits may well be what led community authorities to choose Soraida for the workshop, and the CMP developed strategies to overcome gender biases that made it more difficult for women to participate, but Soraida's experience remains common in the contexts of indigenous media initiatives in both Chiapas and Oaxaca.

Halkin and I were able to compare notes at various times during our overlapping visits in Oaxaca City, notes about some of the salient differences in media projects in Tama and in the Zapatista communities. Aside from this striking sense of clarity and purpose she (and Monteforte) saw in the trainees in Chiapas, there was also a different approach to culture. "In Tama," she thought, "it's the *cultura* [that mat-

FIGURE 5.2. Soraida (Tzeltal) at the first workshop in Ejido Morelia. Photo: Francisco Vázquez. Courtesy of Chiapas Media Project/Promedios.

ters]; media reflect or mirror culture. [In Chiapas,] it's not about that. Culture is part of it. We can videotape a *fiesta* and we can videotape an interview with people that just went to vote and were screwed because their voting place was moved . . . It's part cultural, part political, not a separation."[24] Halkin astutely surmised that this was in part due to the fact that the indigenous Maya of the Altos region of Chiapas migrated there relatively recently and had to adapt culturally and politically to their changing landscape. Stephen confirms, "The shared identity of people within the Lacandon region, for example, is not necessarily based on language or on generations of shared customs. Since many have come to the region within the past forty to sixty years, their shared culture and identity is built out of their political experience and participation in a range of peasant, indigenous—and now guerilla—organizations" (2002, 88). The notion of the electronic mirror was used in the Chiapas training workshops, and documentary was taught as the preferred genre for capturing an underrepresented and re-pressed reality, but the production process was anchored to the shared social and political agenda of the Zapatista movement to achieve indigenous autonomy, rather than the preservation of a particular culture.

Two CMP Programs

Two programs were produced by the Chiapas Media Project / Prome-dios within the context of the project's distribution strategy. The first video, *La familia indígena,* is the first edited program to come out of the project in 1999, and the second, *La tierra es de quein la trabaja / The Land Belongs to Those Who Work It,* is a fifteen-minute documentary, released in 2005, that does a beautiful job of summing up Zapatista practices and the abundant odds they face. Halkin affirmed that as far as what gets captured on tape, "what they record is totally up to them," and according to her, many of the programs produced by the trainees have been "more cultural than anything else."[25] Within the context of the rebellion, making culture visible adds a bit of normalcy to life in a war zone. But, building in part on what seems to be a common "double mode" of producing indigenous video elsewhere in the world, includ-ing in Oaxaca, the Chiapas Media Project produces certain programs for consumption inside the community, and different programs for circulation outside the community. Antonio, a trainee from Oconsingo who participated in the Morelia workshop alongside Soraida in 1999, confirmed that they liked to tape what was interesting about their culture (fiestas, celebrations, etc.), but it was equally important to circulate programs about their collective work (1999). For example, *Mujeres unidas/United Women* (1999, 16 min.) does just that, capturing the way Zapatista women have organized to work collectively in fields, vegetable gardens, and in baking collectives. Working together marks a definite break with "life before the struggle," when women worked alone in their communities. *Mujeres unidas* is perhaps one of the only crossover CMP programs that has been consistently used inside and outside Chiapas, almost as a "how to" video on collective work. The media project currently has twenty-four video programs available for international circulation and hundreds of videos that are used internally by indigenous communities in Chiapas (Halkin 2008, 177).

La Familia Indígena • The first edited program to come out of the Chiapas Media Project is *La familia indígena* (1999), a six-minute documentary shot in Morelia about men's and women's roles in the community. A slow orientation pan, shot from a nearby hillside, of the town of Morelia is accompanied by traditional guitar and violin music. The music fades over an exterior shot of a modest house surrounded by a rickety fence, suggesting that we are moving inside. The program cuts to the interior of the house, to an interview with a woman standing in her kitchen area. She speaks directly to the camera in her modest Spanish; her visible breath reveals the nippy morning temperatures in the highland region. She talks about men's work and how important it is for putting food on the table: "They sow the corn patch, plant corn, beans, cut wood." The rhythmic music comes in again over shots of a man returning from the field with a heavy load of maize on his back, two dogs in tow, demonstrating the woman's matter-of-fact account. It is a man's turn now: "Women's workload is heavier then men's because she does all the housework," he explains. Images show women of various ages cooking, washing, and cleaning. "Men lend work, too, but not as much as women when it comes to feeding the family," he continues. We see women carry impressively heavy bundles of household supplies on their heads and shoulders from a spot along the road to their homes.

Now a man and woman appear together in their kitchen. He sits while she grinds corn. "We go to work to bring firewood," he explains.

"It can take all day—but sometimes we also clean the milpa and if we aren't too tired, we go pick some coffee, and then maybe rest a day. And the next day we may harvest some milpa, but the poor women, they get tired. She has to grind and make tortillas." The first woman returns to the screen and explains, "We can work separately. We can pick some coffee, we can clean a bit of milpa, but we can do it together. I can't always do heavy chores, like cut big trees in dense forest, but I can cut coffee and beans." An older man weaves and the music comes up again over additional shots of men working. A quiet domestic scene ends the program and hand-written credits come into view. The point of the programs is as straightforward as its style. Men and women both work hard to keep a household and a community going.

La familia indígena sold over 150 copies in the first six months of the project. The CMP used the program as their first promotional video in a series of United States tours that have become "a viable model for doing presentations that generat[e] income and rais[e] visibility of the project" (Halkin 2008, 175). The video shows the Zapatistas as corn-growing peasants (not hooded soldiers, as Pérez Rojas remarked), grounding their struggle in the most universal of human tasks, feeding the family. Halkin was clear from the beginning that the project's overall sustainability hinged on economic viability that could not depend on the communities alone. "We entered the project knowing that neither goodwill nor passion would buy us a video camera or a Final Cut Pro editing system. Self-sustainability also requires a media product that can be shown, distributed, and sold" (ibid.). Not wishing to create false expectations in the communities, Halkin addressed this question early on. "When we first began discussion with the communities about the project," she writes, "we explained that the equipment was theirs to do whatever they wanted with, but that if they decided not to produce videos for outside consumption (a product to *sell* to the outside world), it would be hard to maintain financing" (Halkin 2008, 175). With the success of La familia indígena, the Chiapas Media Project opened the doors of an alternative distribution circuit that continues to provide most of the project's operating budget. Through their website and university and festival presentations in the United States, representatives of the project reach a sympathetic public with at least enough cash to buy a program or two. Subsequent videos may not have sold as quickly as La familia indígena, but they sell consistently, presenting the ongoing Zapatista struggle (as well as the dire situation in several indigenous communities in Guerreo State) in a more didactic manner.

La Tierra Es de Quien la Trabaja • *La tierra es de quien la trabaja/ The Land Belongs to Those Who Work It* (2005) is a powerful presentation of the Zapatista struggle and process in a fifteen-minute nutshell. A *corrido*, or Mexican ballad, introduces the theme of struggle and government lies as orientation shots show us that we are in Zapatista territory—the familiar sign warns the viewer that "you are in Zapatista rebel territory," and carved on the trunk of a nearby tree is "EZLN" under the outlines of a ski mask. This program takes place in the northern zone of Chiapas, in the community of Bolon aja'aw, near the impressive Aguas Azules cascades, a nationally recognized tourist site. The crux of the program is an encounter between the Bolon aja'aw community leader and a delegation of government representatives that arrive unexpectedly in their community. The exchange between the two sides exemplifies not only the Zapatista struggle, in practice, but also the obstacles they are up against, which also include Mexico's burgeoning and diverse tourism industry.

Titles fade over two almost identical structures—modest homes almost like row houses, built of wooden planks, with the letters E-Z-L-N written in large chalk on the dirt path out front. Men leave their homes to work, as a narrator explains, "The date we arrived here was March 12, 2003. They were 300 people looking for land to cultivate so they could eat." A series of shots show men working in a cornfield, women milling corn, and the community as a whole attending a funeral, always with their red bandanas in place. A woman continues, "We want to live where the government won't bother us. We are never going to leave because it is here that we will eat with our children. This land wasn't meant to be a tourist attraction. It is the land of our ancestors. It is farmers' land. The government has gotten used to eating with money and living with money. They never worked with a machete. We pick up machetes and work. We don't accept government assistance. We live in resistance." Another man talks directly to the camera about how he was assaulted on the way to Oconsingo, detained by men that were fencing off the road. Something was going to happen.

A block of text introduces the heart of the program: "In April of 2004 a commission from the Chiapas State Government comes to the community without warning." Cameras from the CMP were there to tape the encounter. Wearing shorts and baseball caps, about twelve conspicuously heavy-set men approach the community. A Zapatista community elder blows his whistle to alert the community to gather. Women and children assemble under a makeshift shade structure, and the government representatives are invited to sit on wooden benches and introduce themselves one by one, by name and position. Among them are representatives from the sub-ministry of the interior, the ministry of the environment, the state indigenous affairs office, as well as municipal presidents from neighboring communities and a human rights worker. In general, as one of them explains, "they are looking for an alternative solution to the problem, and invite the community to dialogue." The Zapatista community leader writes everything down in a spiral notebook.

After the introductions (the Zapatistas do not reciprocate by introducing themselves), the Zapatista leader asserts right off the bat that they have no intention of ever leaving. "All of the *compañeros* that are here with their children and their wives are never going to leave. That is the decision. Why? Because we have our demands, to eat, to live. That is the idea. We are not robbing, we are not delinquents. Don't think that we came here just this week, no. We have been here for a year." A man from the delegation (who was not introduced, at least not in the edited program) interrupts, "Brother, may I speak?" Addressing the Zapatista leader in Tzeltal, he says, "Look, I come from Agua Azul. As you said, we should respect each other equally, but in this case, you are not respecting me. I didn't just get this land, we've had it for more than twenty-six years. It is where we have cultivated our crops. We just moved our people from the edge of the river to over there behind the mountain so as not to harm these 500 hectares." The community leader responds, "Brother, what you are saying is fine. If you own the land and you work it, we can work that out later. But if you are asking so that the government will come in here and put in an eco-tourism zone—that we will never permit! But if you really understand what we want, in our hearts as Zapatistas then you will understand that this is Zapatista territory. The government's strategy is to give land to indigenous groups that accept their projects and use them to make it easier because the government knows that it can't." Replaying the history that lead to the Zapatistas uprising, the video depicts how the government pits peasant communities against each other while offering little security for their livelihoods.

The main government representative enters the dialogue. He is Victor Manuel Espinoza Utrilla, from the Secretaría de Gobernación (the Ministry of the Interior). He is the adviser to the subsecretary of political relations. "Like you say, as Zapata put it, the land belongs to those who work it, but every piece of land has an owner, right? So at some point you need to see that, ok? If we talk about rights, that is something else. I understand your ideology, I respect your ideology." The community leader responds forcefully: "I am going to tell you what Zapata said: 'The land belongs to those who work it.' The land is ours because we work it!" Mr. Espinoza, in all seriousness, proposes that the government could acquire a ranch and give it to them. The community leader articulates the history of ignored land requests. The human rights worker brings the discussion to the point at hand: the five hundred hectares on which the community is living are part of an ecological reserve. The community leader challenges him: "These are not untouched forests, gentlemen, but fallow fields. There are some big trees, but they aren't mountain forest. . . . We can protect this environment, this ecology. We can do that." Espinoza wraps up the discussion: "I don't think there is any problem. We are going to leave. Thank you for stating your position." As the group rustles to leave, the community leader asks them to inform their supervisors that the men who came to put up the fence called them "animals, cattle." Addressing the human rights worker directly, he admonishes, "They shouldn't say those things!"

Leaving, Espinoza says, "You pick the date and we will come [to participate in more dialogue]," but the community leader doesn't want to give false impressions. "If the invitation doesn't come, it means we don't want anything." As they shake hands, the women cheer "¡Viva Zapata! Long live the struggle!" A block of text adds to the backstory of this encounter. The Plan Puebla Panama (PPP), a multinational government plan to build infrastructure to improve trade throughout southern Mexico and Central America, uses ecotourism as a community-development proposal. The video ends with text stating, "The PPP uses the false claim of the common good to cover up the real intention to reduce indigenous cosmovision to something that can be bought and sold. Zapatista resistance demonstrates that the land and culture are not for sale, and are not goods to be privatized."

Each side has learned the discourse of their supervisors. The government representative asserts the bottom line—"Every piece of land has an owner, right?"—as he dismisses rights and culture. The Zapatista leader asserts none other than Zapata himself—"The land belongs to those who work it"—and the inalienable relationship that peasants had with land before neoliberalism. The intractable positions upon which history is replayed are plain as day in this documentary. A narrator couldn't have explained it better. Captured by videomakers trained by the Chiapas Media Project, in progress and "on location" (just as conflict resolution in Tama is captured in *Këdung Ajtk*), and then polished in postproduction phases, first at the regional media centers in the Caracol of Robert Barrios and then in the project headquarters in San Cristóbal, the footage is clearly positioned. In this lush territory within earshot of the huge Aguas Azules waterfalls, peasants (whose faces are masked by red bandanas) harvest their corn and build new wooden houses all in a row. When the government representatives approach, the very specter of the city men, who for the most part look like they have never worked a day in a field in their lives, speaks to the palpable mistrust peasants have for the mal gobierno. Vázquez confirmed to me recently that the Zapatista settlers in Bolon aja'aw are still holding their ground, despite the fact that tensions among neighboring ejidatarios became violent after President Calderón's visit to the area in February of 2011, to promote Mexico's "Year of Tourism."[26]

Video work isn't challenged in these settings as it was in Tama during the tequio; rather, it is given a respectful place as an important part of the lucha. As if to cement the relationship between video work, land, and struggle, Vázquez related a story of a Mayan elder who suggested that video is like the peasant's machete. Vázquez explains that the notion of "video machete" aptly reflects the intent behind revolutionary media: "Video can be used like a weapon to defend oneself or like an instrument of construction or creation" (quoted in Köhler 2004, 4). Most Oaxacan videomakers would surely agree with such an analysis, but not all community members are aligned with such a notion.

What this difference makes clear is that while revolutionary media is certainly entangled in relationships of power and influence situated far from communities—Promedios continues to be dependent on a nongovernmental organization based in the United States—the media initiatives that the Chiapas Media Project established are vetted and produced through a social and political structure based on consensual decision making and diffuse leadership.

Halkin herself does not see the regional media centers in the Caracoles ever being fully independent of the support base in the United States. The institutional structure in these community centers is not sufficient to maintain media production without outside help (Halkin, personal communication with the author). Despite this, it is hard to argue with Halkin, who describes the CMP as a "'best practice model' of cooperative, transnational, Indigenous media making" (2008, 161). As with the Zapatista movement itself, having a steady footing of support outside of Mexico is essential to the survival of the CMP's media initiatives, which are stationed in the trenches of "low-intensity" warfare. Indigenous videomakers trained by the CMP have social obstacles to overcome that do not have to do with being at war—being a videomaker is still a new social role in many communities—but, as Monteforte emphasized, discourse about social struggle does not have to be taught or fomented in Zapatista communities. The task of raising awareness of the lucha, which frustrated Radio y Video Tamix producers in Tama, is not present in Zapatista communities, where overt social struggle permeates everyday life. As the anthropologist Shannon Speed argues, "In the Zapatistas' alternative project, rights exist in their exercise," and CMP videos concretely demonstrate how they exercise them to a diverse range of audiences (2008, 172).

Videos like *La familia indígena* and *La tierra es de quien la trabaja* are overtly didactic, almost like how-to videos for living in resistance. They capture how Zapatista civilian communities apply basic revolutionary principles that resist market logic, such as an inalienable relationship to land, to actively protect their autonomy and build their futures. These videos are useful tools for Zapatista audiences as well, but they are also designed to educate outside audiences about life in *rebeldia* and put everyday faces on a movement that has been sensationalized by commercial media. Because of the overtly didactic aspect of CMP videos, they screen to international audiences with very little ambiguity unlike some examples of indigenous video from Oaxaca, which extend problematic issues of representativity and embeddedness to the international stage in ways that highlight the role of Westerners as consumers of indigenous media.

SIX

Conclusions

Indigenous Media on the International Stage

The world of international indigenous film and video festivals is an important aspect of indigenous media. Festivals attune us to issues of consumption and circulation, to indigenous media as material culture, and broadens the social space of indigenous media to include even more actors, organizations, and institutions. It allows us to consider how in moments and circuits of exhibition, "video makers perfor[m] powerful scenes of indigeneity—defining themselves as contemporary indigenous subjects who are active cultural producers engaged with the institutions and technologies of modernity" as Jeff Himpele, the anthropologist and media scholar, asserts (2008, xix). As performative acts, or as "cultural forms about culture" (Guss 2000, 9), indigenous media are constituted in part through their circulation to a range of audiences. In other words, the practice of making culture visible also includes the practice of showing. Festival presentations and screenings are performances of indigeneity—"tournaments of value" (Appadurai 1986) and "value-producing activities" (Myers 1995, 4)—in which audiences actively participate. In a practical sense, festivals offer indigenous producers forms of cultural capital and put indigenous media-makers in touch with each other, as well as with supportive NGOs and funding organizations that can come to play important roles in the sustainability of their craft and postura. What turns community-based media into global events is not only the way programs and their producers articulate issues central to the global indigeneity movement, but the fact that these programs regularly play on international stages, to transnational audiences.

It is important to acknowledge that the range of screening situations that make up the circuits of indigenous media exhibition include local and regional screenings. Tama's Canal 12, Tlahui's Canal 8, and

Comunalidad's station in Guelatao are examples of such efforts. These screening spaces provide local, grounded alternatives to mass media. Members of Ojo de Agua, often in partnership with other organizations, such as the Chiapas Media Project, regularly organize regional itinerant community screenings throughout Oaxaca. Like the community television initiatives mentioned above, these screening tours are about correcting and complementing information available through mass media with less mediated stories from indigenous peoples from other parts of the state, Mexico, or Latin America. Organized around a desire to stimulate solidarity, community tours often include guest videomakers, who present their work in person and engage in dialogue with their community hosts. Exhibitions based in Oaxaca City are organized with the same principles in mind, but set in art-house contexts, they reach out to broader audiences (including students, international tourists, and Oaxaca's growing number of expatriates) in the hope of building support for indigenously produced work and, more importantly, for a variety of indigenous causes.

Urban-based and relatively "big budget" festivals draw audiences that are most likely made up of people very similar to the majority of readers of this book: a mix of indigenous and nonindigenous people that, if not urban-based themselves, are probably not marginalized members of dominant societies. As audiences, we are not passive receivers of information; rather, we produce knowledge with what we see and learn, and our interpretations in turn influence our social worlds. As members of dominant society, we are not only directly implicated in the indigenous work we see. We have a responsibility to think differently and reflect on the ways we are complicit in the systems of power that continue to disenfranchise indigenous peoples.

The oldest international indigenous media festivals are here in the United States. Founded in 1975 and 1979, respectively, the American Indian Film and Video Exhibition, in San Francisco, and the Native American Film and Video Festival of the National Museum of the American Indian, Smithsonian Institution, in New York City, primarily show work by Native Americans from the United States and Canada. Since the mid-1990s, however, these festivals have included an increasing number of Latin American works.[1] Indigenous media festivals in Latin America tend to show little, if any, work from the United States and Canada, but what uniquely characterizes indigenous media festivals in Latin America is the way they deliberately reach beyond urban settings and offer workshops and roundtables to consolidate indigenous mediamakers into a social movement (Córdova and Salazar 2008; Wortham 2002).

Latin America's most prominent indigenous film and video festival —the Festival Americano de Cine y Video de los Pueblos Indígenas— was launched in 1985 in Mexico City, by the Comité Latinoamericano de Cine de los Pueblos Indígenas (CLACPI), an advocacy and training organization that began with an international group of non-Indian Latin American anthropologists and filmmakers with a strong interest in ethnographic film and has since transformed itself into a membership-based organization of indigenous mediamakers and their supporters. The festival has been held in Brazil, Venezuela, Peru, Bolivia, Chile, and Oaxaca, Mexico. Over the years, CLACPI has been transformed from a small group of visionary, nonindigenous filmmakers into a loosely defined, open-umbrella organization with broad indigenous membership spearheaded by the Centro de Estudio, Formación y Realización Cinematográfica (CEFREC), a nonprofit organization based in La Paz, Bolivia, and founded in 1989 to train indigenous mediamakers, as well as to produce and distribute their work. Directed by Ivan Sanjinés, the son of the legendary Bolivian "revolutionary" filmmaker Jorge Sanjinés, CEFREC is the most active, founding-member organization of CLACPI.

International indigenous media festivals like CLACPI's, while not harmonious or unproblematic events, are unique spaces and moments for indigenous mediamakers to grow their network, develop their craft, build their movement, and participate in negotiating the place of indigenous peoples within nation-states through direct contact with mainstream audiences. The media scholars Juan Francisco Salazar and Amalia Córdova note that "CLACPI's festivals have not only consolidated CLACPI as a pan-Indigenous organization, they have also strengthened the social spaces of Indigenous media production and the position of Indigenous media makers in the management of their organizations" (2008, 50). Festival screenings and awards can launch careers and, by reaching audiences, potentially make a difference outside the videomakers' communities and countries. What makes festivals extraordinary opportunities for audiences and artists alike is the fact that the mediamakers are often present, in person, to further contextualize their work, get feedback, and answer questions from the audience. But beyond advocacy and the traditional markers of success that festivals provide, the international stage offers another view of some of the tensions and dilemmas indigenous mediamakers experience in their home communities.

Community belonging and being an embedded social actor is a prerequisite for indigenous mediamakers on the international stage; it is assumed and provides the basis of indigenous media as a valued form. But embeddedness and community representativity are also taken for granted on the international stage, where there is often an uncomplicated shift from identifying as indigenous to identifying in terms of nation—from, say, Mixe to Mexicano, or Aymara to Boliviano.[2] Even the Hopi videomaker Victor Masayesva Jr. admitted to me that he felt like a gringo for the first time in his life at the international Encuentro in Tlaxcala, Mexico, in 1994. Curiously, in the international festival context, nation becomes more relevant than First Nations. There are practical reasons for this shift, of course, having to do with standard geopolitical maps that have deeply colonized our minds, but in the process, local specificities are often lost on international audiences (for the most part), and the cost of this loss constitutes a flipside of indigeneity: audiences are permitted to continue to think of indigenous peoples as "other," as part of an undifferentiated or underdifferentiated category of people, with few internal conflicts and contradictions. *Dulce convivencia/Sweet Gathering* exemplifies this complexity.

Dulce Convivencia

Dulce convivencia/Sweet Gathering (2004, 18 min.) is without a doubt a beautiful piece. The Mixe video program journeyed from the complex and multiple settings of the mediamaker's own sense of attachment to and embeddedness in his community—and his somewhat buried attempt to resolve the acute political conflict between factions in his community—to the international stage, where it won multiple awards and played as an "authentic," lyrical, and "visionary experience" (L. C. Smith 2011, 15). The Mixe videomaker Filoteo Gómez Martinez, who made *Dulce convivencia*, is from the village San Miguel Quetzaltepec, which is in the Mixe sierra, east of and a bit lower in altitude than Tamazulapam. I first met Gómez at the wrap party for the Raiz de la Imagen, a festival in Oaxaca City, in 2006, CLACPI's eighth Festival Americano de Cine y Video de Pueblos Indígenas. At the time, every-

FIGURE 6.1. A still from *Dulce convivencia/Sweet Gathering* (2004, 18 min.).
Courtesy of Filoteo Gómez Martinez.

one's attention was turning to the impending threat of military action
as the teachers' sit-in was poised to turn into a movement of tremendous
dous impact to the city and state.

Gómez left Quetzaltepec in 1997, when he was seventeen years old, to
attend high school in Oaxaca City.[3] There he met his future wife, Laurel
Smith, an American cultural geographer who was doing field research on
Ojo de Agua.[4] He got involved with video through her relationships with
members of Ojo de Agua who encouraged him to learn video production.
tion. Gómez completed two videomaking workshops with the group
and made *Dulce convivencia* in the second workshop.

The video opens with an introductory sequence framed by Gómez
himself, speaking directly to the camera for a moment, but mostly over
a montage of still images of a young boy holding a heavy iron gear of a
grinder up to his eye as a camera, a montage that sets up this piece's
intimate and almost tender perspective (see figure 6.1). Gómez positions
tions himself through the child's close and inquisitive poses.

In Mixe, Gómez explains (as the English subtitles translate), "After
being away for a while, I returned to my village with a video camera.
Through the camera lens I capture the process of producing 'panela' [a

raw brown sugar]. Today I want to share with you what I saw and how the people reacted to being recorded."[5] The little boy mimics a camera person expertly, striking various positions with respect to his subject as he looks though the "viewfinder."

Two separate interviews with Filo's neighbors, Señor Julián Martínez and his wife, Señora Juana Martínez, carry much of the program, though the visual content of the piece is the labor-intensive process of making panela. Mr. Martínez is seated on his patio, addressing the camera directly. A finger raised to the air, he says, "We aren't obliged to copy what comes from the outside. We are obliged to conserve what we inherited from our forefathers and what Mother Earth produces. When I was a boy I helped other people produce their panela. This is why it's good for teaching our children to work for their own good and for the community's well-being." The program smoothly shifts back and forth from Mr. Martínez to images of men, women, and children getting ready for a day's work, loading mules with supplies, tools in hand, people their leaving homes along well-worn dirt paths toward the main road.

Señora Juana Martínez, sitting with a young helper on the floor inside her home, is scraping dry corn kernels off cobs. She looks down at her busy hands and says, "Every year we produce panela with our family. Now my son Robert, he plants his own sugar cane because he knows we use panela every day." We see Roberto leaving with two mules. "We use panela in the morning and we use it in the evening just as we use maize," Mrs. Martínez's voice-over continues as group climbs up a broad dirt road on foot, dogs and mules in tow. The group forges a sizable river at the bottom of the canyon. The mules cross first on their own. Gómez includes a close-up of the mules' steady footing through the river. A reluctant dog yelps from across the river before jumping in to follow the group.

Mr. Martínez's interview continues: "As the saying says 'if you help you will learn something.' After this I started to plant my own sugar cane and I built my *trapiche* [a sugar press]. And now I help other people build their trapiches. I earn my money doing this." By now we are at the site where they will make panela. In a small clearing with a nice view of the valley below, the family has a simple field house, a rudimentary wooden structure. Inside, the *caldo* (broth) is already boiling and women tend to young ones. A young woman places her infant in a hammock for a nap and tenderly arranges its blanket. Mr. Martínez's interview continues over shots of the young mothers swinging the hammock and giggling with the young children at their side: "In the village we don't need money to feed our family. We know how to grow our own food. But there are people who do worry about getting money even though we know that you can't eat money." A man hovering over a corn grinder attached to a tree stump turns the handle repetitively as plastic buckets catch the ground maize. All the activity in this video is captured without moving the camera (though Gómez is fond of zooms), privileging the slow, deliberate, and repetitive motion of his people at work.

Back to Mrs. Martínez's interview, she explains, "Panela has a special taste that is nothing like sugar. Because we made it ourselves we know how it is prepared. On the other hand, we don't know how sugar is prepared or processed." She never looks up to the camera directly, preferring to keep her head down, focused on her work. Back at the field house, we hear Mrs. Martínez's words: "That is why we use panela in all our drinks and in some of our foods." An elderly woman cooks chicken at the field house as young boys arrive with buckets of water. The rest of the group, extended family and friends, arrive at the clearing, chatting about their walk from the village. Gómez inserts his father's whistle to accompany a long shot of Quetzaltenango in the distance, a zoom out gives us the feeling of how far they have walked to reach their cane field.

In the cane field, men and boys cut the tall stalks from the ground and clean off their leaves. Gómez jokes from behind the camera about "how great this is for kids, right?" The boys return comments and laughter as they bundle cane stalks in ropes and carry them back to the field house on their heads with a *mecapal* (forehead strap). Some boys giggle and hold fists up in the air in a joking manner. The older men rest now in the field, as Gómez uses another zoom out show how large the field is that they have harvested. Up at their field house, the cane is unloaded and piled up near a large wooden trapiche. The mules are tied to the trapiche and Roberto gets them going, around and around, as two men feed cane stalks into the press. The distinctive noise of the press sounds like heavy ropes being incessantly stretched. Cane stalks are fed into the press continuously, as the cane juice fills buckets under the trapiche.

The final sequence of the video is shot as carefully and systematically as the first two. No step in the process is missed. Making panela is hard work, involving people of all ages, including elderly women who prepare food for the group. Large metal tubs are placed in huge out-door ovens carved into the hillside, firewood stacked below each one. As the cane juice comes to a boil, it is constantly and expertly scooped with colanders attached to long poles. The beautiful, hand-carved molds come into view. A chunk of gelled panela is cooled in water; Roberto tastes it to see if it is ready. The boiling juice is transferred to clean tubs and cooled with rapid stirring and the molds are filled.

Over a shot of a panela cone that has come from the mold, Mr. Martínez's voice comes back in: "These days lots of people don't know what they eat, how its prepared or the ingredients. They just fill their stomach without thinking about it." The videomaker's own voice comes in now, over images of a family sharing a meal in a home in the village, drinking coffee prepared with panela. A slow pan across hundreds of panela cones wrapped in banana leaves and neatly stacked takes stock of the day's achievement.

Gómez contextualizes the meaning of what we have just seen in terms of indigenous ways of life and survival. The subtitles read: "Convivencia is the way of life in indigenous communities, where everyone shares the work, the good and the suffering while respecting each other. These are the main reasons we carry on as a community. This is what has allowed us to survive as indigenous people. Sweet is working together even though the work is hard. That is what I call sweet gathering, the sweetness of living together." In front of the camera again, Gómez ends the program by saying, "I sure appreciate everyone making time to see this documentary. Thank you."

Gómez is obviously not a stranger to this group. Rather, he is "just another person from the community with a machine stuck to his shoulder," to use Juan José García's words.[6] He is embedded, positioned from the inside looking in. The young people in the video show a playfulness with the camera; elders are rather undisturbed by its presence. The piece is respectful and deliberate, relying on the "codes" of indigenous video to deliver an intimate portrait of a community at work.[7] The pace of the video is common to many indigenously produced videos—it is slow and deliberate; not one part of the process is missed. The use of close-ups and the editing clearly show the hand of a more experienced editor, which is also common in work produced under Ojo de Agua's guidance, while the beautiful photography is evidence of Gómez's natural talents.

Dulce convivencia has had an impressive run on the international stage since its debut in November 2005, at the festival called Geografías Suaves: CINE / VIDEO / SOCIEDAD, in Mérida, Mexico, where it won the Bichito de Maíz award for best work spoken in an indigenous language. In 2006, it won a prize in the same category at the International Cherokee Film Festival, in Talequah, Oklahoma. The panel of jurors at the CLACPI festival described why the video merited such recognition: "For the lyricism and the sensitivity with which the author approaches the community, which represented not only in the beauty and simplicity of his images, but also in the positive and lucid spirit that emanate from the values expressed in collective work, environmental relations, and the traditional productive processes of agrarian peoples" (quoted in Smith 2011, 15). In 2007, the video screened in Los Angeles, at the All Roads Film Festival, held by the National Geographic Society. *Documentary Magazine* covered the festival, and in its issue from January 2007, described *Dulce convivencia* as the "most powerful film in the festival . . . [It] demonstrates how a straightforward subject (making panela, or unrefined sugar) can be treated with such understated reverence as to become a visionary experience." The message of community and self-sustenance is clear in the work: through their collective work, Gómez's community reproduces and reaffirms their way of life. The inside-outside discourse, which clearly prefers what is produced by those inside because it is knowable and tastes better, is a direct critique of globalization and an affirmation of community—"you can't eat money." In this sense, Gómez's video appears to perform indigeneity as beautifully as it is exemplary of the process of making culture visible. Lyricism, sensitivity, and the visionary experience embedded within Gómez's documentary, however, were lost on one critic who berated the documentary as "overly folkloric and therefore disempowering" at an earlier screening, in 2005, in Xalapa, Veracruz, at the Third International Symposium on Ethnographic Film and Video, "Anthropology of Differences: Multidisciplinary Gazes from Film, Video, and Other Communication Technologies."[8]

Indeed, without the backstory of the video, about the violent intra-community conflict that inspired Gómez to make the video in the first place, it is difficult to see how making culture visible mediates and repairs the imposed tension between culture and politics.

Laurel Smith brilliantly captures the roller coaster ride her husband experienced at various international screenings in her article "Decolonizing Hybridity" (2011). In it she explains how Gómez wasn't prepared to respond to the anthropologists' critique at the Xalapa event, but shared his reflections after the fact:

> When he traveled back [to Quetzaltepec] to record the panela harvest, he says he returned not only with our mini-DVD camcorder, but also with the idea that video could serve as a mirror in which the community might see itself. Sensitive to how easily he might be received as an inexperienced upstart who had gone to the city, acquired an education, and then returned to offer unsolicited advice, Filo figured his audience of Quetzaltepecanos merited the utmost respect. In no way should his video shock, scold, or lecture. Focusing on the images, sounds, and rhythms he thought his family and neighbors, young and old, would most like to see, he recorded a common practice of working together in a peaceful and productive manner. His hope was (and is) to spark collective reflection among the residents of Quetzaltepec about place-specific traditions that fostered collaboration. This way *Dulce Convivencia* might contribute to community conversations about the current situation, recent events, and a communal future. (L. C. Smith 2011, 24)

Several familiar aspects of indigenous media are present in Filo's account—the cycle of leaving and returning, the electronic mirror, and the process of reflection that can in turn strengthen community cohesion, and of course the value of collective labor. The "current situation and recent events" that Smith refers to, however, have to do with deep divisions and violence that are specific to Quetzaltepec (but unfortunately not uncommon in the sierras of Oaxaca). I interviewed Gómez not too long ago over the phone, in order to better understand the situation and his reasons for making *Dulce convivencia*.

Gómez made this video for a particular reason—well, two reasons. He had to make something for the video-production workshop and the timing worked out that his extended family and friends were preparing to harvest their cane field and make panela. The second reason has to do with a severe conflict in his community. In 2001, Quetzaltepec suffered a fraudulent municipal election. A teacher, Gómez's cousin, with ties to the PRI was put into the office of municipal president even though the community did not vote for him, evidence that the "era of the teacher" that Genaro Rojas spoke about had reached new heights. There were several retaliatory murders and the community remained deeply divided during the president's three-year term.

Gómez wanted to use video to reconcile his community's divisions, to remind them about what they share and how important it is that they work together. Like tequio, collective work is a social glue and a basis for sustainability and survival. But Gómez did not feel he could address the conflict in a direct way, because "who is he to speak about his community?" He left Quetzaltepec when he was seventeen. Leaving may have permitted a process of reflection that is common among indigenous videomakers; many leave to come back infused with a different level of commitment to their community. But Gómez has never served a cargo or position of authority in his community, so his voice carries little weight at home. As a result, Gómez has only shown his video to the friends and family that appear in the video, and they like it very much, according to him. His mom plays it all the time on her television. But he has never arranged a public screening in Quetzaltepec because, as he said to me, "no me quiero meter en problemas" (I don't want to get in trouble). Gómez isn't fully authorized to speak for his community, an issue that will probably catch up with him at some point, but on the international stage, his voice carries significant weight.[9] Indigenous media on the international stage help us understand these powerful scenes of indigeneity in a more complex way that can only be appreciated if we look at global and local contexts simultaneously, and if we look at a program's content in relationship to its making.

Social and cultural embeddedness is a hallmark of indigenously produced media, what scholars and mediamakers agree makes the work unique. Notions of authenticity, like embeddedness, are constructed, and they are sometimes partial, and even fought for. As the growing number of indigenous media festivals, their funders as well as the foundations that support indigenous media production, affirm, the value of indigenous media lies not just in any presumed authenticity or embeddedness, but in the ways mediamakers imagine social change.[10] Gómez might not be solving any particular problems at home, but he engages indigenous-state discourses as he presents his work to general audiences in Mexico (and beyond) and makes visible the ways indigenous communities survive and stay strong. The backstory of how electoral politics and indigenous autonomy continue to clash, with grave consequences, may not be in the video, but it is now visible as part of the larger process of its making, told in part here and in more detail by his wife, and perhaps now by Gómez himself as he continues to screen his video. In a plural manner, we give evidence of indigenous video's *postura*, and *Dulce convivencia* reminds us that all projects and categories are best understood as situated and positional, mobilized according to specific histories and circumstances. In this way, collectively, we make indigenous media matter.

———————

Indigenous media matters because indigenous people do. Their struggles for autonomy and self-determination remind us that our political structures and power relations are constructed, enforced, and contested in everyday ways, permitting us to zero in on the permeability of narratives that exclude on the basis of difference. As indigenous mediamakers imagine social change, they also reflect it, capturing hard-won degrees of autonomy from and resistance to dominant society that inspire activists and movements seeking more. But indigenous media should not be cast simply as a positive, unproblematic development in the lives of indigenous peoples. Many of the dilemmas involved in making culture visible have less to do with the technology of representation than with the challenging sociopolitical contexts in which indigenous peoples are immersed. Nevertheless, the point is that indigenous media comprise a complex social arena and process wherein struggles for identity and self-determination are played out. Taking a close look at how the technologies of visual self-representation are approached and introduced helps us understand how these technologies influence these processes—processes of reflection and cultural awareness, in particular—and how they are also invested with capacities to effect social change.

Indigenous media in southern Mexico involves a convergence of government institutions (and experimental moments within them), darker state practices of hegemonic control, and variously constituted (local, regional, national, and global) struggles for pluralism, in the form of indigenous self-determination and autonomy. This project of showing a community back to itself, based on a process of reflection embedded in the encounter with visual media, is at the heart of making culture visible. Producing those media reconnects culture with social organization and political action, and demonstrates how communications media are playing an important role in the situated struggles of indigenous people to achieve more control over their lives and resources. Freya Schiwy, cultural studies scholar, comes to a similar conclusion about indigenous works of fiction in the Andean context: "They do not endorse a superficial multiculturalism that exhausts itself in folkloric posturing but instead mobilize the potential of cultural memory to radically alter power relations and forms of understanding that have been hegemonic since the conquest" (2009, 103). In Mexico, indigenous media organizations engage the state and diverse audiences directly, with varying strategies and results, asserting the central role communications media play in achieving self-determination.

The INI "invented" video indígena in the early 1990s and invested it with the potential to signal the end of indigenismo, a nearly century-long state practice bent on assimilating indigenous peoples into the nation. Through the practice of indigenismo, indigenous cultures were depoliticized by the state as they were folklorized, rendered safe and consumable for the nation. The practice of making culture visible in Mexico repairs the rift caused by decades of government-sponsored assimilation programs, a rift between cultural production, on the one hand, and political action and social organization, on the other. Indigenous media mediates this rupture and reempowers culture. Along the way, indigenous media create counterdiscourses and narratives that gain visibility and momentum, and engender alternative public spheres.

Several organizations in Oaxaca turned to televisual media to achieve their goals of solidifying regional autonomy, in part by showing communities how autonomous they already were. On the other hand, engaging with government-sponsored media initiatives like the INI's Transferencia de Medios program in some cases reproduced monopolistic and top-down (and, in most cases, male-dominated) power structures within media organizations, structures that created problems of accountability within community settings.

Revolutionary media in Chiapas helps consolidate and articulate a project of living in rebeldia. Media production mediates the experience of low-intensity war and lends an everyday face to revolutionaries sensationalized by commercial media. Comparing revolutionary media production in Chiapas to indigenous media in Oaxaca emphasizes how versions and visions of cultural identity and autonomy vary according to differently situated histories of marginalization, accommodation, and resistance. The comparison of revolutionary and entangled strategies of media production also stresses how two very different roads arrived at a similar notion of comunicación de lucha.

In Oaxaca, culturally based visions of autonomy—such as the Mixe-

Ayuuk way of carrying out community service or the particular Mixe-Ayuuk practices and meanings invested in corn—contrasts with the direct and practical approaches to building and enacting autonomy in Zapatista civilian communities. While some members of community-based media organizations in Oaxaca continue to insist that language and culture is the defining element of video indígena, as Genaro Rojas does, urban-based organizations with regional representation, such as Ojo de Agua, retreat from the use of "video indígena" today. Video indígena had its moment, as Juan José García said, and from today's perspective seems attached to a legacy of government sponsorship and rigid categorization. Members of Ojo de Agua prefer more inclusive notions like comunicación alternativa or comunicación de lucha, which express a panethnic, proresistance postura that incorporates nonindigenous resistance organizations. The Popular Assembly of the Peoples of Oaxaca (APPO), whose movement in Oaxaca City, in 2006, coincidentally exploded into being just after Ojo de Agua hosted Raíz de la Imagen, the international indigenous video festival, shifted the playing field in significant ways. The APPO, which itself takes one of the defining social institutions of indigenous community-based autonomy, the *asamblea*, as the basis of its decision-making structure, comprises myriad social resistance organizations. While Ojo de Agua was never officially part of the APPO, the work its members carried out as mediamakers during the APPO's takeover of Oaxaca City clearly pushed the limits of "video indígena." Indigenous mediamakers working with the Chiapas Media Project were not handed such terms to appropriate, negotiate, or cast off. With their revolutionary positioning, video was swiftly brought into the service of their specific lucha, or "social struggle."

The role of individual actors—indigenous mediamakers and their supporters—demonstrates the agency and the self-conscious concern for social change at work in the production of indigenous media. Faye Ginsburg, the anthropologist and indigeous media scholar, calls the media producers she studies "cultural activists" (1997) and the anthropologist Maureen Mahon suggests the term "cultural producers" (2000). Both terms—or perhaps a combination of them, "activist producers"—are apt for signaling the self-conscious ways indigenous and nonindigenous activists produce and mobilize culture within broader struggles for self-determination. A focus on individual agency privileges practice, demassifies our understanding of media (as well as of the state) and underscores the fact that even community (not to mention autonomy) is achieved, not given. Indigenous mediamakers, as artists and activists, operate with a deep sense of accountability, an aspect of their positioning that Hopi video artist Victor Masayesva Jr. (1995) deemed essential, but the constructed nature of embeddedness and authenticity affirms that mediamakers lose no legitimacy if their work is a bit untethered from tradition.

With these understandings, the study of indigenous media constitutes a collaborative space in which researchers work alongside other participants, "as a mode of social action and intervention, [that exists] in relation to and collaboration with the projects of those [researchers] study" (Ginsburg 1997, 140). The asymmetrical relationships between indigenous peoples and national governments are not completely realigned in this collaborative space, but they are at least reimagined—in the work itself and through the social relationships established through media production, its exhibition, and this researcher's own "activist imaginary" (Marcus 1996, 6). My focus on indigenous media's audiences serves to remind readers that they are active participants in the social process of making culture visible, just as scholars are.

While the direct benefits of indigenous media production are difficult to measure at the local level, in terms of what kind of specific gains communities or regions make toward fuller autonomy and self-determination, they make clear that the struggle for self-determination is being waged on the fields of media production and consumption. Indigenous media production and consumption act as catalysts, engendering discussions that lead to empowering awarenesses. More concretely, indigenous media claim airtime that was previously inaccessible to native peoples, despite the government's failure to grant indigenous peoples increased access to communications media, as was promised in the San Andrés Accords and the international agreements that frame the global context of this study. A level playing field may yet be a thing of the future, but it is no small matter that indigenous activists are vigorously playing at all, both on their fields and far beyond. The project of decolonizing our imagination is far from accomplished, but the accomplishments of making culture visible bring us further along.

NOTES

Introduction. Making Culture Visible

1 When I write "indigenous media is," as in "indigenous media matters because it is a form of self-determination," I refer to the social process and
practice as a whole, whereas when I write "indigenous media are" (indigenous media matter, too), I am referring to the actual programs producers of
indigenous media make, though the two aspects are obviously separable
only for the purposes of discussion.

2 "Indigenous Peoples," Amnesty International, amnesty.org. Accessed February 4, 2013. www.amnesty.org/en/indigenous-peoples.

3 It deserves to be said that the war in Chiapas is only one example of the ways
the Mexican state has acted rather brutally against its own people. Patterns
of corruption and fraud are often punctuated by cycles of murders and
disappearances that have perhaps not enjoyed the kind of visibility the
"narco" violence of today does, but have nonetheless been steady and
equally horrifying over time. Military and paramilitary forces are to blame
for most of the human rights abuses in Mexico, not to mention the violent
repression of peasant organizations and peaceful movements like the teachers' movement in Oaxaca in 2006. Indigenous people are directly affected by
this brutality, especially in the states covered in this book, but it is the
hegemonic sphere of state penetration with which I am most concerned as I
situate indigenous video in terms of indigenous demands for self-determination.

4 Elsewhere, writing about the production of indigenous identities on tape, I
offer a similar notion that identities are "plurally produced," as a way to
acknowledge the wide range of social actors that participate in video indígena, from indigenous activists themselves to scholars, funders, and bureaucrats (Wortham 2005).

5 Juan José García, interviewed by Cristina Propios, 1999, Oaxaca City, Mexico.

6 The Comisión Nacional para el Desarrollo de los Pueblos Indígenas (CDI),
the post–2003 INI, devotes a substantial amount of its website to their
national network of "cultural indigenous radio stations," or SRCI, which
began in 1979 with the installation of the first indigenous radio station in
the state of Guerrero. Currently the CDI streams radio from twenty of their
stations online, at ecos.cdi.gob.mx/index.html. Antoni Castells-Talens

wrote a thorough doctoral dissertation on the subject of indigenist radio in Mexico (2004). He and Rodriguez Ramos have written some interesting and critical reviews of radio production under the CDI (2010).

7 Cultural objectification through technologies of representation (such as video) has been singled out by some critics of indigenous media as one of the nefarious ways these media wreak havoc on indigenous cultures (or, using Weiner's words, "drive the final nail into the coffin of the non-Western world") (1997, 208). Turner directly confronts the critics of indigenous media by pointing out that the West does not hold a monopoly on representation (1997, 227).

8 Stephen Leuthold's book *Indigenous Aesthetic: Native Art, Media, and Identity* is more about decolonizing aesthetic discussions than pinpointing an indigenous one—or, in his words, recognizing that there are "ideas about art held by indigenous peoples" rather than only "a Western theory of art that seeks to account for art in primitive societies" (1998, 2–3). But he does approach a definition of indigenous aesthetics that closely links its expressions to nature and spirituality (1998, 183). Speaking collectively, the Hopi artist Victor Masayesva Jr. firmly asserts that Indian filmmakers "want to start participating [in] and developing an Indian aesthetic. And there is such a thing as an Indian aesthetic, and it begins with the sacred" (Marubbio 2010, 3). The videomaker and scholar Byrt Wammack Weber, who works with Mayan videomakers in Mérida, Yucatán, has come up with a simple categorization that combines aesthetic considerations with questions of practice for what he calls "video with a Mayan accent" (2011). His typology includes: (1) "Mayan vernacular style," which is "brut video" with no specialized training; (2) "Mayan hybrid style," which incorporates "appropriated aesthetics, film form and/or a narrative structure from television, moving pictures, music videos, video art or experimental film"; and (3) " institutionalized Mayan video," which is "made to comply with quality and content guidelines (and oftentimes conceptions of authenticity) which are established elsewhere" (2011, 28). In his scheme, video indígena produced today by the CDI's Centro de Video Indígena, in Mérida, is institutional Mayan video, whereas the video indígena I discuss would fall under the hybrid category in his scheme.

9 Juan José García, interviewed by the author, 2000, Oaxaca City, Mexico.

10 Even as a Zapotec, García felt hard pressed to call his work "Zapotec video" and was more comfortable with "video Juan José." The tension between community representative and auteur is unresolved and runs throughout video indígena.

11 There are indigenously authored media that have penetrated some of these larger commercial circuits, but by no means do they emanate from them. One example is the work of the Inuit filmmaker Zacharias Kunuk.

12 My colleague Amalia Córdova and her coauthor, Juan Salazar, use the same expression, "making culture visible" in their chapter in *Global Indigenous Media: Culture, Poetics, and Politics* (Pamela Wilson and Michelle Stewart, eds.), which they define as "socially-embedded self-representation" (2008, 40). Córdova and Salazar emphasize and label several important processes involved in indigenous mediamaking, in particular calling it "autonomous collaborative production" (55), but my use of the term does not only emanate directly from my informants' own experiences and language. I use the term with more breadth, complexity, and inclusivity, in order to discuss the social and political movements that underpin indigenous media, the particularities of how indigenous mediamakers were trained in the 1990s, as well as how the notion resonates with a concept of culture that was reshaped in part by my discipline's interaction with visual media.

13 Guillermo Monteforte, interviewed by the author, 2000, Oaxaca City, Mexico.

14 Emigdio has been in Indianapolis since 1998, working in a CD factory to pay off debts he accumulated during three years of obligatory and unpaid community service (a position, or *cargo*, to which he was elected by his community) and, since a *paisano* managed to get his camera to him in 1999, shooting for a video project on migration. Teófila has not made a video since 1995 and her repaired equipment remained at the CVI in Oaxaca City.

One. Global and National Contexts of Video Indígena

1 Rogers et al. assert, "All contemporary discussion about the rights of indigenous peoples in international law is based on the ILO's work on this issue" (2009, 13).

2 This declaration and other UN documents can be found at www.un.org. While the Universal Declaration of Human Rights is not a legally binding document, related covenants adopted in the 1960s, such as the Covenant on Civil and Political Rights and the International Covenant on Economic, Social and Cultural Rights (ICESCR), which are known as the International Bill of Rights, have been ratified by over 130 states and are binding much as treaties. The United States has only signed the ICESPR (and with exceptions) while Mexico has signed and ratified the covenant.

3 Those nations who voted against the declaration are the United States, Canada, Australia, and New Zealand, though Australia and New Zealand now endorse the declaration. The Iroquois chief Oren Lyons, who has worked with the Working Group on Indigenous Populations on the declaration for over thirty years, sees the vote by the United States against it as a kind of "victory": "They are exposed for who they are and have always been . . . against us because we challenge their tenure to land" (www.native americanroots.net).

4 In a similar pattern, the "new communications law" that the accords demanded was trumped when the government did revise its communication law, in 2006, dashing the hopes of many independent mediamakers for more open channels for independent, public, and indigenous media. The new communications law was nicknamed "Televisa Law" to emphasize that it favored the media conglomerate Televisa, which already dominates Mexican airwaves (Tajonar 2011).

5 Juan José García, interviewed by the author, 2000, Oaxaca City, Mexico.

6 Francisco Luna, interviewed by the author, 2000, Oaxaca City, Mexico.

7 Luna, interview.

8 Ibid.

9 I do not review all the proposals for autonomy in Mexico today, such as those among the Huicholes in Jalisco, but rather focus on proposals that are relevant for Oaxaca and Chiapas.

10 See Cortéz (1998) and Robles (2000). Gustavo Esteva, an intellectual active in the autonomy movement, locates autonomy's recent historical roots in the establishment of the National Autonomous University of Mexico (Esteva and Prakesh 1998, 307).

11 The term "self-determination" is usually associated in international legal discourse with the right to an independent nation or statehood. Díaz Polanco feels this perspective is forced onto Latin American groups from United States and Canadian-based indigenous organizations—what he calls "colonial arrogance"—and does not see statehood as the only option for implementing self-determination (1997, 100).

12 A popular rephrasing of solidaridad, using typical Mexican wordplay is "solodarydar," which loosely translates as "only give and give" (Topil 1993).

13 An ejido is a form of pre-Columbian communal landownership that was given legal status during the period of colonial rule in Mexico. Ejidos and other forms of communal landholdings were systematically dismantled during the nineteenth century and restored by law after the Mexican Revolution in the constitution of 1917. Many of today's ejidos were not created until the 1930s and '40s, during the Cárdenas administration.

14 Warman adds that Gamio's vision of science in service to the state turned a "marriage" into "concubinage," a relationship that anthropologists are still "paying for" today (1968, 29).

15 Stavehagen adds another dimension to the "revolutionary" aspect of unification project: "while Europe was regressing to the myth of racial purity and superiority and while white supremacy was still legally enshrined in the US, the idealization of the mixed-blood mestizo in Latin America during the 1920s and 1930s could be considered as something of a heterodox, if not a revolutionary position" (1992, 428).

16 Incorporation or assimilation can also be seen as appropriation: Mexican

mestizo identity was being constructed through the appropriation of indigenous peoples' culture, which in turn was considered the "legitimate inheritance of the state" (Hernández Díaz 1992, 15).

17 In economic terms, of course, the citizen was defined by private property. Thus the liberal project began dismantling the basis of community life: communal lands (including those held by the Catholic Church). Ironically, as Díaz Polanco points out, many indigenous communities had rented lands to private interests and were financially dependent on the income (1991, 90). In the process of privatizing indigenous lands, many communities were tricked out of ownership, giving the *latifundistas* (large landholders) free rein to expand and later become the basis of Mexico's rural economy.

18 See Aguirre Beltrán (1969) for a discussion of indigenismo's contribution to Mexican nationalism.

19 Mexican indigenismo is redundant, according to Nolasco: "El indigenismo es mexicano, hecho en México, para México" (1970, 67).

20 This direct relationship with the executive branch is clearly visible wherever the INI is or goes: "Poder Ejecutivo Federal" is written on all the institution's official decals and signs (from letterhead to vehicles and buildings).

21 San Cristóbal de las Casas, a largely non-Indian city, was chosen for the seat of the first CCI over Mitontic (a Tzeltal community that was Pozas's preference) by Aguirre Beltán who argued that the ladino city was the "heart" of the indigenous region and where interethnic relations flourished (Herrasti 1989, 248).

22 The INI published several puppet theater scripts as cartoons in its magazine, *Acción Indigenista*. One play, with a cast of characters that included Mr. Flea, Mrs. Bedbug, Mr. Lice, Mr. DDT, Mrs. Comb, and Mr. Soap, clearly taught more than Spanish (INI 1955b).

23 Bonfil Batalla articulates a lengthier version of his vision of how Mexico must reclaim its Mesoamerican civilization in his well-known book *México Profundo* (1996).

24 Nahmad actually served a prison sentence for his "crime," but a number of sources—mostly anthropologists and indigenous activists I met in Oaxaca City, where Nahmad is a tenured researcher at CIESAS—told me in informal conversations that he was clearly framed and falsely accused. Nahmad has played a pivotal role in constitutional reform in Oaxaca and is regularly called in to legal proceedings to defend indigenous victims of Mexican law.

25 Having entered office after overcoming the most serious challenge by opposition parties (some say by fraud), Salinas was focused on consolidating the party's support among voters.

26 Hindley is right to juxtapose the amendment of article 4 with the simultaneous reform to article 27 for another reason. The government did not

undertake any broad consultations for the reform of article 27, nor was the
INI invited to participate: "The exclusionary way and speed with which the
new agrarian legislation was formulated and passed was a clear demonstration of executive power" (Hindley 1996, 236).

27 Though the INI's video program is described in the 1994 memorias, it is not
mentioned in this initial list of accomplishments, an omission that attests to
the kind of liminal position of the video program within the INI's administrative structure, a point I will discuss in more detail in the next chapter.

28 Fox attributes their success to the INI's long-standing policy that supported
autonomous self-organization of indigenous peoples, a claim he does not
substantiate, and the fact that the INI was more insulated from the electoral
arena since the PRI did not perceive a risk to its electoral base in indigenous
communities (Fox 1994, 190).

29 Guillermo Monteforte, interviewed by the author, 2000, Oaxaca City, Mexico.

Two. Inventing Video Indígena

1 This is not to say that indigenous media production in Mexico couldn't
have occurred in any other way; it did and it has. I am particularly interested in the context where the INI "invents" video indígena and, along with
it, also from above, the social role of the indigenous videomaker.

2 In this document, Warman lays out the INI's tasks for his term as director.
They include (1) the participation of indigenous pueblos in the planning
and execution of the INI programs which in turn was to culminate in (2)
the transfer of institutional functions to organizations and collectives, and
(3) the coordination of the institute's work with federal, state, municipal,
civil, and international institutions (Warman 1989).

3 Juan José García, interviewed by the author, 2000, Oaxaca City, Mexico.

4 Carlos Cruz, interviewed by the author, 2000, Mexico City.

5 Today the TMA is nowhere to be found on the website of the Comisión
Nacional para el Desarrollo de los Pueblos Indígenas (CDI), the post–2003
INI, though the CDI has continued to fund and support indigenous video
projects through the Apoyo a Proyectos de Comunicación Indígena (Support for Indigenous Communication Projects), which accepts applications
for video productions proposed by members of indigenous communities
who have the support of the community authorities. The CDI has also
maintained four CVIS, but the producers, who originally inhabited the facil-
ities, at least in Oaxaca, maintain a healthy distance from the CDI. Furthermore, the video programs produced at the CDI in Oaxaca today bring
indigenous video production back in line with a safe representation of
indigenous culture that is not threatening to the state.

6 Alfono Muñoz Jimenez, interviewed by the author, 1996, Mexico City.

7 Cruz, interview.

8 The film, *El pueblo Mexicano que camina* (INI 1996), about Mexico's "cult" following of the Tonantzin-Virgin of Guadalupe, took director Juan Francisco Urrusti nine years of heated impasses with the INI to make it the way he envisioned it.

9 Guillermo Monteforte, interviewed by the author, 2000, Oaxaca City, Mexico. This sooner-or-later logic resonates with how Vincent Carelli defends his project Video Nas Aldeas when he is criticized for forcing first contact with media technology in the Brazilian Amazon (Aufderheide 1995). Scholars of indigenous media are generally supportive of this approach, recognizing that indigenous peoples do not live in a vacuum.

10 Cruz, interview.

11 Cruz, interview.

12 Monteforte, interview.

13 Monteforte, interview.

14 Monteforte, interview.

15 Monteforte, interview.

16 Monteforte, interview.

17 Monteforte, interview.

18 Monteforte, interview.

19 Female participants were sought but few attended. In addition to logistical obstacles having to do with who would feed their husbands and care for their children, not to mention all the other chores women are responsible for, media technology was generally perceived as a gendered sphere reserved for men. Teofila Palafox (Ikoods), who participated in the Super-8 workshop in 1985, recounted how the local context for watching movies involved pornography and men only. She had a hard time convincing people in her community that video production could be different. Similarly, as I discuss in chapter 5, Soraida (Tzeltal), a participant in the Chiapas Media Project, had to convince the women in her home community that she was receiving legitimate training in the face of their accusation of having "relations" with other men.

20 María Santiago Ruiz, a Zapotec videomaker from the Oaxaca Central Valley region became for a time a prominent member of the Oaxaca-based video indígena scene. Her video *Buscando bienestar* won several international awards and, with the help of Monteforte, she received a MacArthur Media fellowship in 1998. María regularly accompanied CVI staff in Oaxaca at workshops and on screening outings, and while she rarely made overt contributions as an instructor, her presence as an accomplished videomaker consistently added an important motivational element to the workshops (García, interview; L. C. Smith).

21 Cruz, interview.

22 Cruz, interview.

23 Monteforte, interview.

24 Cruz, interview.

25 Cruz, interview.

26 Cruz, interview.

27 Guillermo Monteforte, interviewed by Cristina Propios, 1999, Oaxaca City, Mexico.

28 Freya Schiwy, in her new book on Andean indigenous media, touches on the use of "commercial cinema's visual codes" by indigenous mediamakers, which poses a stark contrast to Bolivia's tradition of revolutionary cinema of the 1960s. The use of close-ups and melodramatic love stories or talking heads does not dilute the potential of indigenous media: "These conventions are employed, however, as indigenous media turn the gaze toward the inside" (2009, 48). I think it is important to consider both the mediascape of which the indigenous producers are a part—what forms of media they are exposed to in a daily way—and how the technology is taught to them.

29 According to the data gathered for the 2010 census in Mexico, in the state of Oaxaca, which has a population of more than 3.8 million, there were 707,465 homes with television sets. In Tamazulapam del Espíritu Santo Mixe, the community that I focus on in chapter 4, there were 1,074 homes with televisions sets. Tama's population is 7,362. In other words, while the ratio of individuals to televisions set is roughly one to four across the state, it is one to seven in this particular indigenous village. It is interesting to note that while televisions are (not surprisingly) more abundant than computers, they consistently outnumber refrigerators. For example, in the state of Oaxaca, out of 881,250 homes with electricity, 134,557 have computers and 560,275 refrigerators, compared to 707,465 with television sets ("Mexico en cifras," Instituto Nacional de Estadística y Geografía, 2010, www.inegi.org .mx/sistemas/mexicocifras).

30 Inspired by the success of Bolivian indigenous short fiction presented at the Festival Americano video festival in 1999 in Guatemala, many indigenous Oaxacan videomakers returned with plans to shift toward making fiction. But one of the few serious efforts to produce fiction in Oaxaca has been made by María Santiago Ruiz. Her video *Soap Tree* is about the advantages of natural, homemade soap (María Santiago Ruiz, interviewed by the author, 2000, Oaxaca City, Mexico). A Purépecha videomaker from Morelia, Michoacán, Pavel Rodríguez Guillén has made several works of fiction, mostly dramatizations of ancient texts, such as his most recent, *Auikanime: La que tiene hambre/auikanime: The One That Is Hungry* (2010, 37 min.) that screened at the Native American Film and Video Festival, in New York City in 2011.

31 Cruz, interview.

32 Cruz, interview.

33 Donaldo Colosio, the presidential candidate for the PRI, was murdered on March 24, 1994, at a campaign rally in Tijuana, in what many believe was an inside job ordered by President Salinas. Months later José Francisco Ruíz Massieu, president of the PRI party and Salinas's brother-in-law, was also murdered in September of 1994. The president's brother, Raul Salinas, is widely believed to have ordered Ruíz Massieu's killing, though bizarre twists and turns in the lengthy trial, unsuccessful extradition attempts, and turnover in prosecuting attorneys points more to the continued impunity of the politically powerful than to specific evidence, with the exception of a taped conversation with a witness that emerged in 1997 (Julia Preston, "Former Mexican President Is Implicated in Brother's Scandals," *New York Times*, April 10, 1997).

34 Cruz recalls a more integrated expansion strategy that was discussed but not systematically applied: to train and outfit the INI's indigenous radio stations with video production. The team did hold a short workshop at the INI station XEGLO, in Guelatao, Oaxaca, in 1991, which established important relationships in the consolidation of video indígena in Oaxaca. Monteforte tried to revive this idea in 1996 with a proposal to turn video equipment at most INI radio stations into Sub-Centros de Video, but it was never approved (Monteforte, interview, 1996).

35 Cruz, interview.

36 Juan José García, interviewed by Cristina Propios, 1999, Oaxaca City, Mexico.

37 García, interview, 2000.

38 García, interview, 1999.

39 From 1995 through 2002, seven indigenous videomakers who worked directly with the CVI in Oaxaca received Media Arts Fellowships from the Rockefeller Foundation and the John D. and Catherine T. MacArthur Foundation: Teófila Palafox (Ikoods), from San Mateo del Mar, Oaxaca; Emigdio Caballero (Mixtec), from San Antonio Huitepec, Oaxaca; Crisanto Manzano (Zapotec), from Tanetze de Zaragoza, Oaxaca; Hermenegildo Rojas (Mixe), from Tamazulapam Espíritu Santo, Oaxaca; María Santiago Ruíz (Zapoteca), from San Pedro Quiatoni, Oaxaca; Mariano Estrada (Tzotzil) from Bachajón, Chiapas; and Carlos Efraín Pérez (Mixe) from Tamazulapam Espíritu Santo, Oaxaca. Guillermo Monteforte and Carlos Martinez Suarez, a nonindigenous videomaker working in San Cristóbal de las Casas, also received MacArthur grants, in 1999 and 1998, respectively.

40 When the EZLN launched its war against the Mexican government, Cruz, Monteforte, and Gutíerrez predicted the end of the TMA. Seeking ways to continue a project that they came to think of as "their own," they created a nonprofit organization called Dispersión Visual A.C. with the intention of finding and funneling funds toward indigenous video production, filling a

void they felt would soon emerge when the government would shut the project down. Cruz remembered, "The objective [of Dispersión Visual] was to look for private or social alternatives in order to continue sustaining the TMA project outside official channels. We knew that the official side was limited and that the time was going to come that it was going to scare some people [within the INI]. There are always those that are more papist than the pope who were going to be scared by some of the images created by indigenous people. But we didn't make it. It's a bit sad, or very sad, to say it, but we didn't measure our strength well. We were too ingenuous, too romantic. We had too much tenderness and romanticism, and care and tenderness don't translate into money or necessary resources" (interview, 2000).

41 Cruz, interview.

42 Cesar Ramirez, interviewed by the author, 2000, Mexico City.

43 Jaime Martínez Luna, interviewed by the author, 2000, Guelatao de Juárez, Oaxaca, Mexico.

44 Cruz, interview.

45 Monteforte, interview, 2000.

46 Frustrated with the low salary, Yolanda left the CVI in 1996 to run a small store in her hometown of Tlacolula so she could be close to her young children. Despite chaotic beginnings, staff remember Yolanda's efficient and organized manner fondly as they often ponder their own disorganized working style.

47 Monteforte, interview, 2000.

48 Sergio Julián Caballero, interviewed by the author, 2000, Oaxaca City, Mexico.

49 Monteforte, interview, 2000.

50 García, interview.

51 García, interview.

52 García, interview.

Three. Regional Dimensions

1 Juan José García, telephone interview by the author, 2011.

2 Oaxaca is mostly mountainous. Both major sierras that run along the eastern and western sides of the North American continent meet in Oaxaca, forming what is locally referred to as *el nudo*.

3 Many more organizations that I had contact with through the Centro de Video Indígena are also described in Laurel Smith's dissertation "Mediating Indigenous Identity: Video, Advocacy, and Knowledge in Oaxaca, Mexico" (2005). This chapter's section on Ojo de Agua is longer than the first two sections, because I did more extensive field research with that organization, but also because of the detail needed to show how the INI kept CVI staff

from doing the kind of work they were committed to undertaking, causing Monteforte and others to deepen their commitment to media for social change.

4   For good overviews of their work, see their chapters in Bartolomé and Barabas (1998).

5   Taking my informants' lead, I use "Sierra Norte."

6   Indeed, Jaime Martínez Luna's letter to the director of the CDI, written at the institution's invitation to contribute to the CDI Consulta in 2003, defends this notion of microregions (CDI 2004, 105–6).

7   The Mixe leader Regino Montes characterizes XEGLO as the "voice of the state," a comment indicative of the ongoing debate about how "indigenous" the INI's indigenous radio stations really are (Castells-Talens 2011).

8   Jaime Martínez Luna, interviewed by the author, 2000, Guelatao de Juárez, Oaxaca, Mexico. All subsequent quotes attributed to Martínez Luna in this chapter are taken from this interview, unless otherwise noted.

9   Francisco Luna, interviewed by the author, 2000, Oaxaca City, Mexico.

10 The 2010 Mexican census reports that out of 144 private homes in Guelatao, 136 have television sets. Guelatao's population is reported to be 544.

11 In addition to the community television projects in the Mixe region, the Zapotec videomaker Crisanto Manzano also tested television transmission in his community (with a transmitter loaned to him by Cervantes) in 1999. The community responded positively and Manzano was looking for funds to buy a transmitter.

12 Adelfo Regino Montes, interviewed by the author, 2000, Oaxaca City, Mexico.

13 Ibid.

14 García, interview.

15 Alvaro Vásquez, interviewed by the author, 1999, Oaxaca City, Mexico.

16 K-Xhon, Video-Cine Zapoteca, interviewed by the author, 1999, Oaxaca City, Mexico.

17 K-Xhon, Video-Cine Zapoteca, interview.

18 K-Xhon, Video-Cine Zapoteca, interview.

19 Vásquez, interview.

20 "Topil," a Zapotec word widely used by Spanish-speakers, refers to a community peacekeeper, and is the lowest-ranking authority in the civil-religious system of community cargos.

21 Vásquez, interview.

22 Vásquez, interview.

23 Unfortunately, most other K-Xhon videos are not easily accessible today. Some, like *Danza Azteca*, which won recognition at international film festivals, are on outdated formats (Betamax), and others are simply difficult to find, even for Colmenares, whose archives have been strewn by the forces of too many house moves.

24 And the anthropologist Benjamin Maldonado writes that the collective is "widely known for being the first [indigenous organization in Oaxaca] to experiment with video" (1999, 2).

25 Ojo de Agua was constituted legally in 1999 as Comunicación Indígena (COMIN). As further evidence of their "organic" development, the group cycled through other titles prior to 1999 including Objetivo Común (Common Objective) and later Comunicación Alternativa (COMAL). Production credits from this period show all three titles.

26 Used to working for months at a time without salary, Caballero went into debt several times as an INI employee. Supporting his wife—who cleaned the CVI—and two children at the time, he, like many Oaxaqueños, had to rely on loaned remittances from his brothers working in the United States.

27 Sergio Julián Caballero, interviewed by the author, 2000, Oaxaca City, Mexico.

28 Caballero, interview.

29 Caballero, interview.

30 García, interview

31 Luna, interview.

32 Guillermo Monteforte, interviewed by the author, 2000, Oaxaca City, Mexico. The economic consequences of transferring the CVI were significant. While never sufficient, on paper, the CVI's annual budget was 500,000 pesos (approximately $55,000).

33 Awards and festival credits can be found on Ojo de Agua's website: www .ojodeaguacomunicacion.org.

34 I extend a special thank-you to Laurel Smith, who gathered a few more details about Santa Ana's community museum than I did (L. C. Smith 2005, 195–99). Santa Ana's community museum, opened in 1996, was developed by the community with the help of a pair of anthropologists working for INAH. The museum achieved enormous success as an example of the potential of community-run museums, culminating in an international conference in Santa Ana, with representatives from ten Latin American countries in attendance. The conference led directly to the creation of a UNESCO/ Rockefeller fund for community museums.

35 Ojo de Agua share the production credit of the series with Media Llum Comunicación, a media production group in the state of Mexico (www .mediallum.com) that was founded by José Luis Velázquez. Employed by the INI at the audiovisual archive in Mexico City, Velázquez was an indispensable ally to many working in Oaxaca through the INI years and up until his untimely death in 2006.

36 LaNeta S.C., a Mexico City-based Internet provider with a social change agenda helped Ojo de Agua develop and host their website until recently.

37 The hundreds of women involved in the COR-TV takeover marched to the

station, banging on pots and pans. The radio programming they commandeered, which they named Radio Caserola (casserole radio), was mostly an
open-mic forum for people from within the movement to give direct and
personal testimonies about the movement, what led them to it, and their
experiences during the military crackdown of June 14, 2006. Stephen's article grounds radio testimony as a speech act to traditional forms of speaking
(much like testimony) in community assemblies (2011).

38 "Formación," Ojo de Agua Comunicación. Accessed February 3, 2013. www
.ojodeaguacomunicacion.org/index.php/lo-que-hacemos/capacitacion.

Four. Dilemmas in Making Culture Visible

1 Names of Mixe villages reveal histories of conquest. Nahuatl names are
evidence of pre-Hispanic colonization by Nahuatl-speaking Mexica of Mexico's central valley, and saints' names of Spain. In Mixe language, Tamazulapam is *Tu'uk në'ëm* and means "place of water" (Genaro Rojas, field
interview by the author, 2000, Tamazulapam, Mixe, Oaxaca, Mexico). The
Ayuuk word for Tlahuitoltepec, the neighboring Mixe village to the north,
means "warming up near the hearth" (Nahmad Sittón 1965, 20).

2 To place Koruda's description of accelerated change in some context, Nahmad reports only 29 percent bilingualism in the Mixe region in 1965 (compared to Pardo's 50 percent in 1994). Notably, he reports only one bilingual
Spanish-speaker in Tama. Nahmad observed in the mid-1960s that "monolinguism [was] one of the most important problems to resolve in order to
integrate the Mixe into national life" (1965, 36).

3 Kuroda describes the myth as follows: "The Legend of Five Brothers, popular in the highland villages, tells of the affinities of the five villages. According to this legend, a woman and her five sons once lived at a place near the
river of Tamazulapám. From there her five sons left in five directions and
formed the five villages ... The kinship of Tlahui with the other four villages
is not at all fictitious, since these five villages are located near one another
and their dialects are similar within the wide variations of the Mixe language" (1984, 11).

4 Not so little anymore, Silvana and her sister are big girls now. Their Face-
book pages boast their school degrees and healthy social lives.

5 Tama and Mixistlán de la Reforma are the only Mixe municipios known for
pottery.

6 I use lineage somewhat loosely to describe a connection of descent organized spatially around, belonging to, having come from, or having lands in
one of the seven ranchos that surround Tama centro. Residents of each
rancho built a field house in the new fields for the residents to use and
tequio labor is organized (grouped) according to rancho affinity.

7 Tamix is Radio y Video Tamix's television station. The collective often uses " Tamix," "Video Tamix," and "Radio y Video Tamix" interchangeably. For consistency, I use Tamix. "Tamix" stands for Ta(mazulapam) Mix(e), and is also used to identify the town's basketball team in intervillage tournaments.

8 This is the same program K-Xhon video claims to have inspired to adopt video, but the historical context for the Casas del Pueblo program dates back to the 1920s, with the federal government's rural education campaigns, called *missiones culturales*, which were integrationist instruments promoting Spanish literacy (1978, 44). The program under discussion in this chapter, however, began in the late 1980s, as a state initiative under Oaxaca's governor, Heladio Ramirez.

9 May to August is a period of scarcity in the Mixe region (Lipp 1991, 52) throughout Oaxaca, where rain-fed agriculture produces only one main crop cycle a year. Sowing happens in May, when the previous year's corn stock has been mostly consumed, and harvesting happens in September. Thus, May, June, July, and August are typically months of scarce food supply.

10 I was not present in Tama during the momentous occasion. I constructed the event from various accounts told to me and to other attentive listeners at various presentations of Tamix's programs since 1992.

11 Tamix's use of "espacio sagrado" was widely appreciated in video indígena circuits as being exemplary of the positive hybridity of indigenous spiritual sensibilities and modern technology. For example, OMVIAC used an extensive quote from Genaro defining "espacio sagrado" in their promotional brochure.

12 Alcoholism has a long-rooted history in many indigenous villages, dating back to independence, when alcohol was often used to buy villagers' labor and, in turn, create their indebtedness. In Tama, alcoholism was definitely considered a problem, mostly by women, who suffered the most from men's underproductivity and violent behavior.

13 Hermenegildo's real passion has always been music, an important tradition in the Mixe region. Part of the funding he received for video production went to a drum set. During my field research he and his friends had an informal band and they would get together to play and compose rock music. Today, Hermenegildo works as an agent for local talent, sponsoring shows in and doing recordings from the area. He has released several CDs.

14 Genaro Rojas, interviewed by the author, 2000, Tamazulapam, Mixe, Oaxaca, Mexico.

15 Colin Clark, in his ethnography on class, ethnicity, and community in southern Mexico, also makes this point: "A core element in the construction of ethnic identity, within the framework of peasant maize cultivation, is the idea of work" (2000, 162).

16 This member of the community wished to remain anonymous.

17 I was struck, reading Beals, with the possibility of a cultural basis for televisión sin reglas when he writes of Mixe material culture: "Far more important seems the lack of any feeling for style, for doing things the right way" (1973, 8). But this possibility is dashed by Beals's dismissive attitude toward Mixe material culture, calling it "makeshift" and "lacking standards of quality" compared to the Zapotec culture of the valley.

18 Mr. and Mrs. Dominguez asked me to be their middle daughter's *madrina* for her graduation from junior high. After accompanying Nayeli and her parents to church for a blessing I became their *compadre*.

19 Cine Sapito was created as a space for "movies," not for indigenous video, according to Hermenegildo's vision. Given this, I thought Chris Eyre's (Cheyenne-Arapaho) recent film *Smoke Signals*, a big-screen, big-budget indigenously produced film with international distribution, would be perfect for Cine Sapito. I had mentioned the movie several times to Hermenegildo and was glad to present him with a copy of a Spanish-language version (*Señales de humo*) I rented at my local video store in Oaxaca. He seemed grateful, but on the night of the presumed screening, the Hollywood thriller *Snake Eyes* preempted *Smoke Signals*. A bit disappointed, I asked Hermenegildo, "Que pasó?" "People aren't interested in those kinds of movies," he told me. Tama residents want to see action films and the success of his cinema endeavor depended on it.

20 Hermenegildo Rojas, e-mail correspondence with the author, 2011. I also conducted field conversations with Hermenegildo from 1999 to 2000, in Tamazulapam.

21 I was able to catch up with Efraín recently at the Native American Film and Video Festival, in New York City in 2011, where his first solo documentary, *Y el río sigue corriendo/And the River Flows On* (2010, 70 min.) was screening. The documentary is about how multiethnic indigenous communities living in the outskirts of Acapulco, Guerrero, are vehemently resisting the federal government's plan to build a hydroelectric dam that would flood their communities. The documentary is beautifully crafted and presents a powerful story that reflects Efraín's decisive move in the direction of "videomaker," without having lost his activist spirit.

Five. Revolutionary Indigenous Media

1 The Zapatistas are famous for being media savvy, but their on-line presence took a few years and several key partnerships to consolidate (see EZLN's official website, enlacezapatista.ezln.org.mx). When the rebellion first started, the rebel army's communiqués were hand-delivered to the newspaper *Tiempo*, in San Cristóbal de las Casas, which in turn faxed the docu-

ments to *La Jornada*, a newspaper based in Mexico City, which has consistently covered the rebellion since 1994. When *La Jornada* went online, the communiqués appeared online as well, and from there websites devoted to the Zapatistas began to appear.

2 CMP/Promedios is not the only organization that has trained and equipped members of indigenous communities in Chiapas. As Axel Köhler signals in his brief discussion of video production in Chiapas, the State Center for Indigenous Language, Arts and Literature (known by its Spanish acronym CELALI) has an audiovisual department and occasionally offers video workshops, but there is little to no continuity with trainees. The INI trained indigenous videomakers from Chiapas through their TMA program, but only one individual, Mariano Estrada Aguilar, has continued to produce work through the Comité de Defensa de la Libertad Indígena. Finally, an Austrian fellow, Thomas Waibel, has trained indigenous individuals in various communities in Chiapas since 1995, through a project called Kinoki-Iumal (2004).

3 I have worked "alongside" some of the CMP project leaders since the late 1990s and the project's founder, Alexandra Halkin, is a personal friend, but I did only a small amount of field research in Chiapas, following Oaxacan videomakers to Ejido Morelia in 1999 to do a training workshop.

4 In Mexico, presidents serve a one-time six-year term, called a *sexenio*. President Felipe Calderón is the second "opposition" president to rule Mexico after Vicente Fox. Both Fox and Calderón are from the right-of-center PAN party.

5 Subcomandante Insurgente Marcos, "About the Wars: A Fragment of the First Letter from Subcomandante Marcos to Don Luis Villoro, beginning the correspondence about Ethics and Politics," My Word Is My Weapon (blog), March 11, 2011, www.mywordismyweapon.blog.spot/2011/02/about-wars-fragment-of-first-letter.html.

6 The fact that Monteforte served as an adviser to the EZLN while still under the employment of the INI, with no direct consequences to his safety or his job, is yet another illustration of the entangled nature of indigenous media in Mexico.

7 *La Jornada*, one of Mexico's only independent newspapers, was created in 1984. The paper and its left-leaning editorial staff have played a significant role in forcing the government to negotiate with peasant organizations, and the paper regularly publishes editorials that are sympathetic to the EZLN.

8 Mariano Estrada, who had just been trained at one of the INI's first workshops, in 1992, participated and taped the march with equipment the INI transferred to his organization, the Comité de Defensa de la Libertad Indígena. He explained to me that they called it the march of the ants because ants always get excited and protest when they are bothered in their little

house (Mariano Estrada, interviewed by the author, 1999, Oaxaca City, Mexico).

9   "Indigenous Peoples," Amnesty International, amnesty.org. Accessed February 4, 2013. www.amnesty.org/en/indigenous-peoples,

10 Alexandra Halkin, interviewed by the author, 1999, Oaxaca City, Mexico.

11 Halkin, interview.

12 Halkin, interview.

13 "Indigenous People Come Together," David Melmer, accessed October 24, 2005. www.indiancountry.com.

14 Halkin, interview.

15 Halkin related to me that they often encountered the aftermath of organizations that came to Chiapas with good intentions but left behind unusable equipment and disappointed community people. Community members would often not receive adequate training, so cameras and televisions would be left unused, consumed by humidity and poor storage conditions. They saw computers that were so old nobody could use them, even people with basic computer skills. Such good intensions amounted to "stuff," essentially electronic waste that took up space in people's homes and gardens. The resulting skepticism was "spoken very clearly to [Halkin and her coworkers], and [Chiapanecans] tested [the workers] for this at first," Halkin said. In her article, she writes, "The Zapatistas needed good equipment and training, not the castoffs from technology-saturated American consumers" (2008, 169).

16 Francisco Vázquez, phone interview with the author, San Cristobal de las Casas, Chiapas, Mexico [his location], 2011.

17 Halkin, interview.

18 Ibid.

19 Ibid.

20 "Community and Self-Representation," interview with Carlos Efraín Pérez Rojas, conducted by Gabriela Zamorano, www.nativenetworks.si.edu, accessed April 2005.

21 Halkin, interview.

22 This photograph of Soraida, taken by Paco Vázquez, is on the cover of *Global Indigenous Media*. As an iconic signifier of indigenous media today, this image suggests a sharp departure from visual representations of indigenous media in the 1990s, which tended to feature Brazilian tribesmen dressed in full-feathered regalia, holding cameras, or even Radio y Video Tamix's logo of a man holding a camera crafted as an ancient Mayan drawing. This in situ portrait, emphasized by Soraida and her infant's direct address to the camera, complements our more nuanced understanding of indigenous media today, one that sees beyond easy contrasts of the traditional and the modern to realities of indigenous peoples' daily struggles to demand or sustain life on equal terms.

23 Vázquez, interview.

24 Halkin, interview.

25 Ibid.

26 "Chiapas: confrontation over control point at Agua Azul leave one dead and several injured." Blog of the International Service for Peace, sipaz.org, "sipazen .wordpress.com/2011/02/07/chiapas-confrontation-over-control-point-at-agua-azul-leaves-one-dead-and-several-injured/," accessed 5 February 2013.

Six. Conclusions

1 Other U.S. festivals include the American Indian Film and Video Competition (in association with the Red Earth Festival), in Oklahoma City; the Two Rivers Native Film and Video Festival, in Minneapolis (also founded in 1991); and the Imagining Indians Festival, which was a galvanizing node of anti-quincentenary activity in 1992. More commercial, independent festivals that regularly feature indigenously produced work are the Sundance Film Festival, in Park City, Utah, and the Taos Talking Pictures Festival, in New Mexico. In Canada, Dreamspeakers: The First Peoples World Film Celebration, in Edmonton, Alberta (launched in 1991), has gained prominence as a festival, and the more recent Terres en Vue (Land in sight), of Montréal, Québec, is becoming a vital forum as well. There are also a number of festivals in Europe that program indigenous work. In Latin America, aside from CLACPI's Festival Americano, there is the Abya-Yala Festival, sponsored by the Confederación de Nacionalidades Indígenas de Ecuador, which takes place in the capital city of Quito, and a newer festival, Geografías Suaves: CINE/VIDEO/SOCIEDAD, based in Mérida, Mexico. (Visit the Native Networks website, sponsored by the National Museum of the American Indian, for more information about indigenous media festivals: www.nativenetworks.si.edu.)

2 Turner remarks in a couple of articles (1991a, 1992a) that the problematic dynamics or "social effects" of videomaking in indigenous communities are not discussed at film festivals (1991a, 74).

3 Quetzaltepec has about 7,000 inhabitants in the municipality proper, and the village's main productive activity, beyond subsistence farming, is coffee cultivation. I did not do field research in Quetzaltepec, but met Gómez at the festival, where *Dulce convivencia* screened and was given a "Best Work" award. Since then, we have had several conversations regarding his work as a mediamaker and that video in particular.

4 Laurel Smith is also a colleague of mine. Her wonderful article "Decolonizing Hybridity" offers more detail and scholarly contextualization about her husband's video (2011).

5 The program was subtitled into English by Laurel Smith. I use her translation.

6 Juan José García, interviewed by the author, 2000, Oaxaca City, Mexico.

7 Ibid.

8 This critique came from an anthropologist from Argentina who was a participant at the international event, delivering her paper on transgender communities in Buenos Aires (L. C. Smith 2011, 21).

9 In addition to the festivals described in this chapter, *Dulce convivencia* has screened in Santiago, Chile, Washington, D.C., New York, Madrid, Barcelona, and Havana, and it screens with some regularity on Isuma TV, which is a web-based platform launched by the Inuit television station in the Nunavuut territory, in Canada.

10 The challenges Gómez faced as his video screened for international audiences reminded me of my last visit to Tama, in 2000. Rather than scrambling solo off the bus as it slowed to a crawl in front of Doña Jose's house, that day I arrived in the company of Guillermo Monteforte, María Santiago Ruiz (a Zapotec videomaker), my husband, two French museum curators from Parc La Villette, in Paris, and their translator, the French sociologist Yvon Le Bot. The La Villette curators were on an initial research trip for a major exhibition on Mexican indigenous cultures, planned for 2002. Genaro and Hermenegildo greeted us at the TV studio where "Video Tamix–Transmisión Especial—5 de Marzo 2000" was displayed on the television monitor. Radio y Video Tamix had been transmitting television locally since 1992, and the "special transmission" appeared to be in honor of the foreign guests. But the disorienting feeling of seeing myself in the Parisians' shoes—of having my outsider status undeniably reconfirmed as I saw the Rojas brothers "perform" for the curators—had more to do with the oddness of the day's transmission, which never moved past the block of text announcing its "special" status. Missing from the relatively long chat with the curators about how the Radio y Video Tamix collective is an instrument of dialogue in the community was the fact that Radio y Video Tamix was in the midst of a stand-off with the local municipal government, which had accused Radio y Video Tamix of secrecy and fiscal irresponsibility. The special transmission in this context was thus as much of a disclaimer to community authorities as it was a gesture in honor of foreign visitors, but as far as I know the curators were never made aware of Radio y Video Tamix's precarious status.

REFERENCES

Abercrombie, Thomas. 1991. "To Be Indian, to Be Bolivian: Ethnic and National Discourses of Identity." In *Nation-States and Indians in Latin America*. Edited by G. Urban and J. Sherzer, 95–130. Austin: University of Texas Press.

———. 1998. *Pathways of Memory and Power: Ethnography and History among an Andean People*. Madison: University of Wisconsin Press.

Aguirre Beltrán, Gonzalo. 1969. "El indigenismo y su contribución al dearrollo de la idea de nacionalidad." *América Indígena* 29 (2): 397–406.

Alia, Valerie. 2010. *The New Nations Media: Indigenous Peoples and Global Communications*. New York: Berghahn.

Alonso, Ana María. 1994. "The Politics of Space, Time and Substance: State Formation, Nationalism and Ethnicity." *Annual Review of Anthropology* 23: 379–405.

Anaya, S. J. 2004. *Indigenous Peoples in International Law*. Oxford: Oxford University Press.

Anderson, Benedict. 1991. *Imagined Communities: Reflections on the Origin and Spread of Nationalism*. New York: Verso.

Appadurai, Arjun. 1986. Introduction to *The Social Life of Things: Commodities in Cultural Perspective*. Edited by A. Appadurai, 3–63. Cambridge: Cambridge University Press.

———. 1990. "Disjuncture and Difference in Global Cultural Economy." *Public Culture* 2 (2): 1–24.

———. 1991. "Global Ethnoscapes: Notes and Queries for a Transnational Anthropology." In *Recapturing Anthropology: Working in the Present*. Edited by R. G. Fox, 191–210. Santa Fe: School of American Research.

———. 1996. *Modernity at Large: Cultural Dimensions of Globalization*. Minneapolis: University of Minnesota Press.

———. 2000. "Grassroots Globalization and the Research Imagination." *Public Culture* 12 (1): 1–19.

———. 2002. "Deep Democracy: Urban Governmentality and the Horizon of Politics." *Public Culture* 14 (1): 21–47.

Arizpe, Lourdes. 1996. "Chiapas: The Basic Problems." *Identities: Global Studies in Culture and Power* 3 (1–2): 219–33.

Aufderheide, Patricia. 1993. "Latin American Grassroots Video: Beyond Television." *Public Culture* 5 (3): 569–92.

———. 1995. "The Video in the Villages Project: Videomaking with and by Brazilian Indians." *Visual Anthropology Review* 11 (2): 83–93.

Bakhtin, Mikhail. 1981. *The Dialogic Imagination: Four Essays.* Translated by C. Emerson. Austin: University of Texas Press.

Barabas, Alicia. 1998. "Reorganización etnopolítica y territorial: Caminos Oaxaqueños para la autonomía." In *Autonomía, etnicas y estados nacionales.* Edited by A. M. Barabas and M. A. Bartolomé, 343–66. Mexico City: Instituto Nacional de Antropología e Historia.

Bartolomé, Miguel A., and Alicia M. Barabas. 1986. "La pluralidad desigual en Oaxaca." In *Etnicidad y plurarlismo cultural: La dinámica etnica en Oaxaca.* Edited by A. M. Barabas and M. A. Bartolomé, 15–95. Mexico City: Consejo Nacional para la Cultura y las Artes.

———. 1996. *La pluralidad en peligro.* Mexico City: Instituto Nacional de Antropología e Historia and INI.

———. 1998. Introdución to *Autonomías, etnicas y estados nacionales.* Edited by A. M. Barabas and M. A. Bartolomé, 13–30. Mexico City: Instituto Nacional de Antropología e Historia.

Beals, Ralph L. 1973 [1945]. *Ethnology of the Western Mixe.* New York: Cooper Square.

Bedoya, Ricardo. 1995. "El cine tema indígena en Peru." In *Pueblos indígenas de América Latina y el Caribe: Catálogo de cine y video.* Edited by B. Bermúdez Rothe, 61–64. Caracas: Biblioteca Nacional de Venezuela.

Benjamin, Walter. 1978. *Reflections: Walter Benjamin.* Edited by Peter Demetz. New York: Harcourt Brace Jovanovich.

Bermúdez Rothe, Beatríz. 1995. Introduction to *Pueblos indígenas de América Latina y el Caribe: Catálogo de cine y video.* Edited by B. Bermúdez Rothe, 7–20. Caracas: Biblioteca Nacional de Venezuela.

Bhabha, Homi K. 1994. *The Location of Culture.* New York: Routledge.

Bonfil Batalla, Guillermo. 1970. "Del indigenismo de la revolución a la antropología critia." In *De eso que llaman la antropología Mexicana.* Edited by A. A. Warman and A. Warman, 39–65. Mexico City: AENAH.

———. 1978. "Admitimos que los indios no nacieron equivocados." In *INI 30 Años despues: Revision crítica.* Edited by J. Carreño Carlon, 149–50. Mexico City: INI.

———. 1996. *México Profundo: Reclaiming a Civilization.* Translated by P. A. Denis. Austin: University of Texas Press.

Bourdieu, Pierre. 1993. *The Field of Cultural Production.* New York: Columbia University Press.

Boyle, Dierdre. 1992. "From Portapak to Camcorder: A Brief History of Guerrilla Television." *Journal of Film and Video* 44 (1/2): 67–79.

———. 1997. *Subject to Change: Guerilla Television Revisited.* New York: Oxford University Press.

Brígido-Corachan, Anna. 2004. "An Interview with Juan José García, President of Ojo de Agua Comunicación." *American Anthropologist* 106 (2): 368–73.

Brysk, Alyson. 1994. "Acting Globally: Indian Rights and International Politics in Latin America." In *Indigenous Peoples and Democracy in Latin America.* Edited by D. L. Van Cott, 29–51. New York: St. Martin's.

———. 2000. *From Tribal Village to Global Village: Indian Rights and International Relations in Latin America.* Stanford, CA: Stanford University Press.

Cadena, Marisol de la. 2000. *Indigenous Mestizos: The Politics of Race and Culture in Cuzco, Peru, 1919–1991.* Durham, NC: Duke University Press.

Campbell, Howard, Leigh Binford, Miguel Bartolomé, and Alicia Barabas. 1993. *Zapotec Struggles: Histories, Politics, and Representation from Juchitán, Oaxaca.* Washington, DC: Smithsonian Institution.

Carelli, Vincent, and Dominique Gallois. 1995. "Video in the Villages: The Waiapi Experience." Working Paper. Center for Media, Culture and History, NYU.

Caso, Alfonso. 1953. "Beneficencia e indigenismo." *América indígena, Mexico* 13 (4): 259–62.

———. 1978. "Un experimento de anthropología social en México." In *INI 30 Años Despues: Revisión crítica.* Edited by J. C. Carlon, 83–86. Mexico City: INI.

Castells-Talens, Antoni. 2004. "The Negotiation of Indigenist Radio Policy in Mexico." Ph.D. diss., University of Florida.

———. 2011. "¿Ni indígena ni comunitaria? La radio indigenista en tiempos neoindigenistas." *Nueva época* 15 (January–June): 123–42.

CDI (Comisión Nacional para el Desarrollo de los Pueblos Indígenas). 2004. *Consulta a los pueblos indígenas sobre sus formas y aspiraciones de desarrollo: Informe final.* Mexico City: CDI.

CLACPI (Centro Latino). 1999. *Declaración de X'e Lajoj N'oj (Quetzaltenango).* VI Festival Americano de Cine y Video de los Pueblos Indígenas, Quetzaltenango, Guatemala.

Clark, Colin. 2000. *Class, Ethnicity, and Community in Southern Mexico.* Oxford: Oxford University Press.

Cohodas, Marvin. 1997. *Basketweavers for the California Curio Trade: Elizabeth Louise Hickox.* Tucson: University of Arizona Press.

Collier, George A. 2008 [1994]. *Basta! Land and the Zapatista Rebellion in Chiapas.* 3rd ed. Oakland, CA: Food First.

Cook, Scott, and Jong-Taick Joo. 1995. "Ethnicity and Economy in Rural Mexico: A Critique of the Indigenista Approach." *Latin American Research Review* 30 (2): 33–60.

Córdova, Amalia, and Juan Francisco Salazar. 2008. "Imperfect Media and the Poetics of Indigenous Video in Latin America." In *Global Indigenous Media: Cultures, Poetics, and Politics.* Edited by Pamela Wilson and Michelle Stewart, 39–57. Durham, NC: Duke University Press.

Cornelius, Wayne A., Jonathan Fox, and Ann L. Craig. 1994. "Mexico's National Solidarity Program: An Overview." In *Transforming State-Society Relations in Mexico*. Edited by W. A. Cornelius, J. Fox, and A. L. Craig, 3–26. San Diego: Center for U.S.-Mexican Studies, UCSD.

Cortéz, Margarita M. 1998. "Autonomía y diversidad en el mundo mixe." In *Autonomías étnicas y estados nacionales*. Edited by M. Bartolomé and A. Barabas, 461–70. Mexico City: Instituto Nacional de Antropología e Historia.

Cremoux, Daniela. 1997. "Video indígena, dos casos en la sierra Mixe." BA thesis, Universidad Intercontinental.

Cultural Survival. 1999. "The San Andrés Accords on Indigenous Rights and Culture." In *Cultural Survival Quarterly* 23 (1): 33–38.

CVI (Centro de Video Indígena). 1996. *Taller introductorio de video indígena*. Oaxaca City, Mexico: Centro de Video Indígena, INI.

Daes, Erica-Irene. 1993. "Discrimination against Indigenous Peoples: Explanatory Note Concerning the Draft Declaration on the Rights of Indigenous Peoples." United Nations Economic and Social Council, Commission on Human Rights, July 19. UN Document E/CN.4/Sub. 2/1993/26/Add.1. New York.

Díaz Polanco, Hector. 1987. *Etnia, nación y política*. Mexico City: Editor SA Mexicali.

——. 1991. *Autonomía regional: La autodeterminación de los pueblos indios*. Mexico City: Siglo Veintiuno Editores, S.A. de C.V.

——. 1997. *Indigenous Peoples in Latin America: The Quest for Self-Determination*. Boulder: Westview.

Escobar, Arturo. 2001. "Culture Sits in Places: Reflections on Globalism and Subaltern Strategies of Location." *Political Geography* 20: 139–74.

Esteva, Gustavo, and Madhu Suri Prakash. 1998. *Grassroots Post-Moderism: Remaking the Soil of Cultures*. New York: Zed Books.

Estrada, Mariano. 1994. *Marcha x'nich/March of the Ants*. Video.

Evans, Michael Robert. 2008. *Isuma: Inuit Video Art*. Montreal: McGill-Queens University Press.

EZLN (Ejército Zapatista de Liberación Nacional). 2001. Communiqué. April 30, 2001.

Fabregas, Andres. 1978. "El indigenism necesita una nueva teoria y, sobre ella, reelaborar una nueva praxis." In *INI 30 años despues: Revisión critica*. Edited by J. C. Carlon, 131–38. Mexico City: INI.

Faris, James. 1992. "Anthropological Transparency: Film, Representation, and Politics." In *Film as Ethnography*. Edited by P. Crawford and D. Turton, 171–82. Manchester, UK: Manchester University Press.

——. 1993. "Radioactive Waste, 'Indigenous Media,' and Anthropological Transparency: A Response to Terence Turner." *Anthropology Review* 9 (1): 12–13.

Flores y Ascencio, Daniel. 2002. "Bolivian Links: Interview with Julia Mosúa, Albredo Copa and Marcelino Pinto." *BOMB* 78 (winter): 30–35.

Foucault, Michel. 1978. *The History of Sexuality, Vol. 1, an Introduction*. Translated by R. Hurley. New York: Pantheon.

Foweraker, Joe. 1990. "Popular Movements and Political Change in Mexico." In *Popular Movements and Political Change in Mexico*. Edited by A. L. Craig and J. Foweraker, 3–20. Boulder: Lynne Rienner.

Fox, Jonathan. 1994. "Targeting the Poorest: The Role of the National Indigenous Institute in Mexico's Solidarity Program." In *Transforming State-Society Relations in Mexico*. Edited by W. A. Cornelius, J. Fox, and A. L. Craig, 179–216. San Diego: Center for U.S.-Mexican Studies, UCSD.

——. 2000. "Introductory Notes for Framing Our Discussions." Paper presented at the Center for Global, International and Regional Studies. University of California, Santa Cruz.

Fox, Richard G., and Orin Starn. 1997. Introduction to *Between Resistance and Revolution: Cultural Politics and Social Protest*. Edited by R. G. Fox and O. Starn, 1–16. New Brunswick, NJ: Rutgers University Press.

Gamio, Manuel. 1916. *Forjando patria*. Mexico City: Porrua.

——. 1935. *Hacia un México nuevo: Problemas sociales*. Mexico City: Instituto Indigenista Interamericano.

García Canclini, Néstor. 1989. *Culturas híbridas: Estrategias para entrar y salir de la modernidad*. Mexico City: Consejo Nacional para la Cultura y las Artes and Editorial Grijalbo, S.A. de C.V.

——. 2001. *Consumers and Citizens: Globalization and Multicultural Conflicts*. Minneapolis: University of Minnesota Press.

Gillespie, Marie. 1997. "Local Uses of the Media: Negotiating Culture and Identity." In *Media in Global Context: A Reader*. Edited by A. Sreberny-Mohammadi, D. Winseck, J. McKenna, and O. Boyd-Barret, 323–37. London: Arnold.

Ginsburg, Faye. 1991. "Indigenous Media: Faustian Contract or Global Village?" *Cultural Anthropology* 6 (1): 92–112.

——. 1993a. "Aboriginal Media and the Australian Imaginary." *Public Culture* 5 (3): 557–78.

——. 1993b. "Mediating Culture: Indigenous Media, Ethnographic Film and the Production of Identity." In *Fields of Vision: Essays in Film Studies, Visual Anthropology and Photography*. Edited by L. Devereaux and R. Hillman, 256–91. Berkeley: University of California Press.

——. 1993c. "Station Identification: The Aboriginal Programs Unit of the Australian Broadcasting Corporation." *Visual Anthropology Review* 9 (2): 92–96.

——. 1994a. "Culture / Media: A (Mild) Polemic." *Anthropology Today* 10 (2): 5–15.

——. 1994b. "Embedded Aesthetics: Creating Discursive Space for Indigenous Media." *Cultural Anthropology* 9 (3): 365–82.

——. 1995a. "Parallax Effect: The Impact of Aboriginal Media on Ethnographic Film." *Visual Anthropology Review* 11 (2): 64–76.

———. 1995b. "Production Values: Indigenous Media and the Rhetoric of Self-Determination." In *Rhetorics of Self-Making*. Edited by D. Battaglia, 121–38. Berkeley: University of California Press.

———. 1997. "'From Little Things, Big Things Grow': Indigenous Media and Cultural Activism." In *Between Resistance and Revolution: Cultural Politics and Social Protest*. Edited by R. G. Fox and O. Starn, 118–44. New Brunswick, NJ: Rutgers University Press.

———. 2002. "Screen Memories: Resignifying the Traditional in Indigenous Media." In *Media Worlds: Anthropology on New Terrain*. Edited by F. Ginsburg, L. Abu-Lughod, and B. Larkin, 39–57. Berkeley: University of California Press.

———. 2008. "Rethinking the Digital Age." In *Global Indigenous Media: Cultures, Poetics, and Politics*. Edited by Pam Wilson and Michelle Stewart, 287–334. Durham, NC: Duke University Press.

Ginsburg, Faye, Lila Abu-Lughod, and Brian Larkin. 2002. "The Social Practice of Media: An Introduction." In *Media Worlds: Anthropology on New Terrain*. Edited by F. Ginsburg, L. Abu-Lughod, and B. Larkin, 1–37. Berkeley: University of California Press.

Gupta, Akhil. 1995. "Blurred Boundaries: The Discourse of Corruption, the Culture of Politics and the Imagined State." *American Ethnologist* 22 (2): 375–402.

Gupta, Akhil, and James Ferguson. 1997. "Discipline and Practice: 'The Field' as Site, Method and Location in Anthropology." In *Anthropological Locations: Boundaries and Grounds of a Field Science*. Edited by A. Gupta and J. Ferguson, 1–46. Berkeley: University of California Press.

Guss, David. 2000. *The Festive State: Race, Ethnicity, and Nationalism as Cultural Performance*. Berkeley: University of California Press.

Hale, Charles R. 1994. *Resistance and Contradiction: Miskitu Indians and the Nicaraguan State, 1894–1987*. Stanford, CA: Stanford University Press.

———. 2002. "Does Multiculturalism Menace: Governance, Cultural Rights, and the Politics of Identity in Guatemala." *Journal of Latin American Studies* 34: 485–524.

———. 2008. Introduction to *Engaging Contradictions: Theory, Politics, and Methods of Activist Scholarship*. Edited by C. Hale, 1–28. Berkeley: University of California Press.

Halkin, Alexandra. 2008. "Outside the Lens: Zapatista and Autonomous Videomaking." In *Global Indigenous Media: Cultures, Poetics, and Politics*. Edited by Pamela Wilson and Michelle Stewart, 160–80. Durham, NC: Duke University Press.

Hall, Stuart. 1992. "Cultural Studies and Its Theoretical Legacies." In *Cultural Studies*. Edited by L. Grossberg, 277–94. New York: Routledge.

———. 1996. Introduction to *Questions of Cultural Identity*. Edited by S. Hall and P. du Gay, 1–17. London: Sage.

Hannerz, Ulf. 1997. "Notes on the Global Ecumene." In *Media in Global Context: A Reader*. Edited by A. Sreberny-Mohammadi, J. McKenna, D. Winseck, and O. Boyd-Barret, 11–18. London: Edward Arnold.

Harvey, Neil. 2005 [1998]. *The Chiapas Rebellion: The Struggle for Land and Democracy*. 5th ed. Durham, NC: Duke University Press.

Hellman, Judith Alder. 1995. "The Riddle of New Social Movements: Who They Are and What They Do." In *Capital, Power and Inequality in Latin America*. Edited by S. Halebsky and R. L. Harris, 165–83. Boulder: Westview.

Hernández, Rosala Aída, Sarela Paz, and María Teresa Sierra, eds. 2004. *El estado y los indígenas en los tiempos del PAN*. Mexico City: CIESAS, Miguel Angel Porrua, and Cámara de Diputados de México.

Hernández Díaz, Jorge. 1998. "Las organizaciones indígenas en Oaxaca." In *Autonomías étnicas y estados nacionales*. Edited by A. M. Barabas and M. A. Bartolomé, 385–411. Mexico City: Instituto Nacional de Antropología e Historia.

Herrasti, Lourdes. 1989. "Instituto Nacional Indigenista." In *Las Instituciones*. Vol. 7. Edited by M. Mejía Sanchéz, 240–65. Mexico City: Instituto Nacional de Antropología e Historia.

Himpele, Jeff D. 1996. "Film Distribution as Media: Mapping Difference in the Bolivian Cinemascape." *Visual Anthropology Review* 12 (1): 47–66.

———. 2008. *Circuits of Culture: Media, Politics, and Indigenous Identity in the Andes*. Minneapolis: University of Minnesota Press.

Hindley, Jane. 1996. "Towards a Pluricultural Nation: The Limits of *Indigenismo* and Article 4." In *Dismantling the Mexican State*. Edited by R. Aitken, N. Craske, G. A. Jones, and D. E. Standfield, 225–43. London: Macmillan.

ILO (International Labour Organization). 1989. C169: Indigenous and Tribal Peoples Convention.

———. 2009. *Indigenous and Tribal Peoples' Rights in Practice: A Guide to ILO Convention No. 169*. Geneva: International Labour Standards Department.

INI (Instituto Nacional Indigenista). 1955a. *¿Que es el INI?* Mexico City: INI.

———. 1955b. "Teatro Petúl." *Acción Indigenista* 24 (June).

———. 1978. *INI 30 años despues: Revisión crítica*. Mexico City: INI.

———. 1990a. *Hacia un video indio*. Cuadernos del INI 2. Edited by Graciela Anaya. Mexico City: INI.

———. 1990b. "Políticas y tareas indigenistas 1989–1994." *Boletín Indigenista* 2 (4).

———. 1994a. *Instituto nacional indigenista 1989–1994*. Mexico City: INI.

———. 1994b. *Encuento interamericano de videoastas indígenas: Transferencia de medios audiovisuales a organizaciones y comunidades indígenas*. La Trinidad, Tlaxcala: Encuento Interamericano de Videoastas Indígenas.

Joseph, Gilbert M., and David Nugent. 1994. "Popular Culture and State Formation in Revolutionary Mexico." In *Everyday Forms of State Formation: Revolution and the Negotiation of Rule in Modern Mexico*. Edited by G. M. Joseph and D. Nugent, 4–23. Durham, NC: Duke University Press.

Juhasz, Alex. 1995. AIDS TV: Identity, Community, and Alternative Video. Durham, NC: Duke University Press.

Julián Caballero, Emigdio. 1994. "La T.V. no es realidad." In *Muestra interamericana de videoastas indígenas.* 8–9. Mexico City: INI.

Knight, Alan. 1990. "Racism, Revolution and *Indigenismo*: Mexico, 1910–1940." In *The Idea of Race in Latin America, 1870–1940.* Edited by R. Graham, 71–113. Austin: University of Texas Press.

——. 1994. "Solidarity: Historical Continuities and Contemporary Implications." In *Transforming State-Society Relations in Mexico.* Edited by W. A. Cornelius, J. Fox, and A. L. Craig, 29–45. San Diego: Center for U.S.-Mexican Studies, UCSD.

Köhler, Axel. 2004. "Nuestros antepasados no tenían cámaras: El video como machete y otros retos de la video-producción indígena en Chiapas, México." *Revista Chilena de antropologia visual* 4: 391–406.

Kourí, Emilio H. 2002. "Interpreting the Expropriation of Indian Pueblo Lands in Porfirian Mexico: The Unexamined Legacies of Andrés Molina Enríquez." *Hispanic American Historical Review* 82 (1): 69–117.

Kuroda, Etzuko. 1984. *Under Mt. Zempoaltépetl: Highland Mixe Society and Ritual.* Osaka: National Museum of Ethnology.

——. 1994. "Los mixes ante la nación: Retrospectiva y perspectiva." In *Fuentes Etnológicas para el Estudio de los Pueblos Ayuuk (Mixes) del Estado de Oaxaca.* Edited by S. Nahmad Sittón, 543–49. Oaxaca City, Mexico: CIESAS.

Larkin, Brian. 2002. "Indian Films and Nigerian Lovers: Media and the Creation of Parallel Modernities." In *The Anthropology of Globalization: A Reader.* Edited by J. X. Inda and R. Rosaldo, 350–78. Oxford: Blackwell.

Le Bot, Yvon. 1992. *Guatemala: Violencia, revolución y democracia.* Guatemala City: FLASCO, Centro de Estudios Mexicanos y Centro Americanos.

——. 1997. *El sueño Zapatista: Entrevistas con el subcomandante Marcos, el mayor moisés y el comandante tacho del ejercito de liberación nacional.* Barcelona: Plaza y Janés.

——. 2005. "Indian Movements in Latin America: A Historical Reversal." Paper presented at the Centre for Research in Ethnic Relations, University of Warwick, Coventry, England, February 18.

Lee, Benjamin, and Edward LiPuma. 2002. "Cultures of Circulation: The Imaginations of Modernity." *Public Culture* 14 (1): 191–213.

Leuthold, Steven. 1998. *Indigenous Aesthetics: Native Art, Media, and Identity.* Austin: University of Texas Press.

Levi, Jerome. 2002. "A New Dawn or a Cycle Restored? Regional Dynamics and Cultural Politics in Indigenous Mexico, 1978–2001." In *The Politics of Ethnicity: Indigenous Peoples in Latin American States.* Edited by David Maybury-Lewis, 3–49. Cambridge, MA: Harvard University Press.

Mahon, Maureen. 2000. "The Visible Evidence of Cultural Producers." *Annual Review of Anthropology* 29: 467–92.

Maldonado, Benjamin. 1998. "Obstáculos internos para la construcción de autonomías indias: Una perspectiva desde Oaxaca." In *Autonomías étnicas y estados nacionales*. Edited by A. M. Barabas and M. A. Bartolomé, 367–84. Mexico City: Instituto Nacional de Antropología e Historia.

Mallon, Florencia E. 1995. *Peasant and Nation: The Making of Postcolonial Mexico and Peru*. Berkeley: University of California Press.

Marcus, George E. 1995. "Ethnography in/of the World System: The Emergence of Multi-Sited Ethnography." *Annual Review of Anthropology* 24: 95–117.

———. 1996. Introduction to *Connected: Engagements with Media*. Edited by G. Marcus, 1–18. Chicago: University of Chicago Press.

Marés de Souza, Carlos Federico. 1992. "On Brazil and Its Indian." In *Indigenous Peoples and Democracy in Latin America*. Edited by D. L. Van Cott, 213–33. New York: St. Martin's.

Marks, Laura. 1994. "Reconfigured Nationhood: A Partisan History of the Inuit Broadcasting Corporation." *AfterImage* 21 (8): 4–8.

Martín-Barbero, Jesús. 1988. "Communication from Culture: The Crisis of the National and the Emergence of the Popular." *Media, Culture and Society* 10:447–65.

———. 1993. *Communication, Culture and Hegemony: From the Media to Mediations*. Translated by E. Fox and R. A. White. London: Sage.

Martínez Luna, Jaime. 1977. "Aquí el que manda es el pueblo." *Revista Cuadernos Agrarios* 5: 1–16.

———. 1993. "¿Es la comunidad nuestra identidad?" In *Movimientos indígenas contemporaneos en México*. Edited by A. A. Warman and A. Warman, 157–70. Mexico City: Centro de Investigaciones Interdiciplinarias en Humanidades, UNAM.

———. 1995. "Comunalidad y Autonomia." Working Paper. Comunalidad A.C. Guelatao de Juárez, Oaxaca.

Martinez, Wilton. 1992. "Who Constructs Anthropological Knowledge? Toward a Theory of Ethnographic Film Spectatorship." In *Film as Ethnography*. Edited by P. I. Crawford and D. Turton, 131–61. Manchester, UK: University of Manchester Press.

Marubbio, M. Elise. 2010. "Introduction to Native American/Indigenous Film." *Postscript: Essays in Film and the Humanities* 29 (3): 3–12.

Masayesva, Victor, Jr. 1995. "The Emerging Native American Aesthetics in Film and Video." *Felix* 2 (1): 156–60.

Masferrer Kan, Elio R. 1989. "Instituto indigenista interamericano." In *Las Instituciones*. Vol. 7. Edited by M. Mejía Sanchéz, 155–79. Mexico City: Instituto Nacional de Antropología e Historia.

Mattiace, Shannan. 1997. "Zapata Vive! The EZLN, Indian Politics and the Autonomy Movement in Mexico." *Journal of Latin American Anthropology* 3 (1): 32–71.

——. 1998. "Indian Autonomy in Mexico: Alternative Nationalisms and the Politics of Difference." Paper presented at the Annual Meeting of the Latin American Studies Association, Chicago.

Menezes, Claudia. 1995. "La filmografía Brasileña de temática indígena." In *Pueblos indígenas de América Latina y el Caribe: Catálogo de cine y video*. Edited by B. Bermúdez Rothe, 21–30. Caracas: Biblioteca Nacional de Venezuela.

Michaels, Eric. 1985. "Constraints on Knowledge in an Economy of Oral Information." *Current Anthropology* 2: 505–10.

——. 1994. *Bad Aboriginal Art: Tradition, Media, and Technological Horizons*. Minneapolis: University of Minnesota Press.

Miller, David. 1995. *Anthropology, Modernity and Consumption*. London: Routledge.

Miller, Toby. 1993. *The Well-Tempered Self: Citizenship, Culture and the Postmodern Subject*. Baltimore: Johns Hopkins University Press.

Monteforte, Guillermo. 1992. *Pidiendo vida/Petition to Life*. Edited by G. Monteforte. Mexico City: INI.

——. 1996. *INI plan de trabajo 1996–1997*. Oaxaca: Centro de Video Indígena.

Moore, Rachel. 1994. "Marketing Alterity." In *Visualizing Theory: Selected Essays from V.A.R., 1990–1994*. Edited by L. Taylor, 126–39. New York: Routledge.

Morely, David. 1991. "Where the Global Meets the Local: Notes from the Sitting Room." *Screen* 32 (1): 1–15.

Muenala, Alberto. 1995. "Cinema as an Instrument for Indigenous Peoples." *Felix* 2 (1): 154–56.

Muñoz Jimenez, Alfonso. 1990. "Palabras de bienvenida." In *Hacia un video indio*. Edited by Graciela Anaya, 9. Mexico: INI.

Myers, Fred. 1994. "Culture-Making: Performing Aboriginality at the Asia Society Gallery." *American Ethnologist* 21 (4): 679–99.

——. 1996. "Framing Aboriginal Art: The Circulation of Western Desert Acrylic Painting." Seminar Paper, "Material Culture: Habitus and Values," Advanced Seminar, November 3–7, School of American Research, Santa Fe.

Myers, Fred, and George E. Marcus. 1995. "The Traffic in Art and Culture: An Introduction." In *Traffic in Culture: Refiguring Art and Anthropology*. Edited by F. Myers and G. E. Marcus, 1–54. Berkeley: University of California Press.

Nahmad Sittón, Salomón. 1965. *Los Mixes: Estudio social y cultural de la region del Zempoaltepetl y del ismo de Tehuantepec*. Mexico City: INI.

——. 1994a. "Introducción: Visión retrospectiva y prospectiva del pueblo Mixe." In *Fuentes etnológicas para el estudio de los pueblos Ayuuk (Mixes) del estado de Oaxaca*. Edited by S. Nahmad Sittón, 11–49. Oaxaca City: CIESAS.

——. 1994b. "Frontera territorial e identidad etnica de los Mixes." In *Fuentes etnológicas para el estudio de los pueblos Ayuuk (Mixes) del estado de Oaxaca*. Edited by S. Nahmad Sittón, 535–42. Oaxaca City, Mexico: CIESAS.

Neizen, Ronald. 2003. *The Origins of Indigenism: Human Rights and the Politics of Identity*. Berkeley: University of California Press.

Nolasco Armas, Margarita. 1970. "La antropología aplicada en México y su destino final: El indigenismo." In *De eso que llaman antropología Mexicana*. Edited by A. E. A. Warman, 66–93. Mexico City: AENAH.

Ojo de Agua. 2001. *Plan de trabajo: Tres años*. Oaxaca: Ojo de Agua Comunicación A.C.

———. 2009. *Resumen del plan rector, Junio 2009–Mayo 2011*. Oaxaca: Ojo de Agua Comunicación A.C.

———. 2011. *Plan Rector 2010–2012*. Oaxaca: Ojo de Agua Comunicación A.C.

OMVIAC (Organización Mexicana de Videoastas Indígenas). 1994. OMVIAC brochure.

———. 1994. *Organización Mexicana de videoastas indígenas A.C.* Oaxaca City, Mexico: n.p.

Palattella, John. 1998. "Pictures of Us: Are Native Videomakers Putting Anthropologists Out of Business?" *Lingua Franca* 8 (5): 50–57.

Pardo, María Teresa. 1994. "El territorio, la demografía y la lengua de los Ayuuk." In *Fuentes etnológicas para el estudio de los pueblos Ayuuk (Mixes) del estado de Oaxaca*. Edited by S. Nahmad Sittón, 571–612. Oaxaca City, Mexico: CIESAS.

Postero, Nancy Grey. 2007. *Now We Are Citizens: Indigenous Politics in Postmulticultural Bolivia*. Stanford, CA: Stanford University Press.

Prins, Harald. 1989. "American Indians and the Ethnographic Complex: From Native Participation to Production Control." In *Eyes across the Water: The Amsterdam Conference of Visual Anthropology*. Edited by R. B. Flaes, 80–90. Amsterdam: Het Spinhuis.

———. 1993. "Ethnocinematic Self-Fashioning as Cultural Process." Paper presented at the Annual Meeting of the American Anthropological Association, Washington, DC.

———. 1997. "The Paradox of Primitivism: Native Rights and the Problem of Imagery in Cultural Survival Films." *Visual Anthropology* 9: 1–24.

Quintana, Roberto Diego. 1998. "Financiamiento rural social: Los fondos regionales de solidaridad en retrovisión y en perspectiva." *Cuadernos Agrarios* 40 (3): 47–58.

Raheja, Michelle H. 2010. *Reservation Reelism: Redfacing, Visual Sovereignty, and Representations of Native Americans in Film*. Lincoln: University of Nebraska Press.

Recondo, David. 2001. "Usos y costumbres, procesos electorales y autonomía indígena en Oaxaca." In *Costumbres, leyes y movimiento indio en Oaxaca y Chiapas*. Edited by Lourdes de León Pasquel, 91–113. Mexico City: CIESAS, Grupo Editorial Miguel Angel Porrúa.

———. 2007. *La política del gatopardo: Multiculturalism y democracia en Oaxaca*. Mexico City: Casa Chata.

Regino Montes, Adelfo. 1998. "La reconstrucción de los pueblos indígenas." In *Autonomías etnicas y estados nacionales*. Edited by M. Bartolomé and A. Barabas, 415–24. Mexico City: Instituto Nacional de Antropología e Historia.

Rendón, Juan José. 2003. *La comunidad: Modo de vida en los pueblos indíos*. Mexico City: CONACULTA, Dirección General de Culturas Populares e Indígenas Rivera-Salgado.

Rendón, Juan José, and Ballesteros Rojo. 1999. "Welcome to Oaxacalifornia." *Cultural Survival Quarterly* (spring): 59–61.

Rodriquez Ramos, José M., and Antoni Castells-Talens. 2010. "The Training of Indigenous Videomakers by the Mexican State: Negotiation, Politics and Media." *Postscript: Essays in Film and the Humanities* 29 (3): 83–105.

Rogers, Gerry, Eddy Lee, Lee Swepston, and Jasmien Van Daele. 2009. *The International Labour Organization and the Quest for Social Justice, 1919–2009*. Ithaca: Cornell University Press and the International Labour Organization. www.ilo.org/global/About_the_ILO/lang-en/index.htm.

Rony, Fatimah Tobing. 1994–95. "Victor Masayesva, Jr. and the Politics of *Imagining Indians.*" *Film Quarterly* 48 (2): 20–33.

Rosaldo, Renato. 1995. Foreword to *Hybrid Cultures: Strategies for Entering and Leaving Modernity*. Edited by N. García Canclini, xi–xvii. Minneapolis: University of Minnesota Press.

Roth, Lorna. 1994. "Northern Voices and Mediating Structures: The Emergence and Development of First Peoples Television Broadcasting in the Canadian North." Ph.D. diss., Concordia University.

Roth, Lorna, and Gail Guthrie Valaskakis. 1989. "Aboriginal Broadcasting in Canada: A Case Study in Democratization." In *Communication for and against Democracy*. Edited by M. Raboy and P. A. Buck, 221–34. Montreal: Black Rose.

Rouse, Roger. 2002. "Mexican Migration and the Social Space of Postmodernism." In *The Anthropology of Globalization: A Reader*. Edited by J. X. Inda and R. Rosaldo, 157–71. Oxford: Blackwell.

Ruby, Jay. 1991. "Speaking for, Speaking about, Speaking with or Speaking Alongside: An Anthropological and Documentary Dilemma." *Visual Anthropology Review* 7 (2): 50–67.

Saldívar, Emiko. 2001. "Del indigenismo revolucionario al indigenismo neoliberal." Research Seminar, Center for U.S.-Mexican Studies, UCSD.

———. 2008. *Prácticas quotidianas del estado: Una etnografia del indigenismo*. Mexico City: Universidad Iberoamericana Cuidad de México/Plaza y Valdes.

Sámano Chong, Javier. 1992. "La experiencia del video con grupos indígenas en México." Simposio de antropología visual, CLACPI, Cusco, Peru.

Sanjinés, Iván. 1995. "Panorama del cine y video en Bolivia." In *Pueblos indígenas de América Latina y el Caribe: Catálogo de cine y video*. Edited by B. Bermúdez Rothe, 31–44. Caracas: Biblioteca Nacional de Venezuela.

———. 1997. *Proyecto del Plan Nacional de Comunicación Audiovisual Indígena/ Bolivia*. La Paz, Bolivia: CEFREC.

Sarmiento Silva, Sergio. 1991. "Movimientos indígenas y participación política." In *Nuevos enfoques para el estudio de etnias indígenas en México*. Edited by A. Warman and A. Argueta, 411–19. Mexico City: Centro de Investigaciones Interdisciplinarias en Humanidades, UNAM.

Sarmiento Silva, Sergio, and Consuelo Mejía. 1987. *Lucha indígena: un reto a la ortodoxia*. Mexico City: Siglo XXI.

Schiwy, Freya. 2009. *Indianizing Film: Decolonization, the Andes, and the Question of Technology*. New Brunswick, NJ: Rutgers University Press.

SEDESOL. 1994. *Diagnóstico de los Pueblos Indígenas de Oaxaca*. Mexico City: SEDESOL.

Singer, Beverly. 1994. "Replaying the Native Experience." *Independent* 17 (10): 21–24.

———. 2001a. "Video América Indígena/Video Native America." *Wicazo SA Review* (summer): 35–53.

———. 2001b. *Wiping the War Paint off the Lens: Native American Film and Video*. Minneapolis: University of Minnesota Press.

Smith, Carol. 1991. "Maya Nationalism." *NACLA Report on the Americas* 25 (3): 29–33.

Smith, Laurel Catherine. 2005. "Mediating Indigenous Identity: Video, Advocacy, and Knowledge in Oaxaca, Mexico." Ph.D. diss., University of Kentucky, Lexington.

———. 2008. "The Search of Well-Being: Placing Development with Indigenous Identity." In *Global Indigenous Media: Cultures, Poetics, and Politics*. Edited by Pamela Wilson and Michelle Stewart, 184–96. Durham, NC: Duke University Press.

———. 2011. "Articulating Indigenous Video: Diffraction, Audience and the Politics of Place." Unpublished manuscript.

Speed, Shannon. 2008. *Rights in Rebellion: Indigenous Struggle and Human Rights in Chiapas*. Stanford, CA: Stanford University Press.

Speed, Shannon R., Aída Hernández Castillo, and Lynn M. Stephen. 2006. *Dissident Women: Gender and Cultural Politics in Chiapas*. Austin: University of Texas Press.

Spitulnik, Deborah. 1993. "Anthropology and Mass Media." *Annual Review of Anthropology* 22: 293–315.

Sreberny-Mohammadi, Annabelle, and Ali Mohammadi. 1994. *Small Media, Big Revolution: Communication, Culture, and the Iranian Revolution*. Minneapolis: University of Minnesota Press.

Stavenhagen, Rodolfo. 1978. "Clase, etnia y comunidad." In *INI, 30 años despues: Revisión crítica*. Edited by J. Carreño Carlon, 97–100. Mexico City: INI.

———. 1988. *Derecho indígena y derechos humanos en América Latina*. Mexico City: El Colegio de México and Instituto Interamericano de Derechos Humanos.

——. 1990. "Derecho consuetudinario indígena en América Latina." In *Entre la ley y la costumbre*. Edited by R. Stavenhagen and D. Iturralde, 27–46. Mexico City: Instituto Indigenista Interamericano.

——. 1992. "Challenging the Nation-State in Latin America." *Journal of International Affairs* 34 (2): 421–40.

——. 2001. "Cuidadanía Multicultural en México." Cuidadanías Excluidas, Center for U.S.-Mexican Studies, UCSD.

Steiner, Christopher. 1994. *African Art in Transit*. London: Cambridge University Press.

Stephen, Lynn. 1996. "Redefined Nationalism in Building a Movement for Indigenous Autonomy in Mexico: Oaxaca and Chiapas." Paper presented at the Annual Meeting of the American Anthropological Association, San Francisco.

——. 1999. "Indigenous Rights and Self-Determination in Mexico." *Cultural Survival Quarterly* 23 (1): 23–26.

——. 2002. *Zapata Lives! Histories and Cultural Politics in Southern Mexico*. Berkeley: University of California Press.

——. 2009. "Review of *El Estado y los indígenas en tiempos del PAN: Neoindigenismo, legalidad e identidad*" [edited by Rosalva Aída Hernández, Sarela Paz, and María Teresa Sierra, eds. Mexico City: CIESAS, Miguel Angel Porrua, and Camara de Diputados de Mexico, 2004], *PoLAR: Political and Legal Anthropology Review* 32 (1): 127–32.

——. 2011. "Community and Indigenous Radio in Oaxaca: Testimony and Participatory Democracy." Unpublished manuscript.

Tajonar, Héctor. 2011. "La máscara y el botín: Obstáculos para la consolidación democrática en México." Working Paper. Center for U.S.-Mexican Studies, UCSD.

Thomas, Nicholas. 1991. "Against Ethnography." *Cultural Anthropology* 6 (3): 306–22.

Topil, El. 1993. "Medios de Comunicación." *El topil* 12 (50).

——. 1994. "Autonomía." *El topil* 13 (52).

——. 1999. "Antecedentes para ayudar a entender la próxima consulta del EZLN." *El topil* 19 (56).

Turner, Terence. 1991a. "The Social Dynamics of Video Media in an Indigenous Society: The Cultural Meaning and Personal Politics of Video-making in Kayapo Communities." *Visual Anthropology Review* 7 (2): 68–72.

——. 1991b. "Representing, Resisting, Rethinking: Historical Transformations of Kayapo Culture and Anthropological Consciousness." In *Colonial Situations*. Edited by G. Stocking, 285–313. Madison: University of Wisconsin Press.

——. 1991c. "Visual Media, Cultural Politics and Anthropological Practice: Some Implications of Recent Uses of Film and Video among the Kayapo of Brazil." *Independent* (January/February): 34–40.

——. 1992a. "Defiant Images: the Kayapo Appropriation of Video." *Anthropology Today* 8 (6): 5–16.

——. 1992b. "The Kayapo on Television: An Anthropological Viewing." *Visual Anthropology Review* 8 (1): 107–12.

——. 1995. "Representation, Collaboration and Mediation in Contemporary Ethnographic and Indigenous Media." *Visual Anthropology Review* 11 (2): 102–6.

——. 1997. "Misrepresenting Indigenous Representation: Comment on Wiener." *Current Anthropology* 38 (2): 226–29.

——. 2002. "Representation, Politics and Cultural Imagination in Indigenous Video: General Points and Kayapo Examples." In *Media Worlds: Anthropology on New Terrain.* Edited by F. Ginsburg, L. Abu-Lughod, and B. Larkin, 75–89. Berkeley: University of California Press.

Urban, Greg, and Joel Sherzer. 1991. Introduction to *Nation-States and Indians in Latin America.* Edited by G. Urban and J. Sherzer, 1–18. Austin: University of Texas Press.

United Nations. 2007. *United Nations Declaration on the Rights of Indigenous Peoples.* New York: United Nations.

Van Cott, Donna Lee. 1994. "Indigenous Peoples and Democracy: Issues for Policymakers." In *Indigenous Peoples and Democracy in Latin America.* Edited by D. L. Van Cott, 1–27. New York: St. Martin's.

——. 2001. "Explaining Ethnic Autonomy Regimes in Latin America." *Studies in Comparative International Development* 35 (4): 30–58.

Varese, Stefano. 1983. "Multiethnicity and Hegemonic Construction: Indian Plans for the Furture." In *Ethnicities and Nations: Processes of Interethnic Relations in Latin America, Southeast Asia and the Pacific.* Edited by R. Gudidieri, F. Pellizi, and S. J. Tambiah, 57–77. Austin: University of Texas Press.

Wammack Weber, Bruce. 2011. "(Re)Imagining Diaspora: Two Decades of Video with a Mayan Accent." Unpublished manuscript.

Warman, Arturo. 1970. "Todos santos y todos difuntos: Crítica histórica de la anthropología Mexicana." In *De eso que llaman antropología Mexicana.* Edited by A. Warman, M. Nolasco Armas, G. Bonfil Batalla, M. Olivera de Vazquez, and E. Valencia, 9–38. Mexico City: AENAH.

——. 1978. "Se ha creido que el indigenismo es un apotolado, no una acción polítcia." In *INI, 30 años despues: Revisión crítica.* Edited by J. C. Carlon, 141–44. Mexico City: INI.

——. 1989. "Políticas y tareas indigenistas (1989–1994)." *Boletín indigenista* 2 (4): 2–5.

Warman, Arturo, Margarita Nolasco Armas, Guillermo Bonfil Batalla, Mercedes Olivera de Vazquez, and Enrique Valencia, eds. 1970. *De eso que llaman antropología Mexicana.* Mexico City, Mexico: AENAH.

Warren, Kay B., and Jean E. Jackson. 2002. "Studying Indigenous Activism in

Latin America." In *Indigenous Movements, Self-Representation and the State in Latin America*. Edited by Kay B. Warren and Jean E. Jackson, 1–46. Austin: University of Texas Press.

Weatherford, Elizabeth. 1990. "Native Visions: The Growth of Indigenous Media." *Aperture* 119: 58–61.

——. 1992. "Starting Fire with Gunpowder." *Film Comment* 28 (May/June): 64–67.

——. 1995a. "Native Media-making: A Growing Potential." *Native Americas* 13 (1): 56–59.

——. 1995b. "Film and Video Arts." In *The Native American Almanac: A Portrait of Native America Today*. Edited by A. Hirschfelder and M. Kreipe de Montaño, 177–88. Upper Saddle River, NJ: Prentice Hall.

Weinberg, Bill. 2000. *Homage to Chiapas: The New Indigenous Struggles in Mexico*. New York: Verso.

Weiner, James. 1997. "Televisualist Anthropologist: Representation, Aesthetics and Politics." *Current Anthropology* 38 (2): 197–211.

Williams, Raymond. 1975. *Television: Technology and Cultural Form*. New York: Schocken.

Wilson, Pamela, and Michelle Stewart. 2008. "Indigeneity and Indigenous Media on the Global Stage." In *Global Indigenous Media: Cultures, Poetics, and Politics*. Edited by Pamela Wilson and Michelle Stewart, 39–57. Durham, NC: Duke University Press.

Womack, John, Jr. 1999. *Rebellion in Chiapas: An Historical Reader*. New York: New Press.

Worth, Sol, and John Adair. 1997 [1972]. *Through Navajo Eyes: An Exploration in Film Communication and Anthropology*. Albuquerque: University of New Mexico Press.

Wortham, Erica. 1998. "Documentary as a Tool for Cultural Conservation." In *Sights of the Turn of the Century II: New Tendencies in Documentary Cinema*. Edited by J. F. Urrusti, A. Stavenhagen, and A. G. Castro, 61–73. Mexico City: Centro de Capaciatación Cinematográfica and CONACULTA.

——. 1998. *Video América Indígena/Video Native America: Final Report to the Fidecomiso para la Cultura US-Mexico*. New York: National Museum of the American Indian, Smithsonian Institution.

——. 2000a. "Building Indigenous Video in Guatemala." *Jump Cut: A Review of Contemporary Media* 43: 116–19.

——. 2000b. "News From the Mountains: Redefining the Televisual Borders of Oaxaca." *World Studio Sphere* 5: 32–33.

——. 2002. Review of *Democracia Indígena*, documentary. *American Anthropologist* 104 (4): 1205–7.

——. 2004. "Between the State and Indigenous Autonomy: Video Indígena in Mexico." *American Anthropologist* 106 (2): 363–67.

———. 2005. "Mas allá de la hibridad: Los medios televisivos y la producción de identidades indígenas en Oaxaca, México." *LIMINAR: Estudios Socials y Humanísticos* 3 (2): 34–47.

Yúdice, George. 2001. "From Hybridity to Policy: For a Purposeful Cultural Studies." In *Consumers and Citizens: Globalization and Multicultural Conflicts.* Edited by Néstor García Canclini, ix–xxxviii. Minneapolis: University of Minnesota Press.

INDEX

235n1, 235n3, 235n6, 236n12, 241n11.
See also Radio y Video Tamix
Tejiendo mar y viento (INI), 65
tequio (communal labor), 32, 36–37, 71,
98, 109, 121–22, 137, 139–42, 149–50,
157–60, 167–69, 172, 193, 205, 217,
235n6
Transferencia de Medios Audiovisuales
(TMA), 2, 16, 17, 20–21, 94, 100, 106,
114, 130, 145, 150–51, 162, 172, 196;
demise of, 118–19; history of, 60–65;
video center, 77–88; video workshops, 65–77
Turner, Terrence, 2, 5, 8, 224n7
Tzeltal, 182–84, 203. See also La tierra es
de quein la trabaja/The Land Belongs
to Those Who Work It (CMP); Soraida
Tzotzil, 182, 184, 193. See also Estrada,
Mariano

United Nations Declaration of the
Rights of Indigenous Peoples, 25, 27,
28–29, 30
usos y costumbres (self-government),
35, 105, 138

Varela, Bruno, 121. See also Ojo de Agua
Vásquez, Alvaro. See K-Xhon Video-
Cine Zapoteca
Vázquez, Francisco (Paco), 191–92. See
also Chiapas Media
Project/Promedios
video indígena, xiii, 2–3, 20, 178, 219–20,

223n4; autonomy and, 37; beyond
state sponsorship, 93–129; circulation, 5–6, 15, 19, 200, 207–8; definitions of, 11–13; documentary genre,
20, 22, 58–59, 72, 169, 179, 199; festivals and exhibition, xi, 16–18, 60, 82,
84, 131, 172, 207–10, 215, 217, 220,
240n1, 240n3; fiction genre, 9, 72, 157,
219, 230n30; funding for, 17, 151, 159,
165, 231n39; gender biases, 67, 169,
197, 229n19; history, 30–31; inventing,
58–89
video indio, 9, 62, 96, 144

Wammack Weber, Byrt, 224n8
Warman, Arturo, 42, 46, 48–50, 53–55,
60–63, 74, 96, 113, 228n2
Worker-Peasant-Student Coalition of
Tehuantepec (COCEI), 95

XEGLO, Radio Guelatao, 86, 97, 99–104,
121, 123, 144, 231n34, 233n7

Yalalag, Oaxaca, 112. See also K-Xhon
Video-Cine Zapoteca

Zapoteos, 16. See also Fundación Com-
unalidad, A.C.; García, Juan José;
Hipolito, Cheve; K-Xhon Video-Cine
Zapoteca; Manzano, Crisanto; Mar-
tínez Luna, Jaime; Ruiz, Maria
Santiago